The Complete Guide to Pitching

Derek Johnson

Human Kinetics

Library of Congress Cataloging-in-Publication Data

Johnson, Derek, 1971-
  The complete guide to pitching / Derek Johnson.
    p. cm.
  Includes bibliographical references.
  1. Pitching (Baseball) I. Title.
  GV871.J647 2013
  796.357'22--dc23

                                        2012041426

ISBN-10: 0-7360-7901-7 (print)
ISBN-13: 978-0-7360-7901-3 (print)

Developmental Editor: Laura Floch; **Assistant Editor:** Elizabeth Evans; **Copyeditor:** Pat Connolly; **Indexers:** Robert and Cynthia Swanson; **Graphic Designer:** Nancy Rasmus; **Graphic Artist:** Kim McFarland; **Cover Designer:** Keith Blomberg; **DVD Face Designer:** Susan Rothermel Allen; **DVD Producer:** Gregg Henness; **Video Production Coordinator:** Amy Rose; **Photograph (cover):** John S. Peterson/Icon SMI; **Photographs (interior):** © Human Kinetics; p. 1 VJ Lovero/SI/Icon SMI; p. 77 Zuma Press/Icon SMI; p. 167 Mark LoMoglio/Icon SMI; **Photo Asset Manager:** Laura Fitch; **Visual Production Assistant:** Joyce Brumfield; **Photo Production Manager:** Jason Allen; **Art Manager:** Kelly Hendren; **Associate Art Manager:** Alan L. Wilborn; **Illustrations:** © Human Kinetics; **Printer:** United Graphics

We thank Vanderbilt University and Lipscomb University in Nashville, Tennessee, for assistance in providing the location for the photo shoot for this book.

Human Kinetics books are available at special discounts for bulk purchase. Special editions or book excerpts can also be created to specification. For details, contact the Special Sales Manager at Human Kinetics.

The contents of this DVD are licensed for private home use and traditional, face-to-face classroom instruction only. For public performance licensing, please contact a sales representative at www.HumanKinetics.com/SalesRepresentatives.

Printed in the United States of America   10   9   8   7   6   5   4   3   2   1

The paper in this book is certified under a sustainable forestry program.

Human Kinetics
Website: www.HumanKinetics.com

United States: Human Kinetics
P.O. Box 5076
Champaign, IL 61825-5076
800-747-4457
e-mail: humank@hkusa.com

Canada: Human Kinetics
475 Devonshire Road Unit 100
Windsor, ON N8Y 2L5
800-465-7301 (in Canada only)
e-mail: info@hkcanada.com

Europe: Human Kinetics
107 Bradford Road
Stanningley
Leeds LS28 6AT, United Kingdom
+44 (0) 113 255 5665
e-mail: hk@hkeurope.com

Australia: Human Kinetics
57A Price Avenue
Lower Mitcham, South Australia 5062
08 8372 0999
e-mail: info@hkaustralia.com

New Zealand: Human Kinetics
P.O. Box 80
Torrens Park, South Australia 5062
0800 222 062
e-mail: info@hknewzealand.com

E4677

This book is dedicated to my A-plus wife, Tasha, and our children, Teague and Taite. Thank you for your patience and love throughout the writing of this book and for letting me follow my dream.

I'd also like to dedicate this book to Jim Scott, my high school baseball coach; Dan Callahan, my college coach; and Tim Corbin, whom I worked for at Vanderbilt. Thank you for teaching me about the game and about life.

Thanks to Dana Cavalea, strength and conditioning coach for the New York Yankees, for writing chapter 10 on strength and conditioning; thanks for providing wisdom where I couldn't. And lastly, a heartfelt thank you to Ron Wolforth, Paul Nyman, and Brent Strom—all wonderful friends who have graciously allowed me to "borrow" ideas and programming from them. Thanks to all the pitchers who have taught me as much or more about pitching than I have taught them. Finally, to Mom and Dad for giving me all the opportunities to better my game and allowing me to find my passion.

CONTENTS

DVD Contents   vi
Foreword   vii
Introduction   ix

PART I   **The Science of Pitching**

ONE   **Foundation**   **3**

TWO   **Pre-Mechanics**   **13**

THREE   **Upper-Body Mechanics**   **37**

FOUR   **Lower-Body Mechanics
           and Finish**   **59**

PART II **The Art of Pitching**

FIVE   **Developing an Arsenal**   **79**

SIX   **The Role of the Catcher**   **107**

SEVEN   **Pitching With a Plan**   **115**

EIGHT   **Fielding the Position**   **133**

NINE   **The Mental Game**   **157**

PART III Conditioning for Pitching

TEN   **Arm Strength and Injury
             Prevention**   **169**
             Dana Cavalea

ELEVEN   **Total-Body Conditioning
             for Pitchers**   **213**

TWELVE   **In-Season Throwing
             Routines**   **227**

THIRTEEN   **Year-Round Programming**   **243**

Afterword   256
References   257
Index   258
About the Author   262

DVD CONTENTS

INTRODUCTION

THE SCIENCE OF PITCHING

Pre-Mechanics
Taking Care of the Mound
Posture of the Pitcher's Spine
Pitcher's Lean
Hit the Spot Drill
Stretch Mechanics
Sandy Koufax Exercise
Windup Mechanics
Modified Hand Bump Exercise

Upper-Body Mechanics
T-Drill
Arm and Glove Synchronization
Slow-Medium-Fast Arm Interaction
  Exercise
Upper-Body Finish

Lower-Body Mechanics
Partner Push Drill
K Board Drill
Double Lift and Throw Drill
Backward-Feet Drill
Half-Kneel to Standing Throws Drill

THE ART OF PITCHING

Developing an Arsenal
Fastball
Changeup
Changeup Drill–Ball Flip
Changeup Drill–Open Stride
Curveball
Curveball Pressure Drill
Slider

Fielding the Position
Pitchout
Pickoffs
Right-Handed Pickoff Exercises
Left-Handed Pickoff Exercises
Pickoffs at Second Base
Pitcher's Fielding Practice (PFP)

CONDITIONING FOR PITCHING

**Arm Strength and Injury
  Prevention**
Straight-Arm Horizontal Adduction
Straight-Arm Horizontal Abduction
Bent-Arm Internal Rotation
Bent-Arm External Rotation
Backward Straight-Arm
  Hyperextension
Overhead Triceps Extension
Forward Side-to-Side
Backward Side-to-Side
Forward Pitcher
Backward Pitcher
Pitcher Stretches
Catch Play Routine
Long-Toss Routine
Velocity Training
Arm Care Exercises–Day 1 ACE
  Routine
Arm Care Exercises–Day 2 ACE
  Routine

The DVD included with this book will enhance your knowledge of pitching. This DVD demonstrates the techniques and drills discussed in the book. The techniques and drills that appear on the DVD are marked with a symbol in the margin:

FOREWORD

July 4, 2009, was the date of my 10th Major League start. My previous start had been my very first high-quality start of my Major League career. I had gone six and one-third innings against the Florida Marlins, giving up only one run and recording my second win of the season. I was pitching at Ameritrade Field, also known as The Ballpark at Arlington, which was the home field for the Texas Rangers.

I looked back at the box score, and it showed the game-time temperature as 100 degrees Fahrenheit. It felt even hotter on the field. Growing up in the South, I have never minded pitching in hot weather, but this was a little ridiculous.

My team, the Tampa Bay Rays, batted in the top of the first inning against Texas pitcher Derek Holland. Carl Crawford hit second for us and managed a double to deep center field, but Holland was able to get three outs without Carl's hit making a difference.

Then it was my turn on the mound. Ian Kinsler led off for the Rangers and I was able to get him swinging for a strikeout on a 1-and-2 pitch. Next up was Michael Young. He worked me to 3-and-1 and then I walked him. Marlon Byrd then came to bat and the same thing happened—a 3-and-1 walk. The cleanup hitter for the Rangers that day was Andruw Jones, whom I grew up watching. Living in Tennessee, I was an Atlanta Braves fan and Andruw had his best seasons with the Braves. My first pitch to Andruw was called a strike. It felt good to go ahead 0-and-1. Then on my next pitch, Andruw hit a long fly ball to left-center field. It quickly became clear the park wasn't going to hold it and I had to watch as Kinsler and Young scored in front of Jones rounding the bases for a home run. I was losing 3-0 with only one out in the bottom of the first. I was able to get Hank Blalock to hit a slow ground ball to our shortstop Jason Bartlett for the second out, and then Nelson Cruz struck out swinging on a 2-and-2 pitch. I was out of the inning with no further damage.

In the top of the second, Bartlett hit a solo home run for us off of Holland to make the score 3-1 as I went back out to pitch my half of the second inning. It's always a good feeling when my team scores for me, so I felt charged as I went back to the mound.

David Murphy was first up for the Rangers and I was able to strike him out looking on an 0-and-2 pitch. That was a nice way to start the inning. The rest didn't go so well.

Texas' catcher Taylor Teagarden hit a double off of me to deep center. I then walked Elvis Andrus and walked Kinsler to now have the bases loaded. Michael Young then hit a line drive on a two-and-oh pitch that went in for a double, scoring all three base runners. Marlon Byrd followed Young again. After I worked him to a full count, I walked him for my fifth walk of the game. Byrd would be the last hitter I would face. Our manager, Joe Maddon, slowly walked out into the Texas heat to pull me from the game.

My line for the day: 1.1 innings pitched, 3 hits, 6 runs, 6 earned runs, 5 walks, and 3 strike-outs. To this day that is definitely the ugliest game of my career. I hope it remains that way.

After the game, I started walking back to the team hotel. I didn't know what to think. Did I even belong in the Major Leagues?

Just a few steps into my walk, I dialed the phone of Derek Johnson, or DJ, as I call him. We talked during my entire walk to the hotel. He told me I was *the* guy—the number one starter, the starting quarterback—and that I always needed to think that way no matter how things were going, good or bad. He told me that it was all a mind-set and the difference between great big-leaguers and average big-leaguers is all mental. He said I needed to put myself above everyone else in my mind.

You see, DJ had started telling me to be *the* guy the second I stepped on Vanderbilt's campus in 2004. It was like he saw something in me that I didn't know was there. He helped to bring that guy out of me. And for that, I am forever thankful to Derek "DJ" Johnson.

DJ has an insight into pitching like no one else. His thoughts on the mental side, on the mechanical part, and on strategy have helped me in every game I've pitched for the last eight years. He laid the foundation for the pitcher I am and continues to help as I grow to be the pitcher I want to become. Derek Johnson is truly the best.

David Price
Tampa Bay Rays

INTRODUCTION

It has often been said that hitting a baseball thrown at 90-plus miles per hour is the most difficult thing to do in all of sports. As a former pitcher, I can attest that being on the other end of that equation isn't exactly easy either. And, just like baseball, writing this book wasn't a piece of cake, but it was sure a lot of fun.

Baseball is a simple game, or so I thought when I first started playing. I didn't analyze how I held my bat; I simply gripped it and swung hard. Similarly, it never occurred to me that there was a "proper way" to grip a ball or lift my leg when throwing. I just threw the ball as hard as I possibly could over and over again. But as every kid who has donned a uniform eventually learns, the game of baseball becomes increasingly more difficult as players advance to higher levels. In many ways, the same can be said of coaching. Mastering something involves taking the complex and comprehending it so thoroughly that it becomes simple. With this book, my intent is to simplify the complex things about pitching.

When my collegiate career came to a close, my former coach and very dear friend, Dan Callahan, provided me with an opportunity to coach. Initially, my coaching consisted largely of relaying instruction and information that I had learned from my coaches through the years. Most of the pitchers whom I worked with were fairly talented and made modest improvements during their time with me. I pointed to them with pride, thinking that I had influenced their development. And for those who did not develop, I convinced myself that I could not be at fault because they were "uncoachable." Deep down though, I knew that this wasn't always the case. Deep down I felt as if I had failed myself, and more important, I had failed the pitchers. Because of those players who didn't succeed, I began to question what I was teaching and how I was teaching it. Those questions drive me now, and I believe they should drive anyone who coaches young people.

I began searching for answers and found others who were more than willing to help. Ron Wolforth, owner and operator of the Athletic Pitcher Pitching Ranch in Houston, Texas, was instrumental in my quest. He introduced me to great pitching minds such as Brent Strom, Paul Nyman, and Tom House. I learned as much from these men as I possibly could. I built on and adapted aspects of that knowledge while developing an approach that fit my experience, observations, and personality. This approach has yielded fairly good results, which would not have been achievable without the generosity of fellow coaches who were willing to share their experiences—along with good recruiting from the men with whom I've shared an office. It is my hope that with this book I can repay the favor and help coaches and players more fully understand the art and science of pitching.

So what is that approach? In writing this book, I spent a great deal of time pondering that very question. It would be easy to focus on the individual aspects of development, such as a pitcher's mechanics, arm strength, intensity, commitment, and dedication. Of course, these are all important ingredients in the recipe for any successful approach. However, for the recipe to be a success, ingredients must be added in the proper amounts and at the right time—for the recipe to taste right, some must be added before others.

And this concept also applies to my approach to pitching. I believe that to be successful, a pitcher must first possess and exhibit four essential traits: (1) a work ethic that will not take "no" for an answer; (2) the ability to prepare at a championship level every day; (3) accountability for himself and his career; and (4) a sense of humility for himself and the game. In turn, these traits create a mind-set, a mentality. The pitcher must have the mind-set of a champion—the mind-set of a warrior.

All four traits must be present before a pitcher, or coach, can devote the time and effort to the development of the physical skills. That is not to say that the skills are not important; they are, and they will be covered extensively in this book. However, I've seen many pitchers with great mechanics and overpowering stuff who struggled, fizzled, and faded into oblivion. Alternatively, I've watched while players with fewer tools and less stuff succeeded at the highest levels of the sport. Why? I firmly believe it is because of these essential traits.

It is not uncommon for a coach, teacher, or parent to harp on the importance of developing a solid work ethic supported by organization, dedication, and discipline. With my pitchers, I focus on a model of a work ethic that is different in nature but still supported by these attributes. This work ethic requires an unquenchable thirst for knowledge, specifically pitching knowledge. If a pitcher wants to be the best, he must work when no one else is working, train uniquely, seek ways to improve his training, be comfortable in an uncomfortable setting, and go where no one else dares to go. I will often paraphrase this old saying: "Most people know what to do and how to do it, but very few are actually willing to do it." I want a truly willing pitcher on my side. Those guys will win more games than the other guy.

As the pitcher continues to gain knowledge, he must then understand how to best train based on what he has learned. This is preparation. Most teams and players at any level prepare for a season or a game, but what separates a "have" from a "have not" is the *way* he prepares and the confidence he builds as a result of the training. He might ask himself, "If I truly prepare, then how can I fail?" Or even better, he might say, "If I prepare judiciously and purposefully, then I *will not* fail." Teams and players do not win simply by having more talent than the opposition. Winners have a purpose for doing what they do, they have a defined time for when they do it, and they leave nothing to chance. No stone is left unturned. Everything counts. This is purposeful preparation!

Another quality that is essential for a pitcher is the willingness to take responsibility for his own success, his failures, and most important, his career. We live in a "transfer of blame" society—failure always seems to be someone else's fault. Parents invest more time and money in their youngster's career than ever before, so if "Little Johnny" doesn't become a star, it must be someone else's fault. The player doesn't develop into a high-level performer because of poor coaching or not enough playing time. Although some of these outside reasons do exist, the player should look inward first. Baseball is a game of failure, but the failures are really the opportunities that the game presents to better yourself. Good players take responsibility—bad ones blame something or someone else.

The last quality that a pitcher must possess in order to become extraordinary (extraordinary is what we are looking for) is a sense of humility. Two types of players play the game of baseball—the humble player and the player who is about to be humbled. The humble player leads by example and serves other people before serving himself. He recognizes that everyone around him has an important role, and that he is a small part of a bigger thing—the team. He wins with humility and loses with honor. He lets his actions and accomplishments speak for themselves, and he plays the game with joy and unbridled passion. He is slow to speak, but quick to listen.

Throughout this book and DVD, you'll find advice, guidance, and instruction on nearly every aspect of pitching. You'll learn how a pitcher can refine his mechanics, develop new pitches, improve physical conditioning, recognize a hitter's weaknesses, shut down a running game, and much, much more. What you will not find are instructions for developing character, accountability, and commitment. The development of those traits is the responsibility of the pitcher alone.

PART I

The Science of Pitching

Foundation

Let's get something straight from the very beginning: Becoming a skilled pitcher is very difficult! I'm not trying to sound pessimistic, but pitchers need to understand from the beginning that they must master many layers of proficiency in order to become successful at the highest levels. This is a fact that overwhelms even the greatest athletes, because what works at the present level might not work at the next. If pitching were easy, everyone would do it. The same can be said about the game of baseball. I have spent a lifetime pursuing knowledge of the many layers of pitching, and I suspect that I will spend many more years fitting the pieces together moving closer to what I consider "right."

When teaching young athletes the art of pitching, most coaches would agree that the first step is to lay a foundation of guiding principles. The coach can then build on this foundation while teaching the skills and techniques that pitchers must master to be successful. Foundations create expectations, foster a mentality within the group, set guidelines, and provide a general map on where to go, how to get there, and why. Just as important, foundations give the pitcher a resource to go back to when things aren't going as planned. And if you've ever spent any time around baseball, you undoubtedly understand that things often go awry. A good foundation can provide remedies for many flaws and can keep the pitcher on track as he works to acquire skill. Figure 1.1 represents the seven foundational elements of a pitching program. Although other things could certainly be considered foundational, these seven philosophical concepts provide a solid foundation and should be taught on a regular basis:

1. Joy
2. Balls and strikes
3. Me versus me and me versus you
4. Intent
5. Skills and abilities
6. Balance
7. Training versus trusting

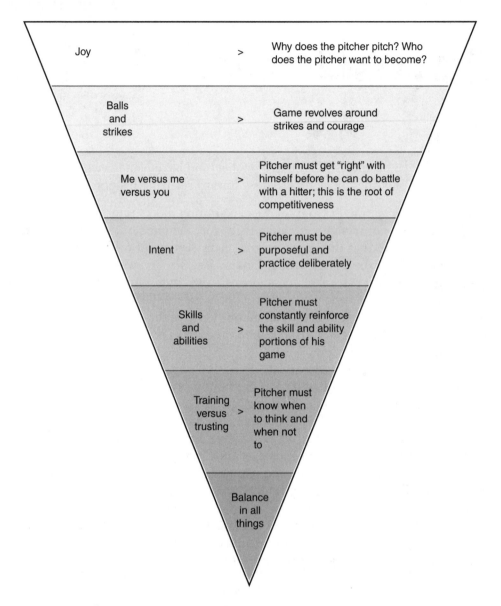

Figure 1.1   Conceptual model of the seven elements of a pitching foundation.

First Principle of the Pitching Foundation: Joy

Joy, or enjoyment, is what drives people in their pursuits. We seek happiness, and therefore we do things that make us happy and generally stay away from things that do not. So, the first principle of the pitching foundation is to find joy in pitching and in the game of baseball.

The first question that a pitcher needs to address within this foundation is "Why do I pitch?" It may seem funny and too elementary to even ask such a question; however, if the pitcher is being totally honest with himself, he might be surprised at some of the answers. This question is important because the answer provides the pitcher with insight into two other questions that can greatly impact the success of a pitcher: "Who am I?" and "Who do I want to be?" Outside of baseball, philosophers have wrestled with these fundamental questions for centuries, and the baseball pitcher should be clear in his answers. When a pitcher has a solid understanding of who he is currently (when he knows himself as a pitcher) and has a plan for who he wants to be as a pitcher, only then does he progress toward realizing his potential. In other words, the pitcher keeps perspective on where he is currently and what he needs to do to take the next step.

So, the question "Why do you pitch?" becomes a search of the soul and brings deeper meaning to the pitcher's pursuit of becoming skilled. You may be thinking that this question is too deep for a young pitcher to comprehend or relate to, but I would politely disagree because the answer is alarmingly simple—the answer should be that he pitches because he experiences a deep and profound joy when he pitches or when he is working on the skills of pitching. Joy, pure joy, provides the pitcher with the fuel needed to find out who he is currently (the style or essence of the pitcher) and a plan for who he wants to become. Joy is natural and comes from within. It is unforced by any outside stimuli (e.g., parents or coaches) and can be seen on the beaming faces of youngsters playing a game of catch in the backyard or hitting their first home run. When true joy is present, playing the game becomes easier, and the work needed to acquire skill doesn't seem like work at all. It seems much more like fun. It comes from the gut, and lives in the heart. Therefore, the first principle involves pursuing the art and craft of pitching with unbridled joy.

Second Principle of the Pitching Foundation: Balls and Strikes

The second principle is also easy to understand and goes right to the heart of the game. This principle is a word play on one of the most fundamental aspects of the game—balls and strikes. In baseball, the pitcher throws the ball across the plate, and the hitter attempts to hit the thrown ball somewhere on the field of play, thereby starting the action of the contest. Without strikes, the game cannot be played. To have the best chance of succeeding, the pitcher must develop the ability to consistently throw strikes in different areas of the strike zone, making it more difficult for the hitter to hit. Throwing to these areas requires great skill and precision, and it is difficult to do consistently.

Unfortunately, other factors come into play that make the pitcher's task more difficult. Pressure (both internal and external), inconsistent mechanics and mentalities, and general fear can prevent the pitcher from throwing strikes. He becomes scared of what the outcome might be or the consequences of failing and becomes unable to make pitches. He throws balls. Of course, not all balls are thrown out of fear or ineptness—balls also occur because pitching is a difficult skill to master. In addition, sometimes the pitcher *wants* to throw balls so that he can set up the next pitch, or he may be trying to get a hitter to chase a ball out of the zone. This too is all part of the game. But the definition of the word *balls* that I am referring to here deals with the intestinal fortitude of the pitcher. It takes courage to throw strikes! If the pitcher has the courage to throw the ball across the plate and do so repeatedly, he will give himself and his team a much better chance to win the game.

Third Principle of the Pitching Foundation: Me Versus Me and Me Versus You

The third principle builds directly on the first two. The pitcher must find joy in his heart to have any chance of identifying why he pitches, who he is, and who he'd like to become. As the pitcher moves through this process, many things happen to impede his progress. He will fail and succeed while competing at the game, and his mind and ego are like a bank account that involves a large number of transactions—confidence deposits and debits. With a good outing, a pitcher's confidence usually gets better, while a poor outing can sometimes destroy the poise of the pitcher. This is the nature of the game and always will be.

Essentially then, the pitcher is battling two opponents at all times—not just the opposing batter, but also himself. Me versus me is the pitcher's battle against himself, and me versus you is the pitcher's battle against the hitter. It is the battle within as well as the battle on the outside. Ultimately, pitching becomes easier when the focus is less internal and the pitcher learns to manage his emotions so that he has a stronger commitment to simply executing pitches and doing battle with the hitter. Put another way, the pitcher learns how to conquer fear and how to "get out of his own way" (me versus me), and he condenses pitching into simply making pitches and doing battle with the hitter (me versus you). This is the root of competitive behavior—a need to prove oneself in a sport arena. The hitter tries to take something from the pitcher (i.e., get a hit, score a run, or win the game), and the pitcher proactively tries to stop the batter from achieving that goal.

Me versus me and me versus you will also create a mentality for the individual pitcher as well as an entire pitching staff. Pitchers need to have an edge about them when they do battle with a hitter. This desire starts in practice and progresses to the game and potentially their life. Pitchers need to feel as if a hitter is trying to take something away from them—and they have to do something about it. This needs to be a confrontational battle. It needs to be personal. In short, the pitcher knows why he pitches (joy), who he is, and who he wants to be. He throws strikes with courage, and he learns to manage the battle within so that his primary focus can be on battling the hitter.

Fourth Principle of the Pitching Foundation: Intent

The fourth principle for building a foundation is based on one word: *intent*. Intent is connecting the mind to the task at hand, providing purpose and meaning. This makes it easier for a person to take determined action toward a goal. The easiest way to understand the word *intent* as it pertains to pitching is to remember a time when you were doing an activity and it seemed as if time stood still. Nothing else mattered, and your mind was completely connected to the activity you were pursuing. That is intent. It is the objective or purpose behind pitching. Skill acquisition starts and ends with *purposeful intent*. For example, we know that arm speed (the speed at which the arm moves) directly correlates with velocity. So if a pitcher is to build velocity, his mind must be connected to the task of training his arm to move faster than it currently moves. During throwing sessions, this intent becomes a powerful training aid and forces the pitcher to pursue his goals with fervor.

One of the best characteristics of intent is that it can be used in every phase of pitcher training. From playing catch to bullpen work, arm care, and weight training, the pitcher must have an intention (purpose or goal) in order to maximize development. Even when the pitcher is pitching on the mound, intent is required for him to compete and execute at a maximal level. Intent provides a connection from the mind to the task—executing pitches and getting outs—so that the pitcher can reach the goals that he has set for himself and can ultimately reach team goals. Intent is purpose, focus, and being "present" for the current activity.

Fifth Principle of the Pitching Foundation: Skills and Abilities

So far, we have focused on the foundational elements that help create an aggressive mentality (me versus you), create harmony within (me versus me and Why do I pitch?), and connect the mind with training in pursuit of specific goals that will enhance development (intent). But pitching is more than just mental proficiency. It also involves physical talent, which can be split into two categories: skill and ability. Abilities are the athletic qualities that a pitcher possesses, and skill is what makes him a baseball player. For example, ability is the physical (and mental) athleticism that a pitcher possesses and seeks to develop. Throwing is an ability, while pitching is more of a skill. Using this example, it is obvious that the two are very connected. By becoming better at throwing—through daily catch with a plan, long toss, and so on—the pitcher puts himself in a position to become more skilled. Another way of looking at this is that as the pitcher's athletic ability is developed through throwing (i.e., as the pitcher is getting bigger, faster, and stronger), his potential skill for pitching increases as well. The two go hand in hand, and one cannot happen without the other.

But even though they are similar to abilities, athletic or pitching skills might include the delivery of the pitcher, the way that his ball moves, the command of his pitches,

PEN SESSION   Using a Proper Training Progression

Teaching mechanics to young pitchers can be very difficult. Coaches who coach this age group often employ a step-by-step approach to teach different parts of the delivery; this is a good approach, at least initially. Step 1 may be the rocker step or the initial step of the stretch position, step 2 may be the proper leg lift, and so on. The problem with this type of teaching is that it teaches positions rather than movements. So much of pitching requires "connecting" two simultaneous positions together, which in turn creates a movement. The movements all flow together, creating momentum and synergy to deliver the ball maximally. The end result is often referred to as looking athletic or powerful. This type of delivery is what you will likely see when watching a big-league pitcher. So, it is appropriate to teach the parts of the delivery to the novice in a step-by-step manner, but as the pitcher matures fundamentally, the coach should teach the movements of the delivery in a more ballistic manner. One such method is called backward chaining. The basic principle behind backward chaining is to position the pitcher just past the critical point of movement—for example, at the release point if working on arm action—and then work back through the path of the arm action ballistically in a backward and then forward motion. This method makes it easier to alter or adjust the movements. A coach must teach movements and not just positions.

and what type of pitches he throws. They also involve his competence in fielding his position or executing pickoffs to bases. Skill might also be the mental talent to "slow the game down" and the knack of making good pitches in pressure situations. Developing routines such as a prepitch routine, either in practice or games, would be considered a skill as well. Like abilities, skills can be learned, developed, and improved. Table 1.1 shows that skills deal with the elements that happen within the game, whereas abilities are usually traits characterized by physicality or athleticism. Also note that some additional skills and abilities (not listed in the table) lie in the mental realm of baseball and pitching. For example, concentration might be thought of as an ability, whereas being able to slow the game down and make a pitch might be thought of as a skill.

It has been my observation that most players excel in one area, either skill or ability, but not in both. Players have a tendency to gravitate toward practicing things that they are already skilled in, but they often shy away from working on weaknesses. A pitcher may already be very skilled on the mound, but he may lack the physical abilities to take his performance to the next level. This pitcher may despise the weight room or might never play catch with intent or purpose. Conversely, another pitcher may love the weight room, the long toss, and any other activity besides actually getting on the mound and working on his craft. He may believe that his training will magically produce pitching skill. Neither of these pitchers will develop maximally.

The same can be said about coaches. Most coaches are comfortable "knowing what they know," and they teach the game based on their strengths. This can be a solid approach because it helps the teacher and the player trust what is being taught.

Table 1.1   Examples of Pitching Skills and Abilities

Skills	Control or command of pitches
	Types of pitches (mastery of the movement; manipulating the ball execution of the pitch or a set of pitches)
	Pitch acquisition or development
	Delivery enhancement
	Quickness to the plate; Holding runners
	Pickoff moves
	Fielding position
Abilities	Strength and weight training
	Throwing (daily catch; long toss; arm care to promote athleticism)
	Conditioning
	Nutritional discipline
	Daily routines
	Approach to the game (which can be enhanced through training)
	Perspective and evaluation

Players can see right through a coach who doesn't know what he is talking about—it is usually very obvious. However, every coach has a duty to diligently pursue and acquire knowledge about the subject he teaches, just as players are expected to become more complete. So instead of regarding themselves as "mental guys" or "mechanics guys," coaches should educate themselves in all facets of the game and should become proficient at teaching all aspects.

Sixth Principle of the Pitching Foundation: Balance

Just as understanding yin and yang as an illustration of symmetry is important to many cultures, balance is extremely important in any discussion of pitching (see figure 1.2). Although I consider balance to be another key fundamental, I do not think of it in the traditional sense of a balance point in the pitching delivery; rather, I teach balance as an aspect of equilibrium and athleticism. Too often, a pitcher is taught mechanics by going from step 1 to step 2, and so on. This way of teaching has value initially, but as the pitcher progresses, it can jeopardize the pitcher's ability to use his athletic ability within his delivery.

Figure 1.2 Yin and yang represent balance in all things. The pitcher should strive to be balanced in the way that he approaches his game, the process, and the way he views himself.

PEN SESSION   Understanding Connection and Balance

Understanding what balance really means in pitching is extremely important. Conventional teaching suggests that there is a balance point—a point where the pitcher essentially gathers or perhaps even stops to stay balanced. Taken literally, static balance will destroy any momentum that the previous movements in the delivery have created, and it can also negatively affect the rhythm and timing of the pitcher and his pitches. The balance that I am referring to here—dynamic balance—might best be described as the connection between movements. Timed, rhythmical, symmetrical movements that exhaust themselves into further movements down the kinetic chain are what the pitcher should strive for. This is a key for the delivery to be athletic, balanced, and connected.

The choreographed mechanics may be easy to teach and easy to comprehend, but they can sometimes lead to a lack of athleticism and individual style. The pitcher needs to be free and easy with his delivery—unrestricted, in rhythm, and on time. His movements should be connected, as should his mind. He should be free to use his athleticism and develop a style that is unique to him. If this happens, the pitcher will have most likely achieved dynamic balance throughout the delivery, connection will have been achieved, his athleticism will prevail, and no further discussion or training will be required.

The second part of the balance premise is that the pitcher must try to become as complete as possible. Only through balancing all aspects of pitching can this be achieved. The pitcher stays balanced in his delivery by keeping his movements connected, staying balanced in his pursuit of all phases of the game, and maintaining balance in his life by prioritizing, planning, and organization. As noted earlier, the pitcher must spend equal time on the physical, mental, mechanical, and emotional parts of the game. No single aspect is more important than the others; rather, the sum of the parts equals a whole. Balance in all things will play a significant role in making the pitcher complete. The pitcher must also have balance in his life outside of baseball. Unfortunately, life gets in the way all too often and can impede the pitcher's progress. Family and school issues, romantic problems, and social activities can all take a toll on the pitcher. The key is to find the correct balance between all of these areas and to prioritize their importance. Planning and organization help achieve balance.

Seventh Principle of the Pitching Foundation: Training Versus Trusting

The final foundational concept is based on the idea that both pitcher and coach will be in specific modes through the course of the training year. For our purposes, we will call it training versus trusting modes. Though this is the last concept described for the foundation, training versus trusting will actually encompass the entire foundation of a pitcher's training.

In the training mode, a pitcher and coach have the ability to adjust, alter, and think through a specific skill or ability. In the trusting mode, the pitcher and coach "get out of their own way" and allow the pitcher to feel the skill or ability. To help you understand this concept better, let's first define the two modes (training and trusting) and discuss the importance of each. These words describe what mode a pitcher is in at any given time. If he were in training mode, the pitcher would be learning and working on getting a feel for a skill or ability. His movements and techniques are being adjusted or altered, and he very well may be thinking too much; that is to be expected in this mode if change is to occur. The goal in this mode is to change a habit or to make a movement or series of movements (the delivery) more efficient. The brain directs traffic, and the coach provides verbal and nonverbal cues and instruction to guide the pitcher through the alteration. This is the mode that a player and coach would use when changing the delivery, developing a pitch, or working on a specific facet of the game.

In the trusting mode, however, nothing physically or mentally is being adjusted or altered except for the normal execution adjustments that every pitcher must make, and the pitcher's brain is on automatic pilot. His intention is to throw strikes and get outs. In a bullpen or drill setting, the pitcher's intention is to simply feel his delivery and pitches and to find rhythm and timing. He readies his mind for the game with a quiet and relatively thoughtless demeanor. In the trusting mode, the coach's role should be limited and less invasive than in the training mode. This is the time for both parties to get out of their own way. It is the time to compete. The trusting mode happens when all the work is done, and it is simply time to pitch. This mode can occur in both a practice and game setting.

The pitcher and the coach must understand the important distinction between the two modes. Too often, a coach interferes at the wrong time, or a player inappropriately thinks about his delivery or a specific skill when he is competing. In turn, this makes the game much more complex than it should be. These modes serve as the rules of engagement for when the pitcher should think, train, and interact or when a quiet and competitive spirit should take over.

The foundational principles discussed in this chapter provide both general and specific goals throughout training. These principles encompass the body of work needed to be a successful pitcher. They help the pitcher develop a belief system regarding the manner in which he should train and compete, as opposed to relying on luck or circumstance. When addressed correctly, these principles help clarify roles and enhance a pitcher's ability to move to a higher level of baseball. In short, the pitching foundation sets the tone for the heart and soul of training.

Pre-Mechanics

When it comes to delivering a baseball, many different body parts must synchronize and mesh together in order for a pitcher to achieve a successful result. For our purposes, at this juncture we will define a successful result as applying the maximum force to the baseball while arriving at a consistent release point (i.e., being "on time"). When a hitter makes contact with a pitch on the sweet spot of the bat, he feels nothing. The ball seems to jump off the bat, and the hitter feels little, if any, negative resistance. When this happens, the hitter has generated perfect timing. For a pitcher, being on time is very similar in that the ball, when released, seems to jump out of his hand. This occurs because his body and arm are in perfect harmony during the delivery portion of the throw. But if improper or poorly timed movements occur early in the delivery, they will usually adversely affect subsequent movements and affect the timing of the pitch.

This seems to be common knowledge among pitchers and pitching coaches alike, yet they often overlook or ignore many of these early movements. Because every pitcher brings a unique and personal style to the table, any changes made to mechanics need to achieve the proper balance of efficiency and individuality. Remember, style is what makes the pitching world go 'round, and if every pitcher threw the same way, hitting would be easy(ier). We certainly don't want that! Part of what is referred to as style or uniqueness in a pitcher may actually result from physical limitations or constraints caused by genetics, past injuries, or the pitcher mimicking what he has seen in the past. Observing babies crawl and then walk can provide us with an illustration of these constraints, because the early locomotion of most babies looks quite similar. As children grow older, they imitate what they see, and some may suffer injuries that affect their movement pattern. My son Teague is a good example of a child developing movement patterns through mimicking. He has observed me run countless times on and off the field; now he runs very similar to the way I do, though he didn't start out running this way. Because of individual constraints (related to genetics or injury) and mimicked movement patterns, it becomes difficult for the coach to know what can be rewired and what cannot.

On the pages that follow, the focus is primarily on starting positions—particularly the factors that influence the subtle, often overlooked starting movements of a pitcher. We'll refer to these movements as pre-mechanics. For some, these subtle movements are quite intuitive and do not need to be addressed, but for others, pre-mechanics could possibly provide clues to problems that occur later in the delivery.

Before the Pitch

Addressing the next four subjects in a mechanics chapter is admittedly unorthodox; however, these subjects are included here because they are all "starting points" for the pitcher and can have an enormous influence on the outcome of the most important pitch—the next pitch!

Taking Care of the Mound

Every pitching mound has its own subtleties and complexities that make it unique. This uniqueness can make a pitcher extremely comfortable or extremely uncomfortable depending on the mound's formation and the way the pitcher throws. Every pitcher's goal should be to start with a solid base on the back foot, make a strong first move when he lifts his front leg, and land solidly on his front foot. Therefore, the pitcher must know how to manicure a mound to his liking during a game. This is important knowledge for a pitcher because the opposing pitcher is also using the same mound and may be creating different landing holes and causing ridges and other unsettling "land mines" that might disrupt the pitching motion.

The two sections of the mound that are of primary concern for the pitcher are the area just in front of the rubber and the landing area. Compacted clay is used to fill in those two areas between contests, and it doesn't take long for these areas to be dug out or worn down during a game. The pitcher needs to monitor these areas and excavate them if necessary, as shown in figure 2.1. In some cases, he will have to further repair the hole with his spikes, ridding it of pesky ridges or fault lines so that he can maintain balance or land flatly. At other times, he will have to fill these holes in and compact them for a smoother landing. If the pitcher intends to repeat his delivery and make each pitch count, this is a very necessary skill to master.

Breathing

In baseball circles, you often hear coaches and players talking about the next pitch being the most important. A good player focuses intently on the next pitch and on being in the moment. The antithesis of being in the moment is letting your thoughts, emotions, or what has just happened in the game cloud your mind for the next pitch. This can cause the game to speed up and cause the pitcher to get lost in an emotional downward spiral.

To counteract this, a pitcher should learn to command and use his breathing to bring his focus back to the task at hand—throwing the next pitch and throwing it well! As much as anything, the deep breath is the line of demarcation between what has just happened and what happens next. It should serve as a reminder for the pitcher to get out of the past and into the present moment.

Breathing is a simple, automatic process, but the quality of a pitcher's breathing during tough times in a game can be so shallow and tight that it actually restricts his ability to coordinate the timing of his delivery. This feeling is also known as "choking". Choking puts the pitcher at risk of not executing at the most critical times. For these reasons, the pitcher should develop the routine of taking a deep breath after

Figure 2.1   Pitcher excavating the mound.

getting the sign from the catcher. This breath signifies passage from past to present and provides the best opportunity for the pitcher to relax and execute the next pitch properly. I like to refer to this process as being "all in" for the next pitch—present, in the moment, and ready to go. Breathing in this manner should be thought of as part of a prepitch routine and should be practiced religiously.

Eyes and Focus

The eyes are one of the most important elements for controlling the baseball. The reason for this is simple—the body follows the eyes. This extends to alignment as well as to the direction of the body during the pitcher's delivery. Simply put, the eyes are the bridge between the mind and the body. Further, for a pitcher or coach, recognizing and correcting an issue with the eyes will often be a quick fix that is better than adjusting, tweaking, or reworking other aspects of the delivery.

Many coaches talk abstractly about concentration and focus, yet few explain to pitchers how to accomplish these. Focus starts with the eyes. A pitcher must train his eyes to see what he wants them to see. This concept is important because a pitcher must not only throw a strike, he must also hit a particular spot within the strike zone (e.g., low and away on the outside corner of the plate to a right-handed hitter). If the pitcher can remain focused on that small target while blocking out other distractions, he will increase his chances of hitting the desired location. This is more difficult than it sounds, however. Because of the twists and turns of a delivery—not to mention additional movements and adjustments necessary for holding runners on base—the pitcher's ability to focus his eyes on a particular spot becomes compromised. More often than not, this results in the pitcher missing the target. Therefore, training the eyes properly will improve the consistency of mind–body connections, and in turn, will produce favorable results. See figure 2.2 for an example of good eyes versus bad eyes.

The eyes are also important because of balance and direction. Try walking a straight line with your eyes wandering aimlessly or looking down at the ground. At the end of the line, you will most likely have veered far from your intended course. If a pitcher does the same thing when beginning his delivery, he will likely lean one way or the other when he lifts up his leg, causing poor posture and direction to the plate. This can cause potential problems with controlling the ball from one side of the plate to the other (see figure 2.3).

Figure 2.2   (a) Pitcher with good eyes and (b) pitcher with bad eyes.

Figure 2.3   *(a)* Pitcher leaning at the beginning of his delivery versus *(b)* pitcher staying upright.

This kind of lean can force the body to compensate at some other point during the delivery in order to correct the faulty movement. I have observed several pitchers throw across their body or step to the open side of the mound—both potentially major faults—simply because that was where their eyes took them. When this happens with right-handed pitchers, they step toward the third-base side; left-handed pitchers step more toward the first-base side, as shown in figure 2.4. In many cases, the simple fix to this problem is to train the pitcher to control his eyes.

Figure 2.4   At landing, a left-handed pitcher *(a)* throwing across his body because of a lean versus *(b)* throwing on a straight line when remaining upright.

PEN SESSION   Training the Eyes

Some pitchers claim that if they look at the catcher's mitt for too long or with too much focus, the target starts to fade or appear fuzzy to them. Each pitcher should be allowed to find his own way in terms of training the eyes. The eyes should focus intently on the target as the pitch is being released, but at the beginning of the delivery and then after release, the eyes may go in various directions based on the pitcher, his style, and perhaps his mechanics. The important thing is for the pitcher to get a "blueprint" of the target, an image of the target in his mind. Then, after release, the eyes can essentially follow where the body takes them. The pitcher needs to stay away from two things in terms of eye mechanics: He should not follow the path of the ball while it is in the air and on the way to the plate, and he should not let the eyes stop the body from fully rotating once the release occurs. In the first situation, the pitcher will watch the flight of the ball after it leaves his hand. Many pitchers who employ this method do not have good command, especially on breaking balls. In the second situation, if the head stays on the target too long after release, it will impede the full rotation of the shoulders around the spine. This will decrease the range of motion to decelerate the arm and will essentially cut off the path of the throwing arm. Cutting off the throwing motion can lead to long-term injury.

So, how exactly can a pitcher control his eyes? Often, this can be accomplished through simple intervention. At the highest point of the delivery (usually the highest point of the leg lift), the pitcher should "get inside the glove" with his eyes. This means he should pick out a small target inside the catcher's mitt and throw to that target. Getting inside the glove allows the pitcher to sharpen his sight and mental focus. It also forces him to aim at a smaller spot, which increases his awareness and concentration. This takes practice, but it is a simple fix that has produced amazing results, including improving command and eliminating mechanical faults such as stepping across the body during delivery.

All in all, training the eyes is about helping the pitcher maximize his chance of hitting the target—that is, the glove. The more often the pitcher hits the glove, the better chance he has to be successful in the short run (against the hitter or for the game) and in the long run of his career. In the end, it all goes back to "balls and strikes." I have seen many pitchers have decent command and control of the pitches they make without the aid of good eye mechanics, but I have seen many more improve their command by emphasizing the eyes.

Hit the Spot Drill

This drill promotes visual awareness and trains the eyes to focus on a specific target.

Setup

Coaches will need a package of round, bright colored labels. Players can be paired with other pitchers or with catchers. The drill can be performed on flat ground during warm-ups or on a mound in the bullpen.

Procedure

1. Affix a brightly colored label (preferably orange) in the palm of each pitcher's glove and each catcher's mitt.
2. Pitchers begin their pitching motion.
3. As the pitcher's leg lift reaches its highest point in the pitching motion, the pitcher should sharply focus on the orange spot in the partner's glove.
4. The pitcher finishes his throwing motion and throws the ball to the partner while focusing on the orange spot.

Pitching Point

Because focus is difficult to maintain for long periods, coaches should make sure that pitchers are not staring at the spot from the very beginning of the pitching motion, unless control does not seem to be affected.

Modifications

Coaches need to treat vision as a priority in pitching training. Young players need to be consistently reminded of the importance of focus and how improving their vision will help them gain more command of their pitches.

Head

As one of the heaviest part of the pitcher's body, the head plays a major role in keeping him on line to the target. The center of the body (i.e., the core) is the energy source of movement and is most responsible for how the body moves in space, but the head should be thought of as the stabilizer because it helps control the posture of the pitcher.

If a pitcher is pulling off his target, which is a common occurrence for many pitchers, he should focus first on his head. More specifically, he should ensure that he is taking his nose to the catcher's mitt as he releases the ball. This quick fix is effective because when a pitcher focuses on keeping his nose going toward the mitt, he's engaging the center of his body and placing the onus on his core rather than the head itself. The head's function is to stay relatively still so that a proper posture of the spine can be created (see figure 2.5). Again, it is not necessary for the pitcher to keep the head completely still or become robotically stiff, but the less the head moves early in the delivery, the more stable the base will be

Figure 2.5 Posture of a pitcher's spine.

for the pitcher to work from. The head is the "captain of the ship" and is responsible for steering the boat.

Once a pitcher masters these processes—caring for the mound, keeping the eyes and head on the target, and learning to control breathing—the coach can then focus more directly on the mechanics of the pitching motion, always keeping in mind how important these nonmechanical actions are.

QUICK PITCH

Ultimately, the head does not necessarily create specific mechanical problems in the delivery. Rather, the head position is a by-product of another movement that affects the angle or positioning of the spine and can affect posture. As mentioned earlier, a quick fix is to take the nose to the target until release of the pitch. At ball release, the pitcher may then move the head to the side and let the arm finish its intended path, which is important so that the natural rotation of the shoulders and the hip can take place.

Setup Positions

As the saying goes, "there are many ways to skin a cat," and there are probably just as many ways to initiate the pitching motion. The key to effective starting positions in the stretch and windup is twofold: First, these positions must put the pitcher in the very best position to efficiently and optimally throw the ball. Second, these positions should promote athleticism within the delivery itself. Athleticism can also be referred to as "connection" because it snaps movements together, creating a one-piece, free flowing delivery. These two keys are certainly related, but the human body and its movements are so unique to their owners that what is efficient for one person may not be efficient or effective for another. Optimally, the pitcher wants to set a solid foundation by having a strong back foot, a strong first move into his lift, and a strong front foot when he lands. These starting positions help promote a strong foundation.

Stretch Mechanics

"Runner on first with no one out, pitcher goes to his stretch, here's the pitch . . . strike 1 on the inside corner." This is a familiar call made by announcers of games from Little League to the big leagues. Anyone who has ever pitched a baseball will tell you that it is much easier to pitch with no runners on base versus pitching when there are runners on base. With no runners on base, pitchers have the freedom to use the windup, which may include as much or as little movement as the pitcher desires. When runners are on base, the windup must be cut in half so that the runners will stay at their respective bases (not steal), but the pitcher still needs to be able to throw the ball with fury to the plate. This half windup is known as the stretch. The following sections identify some solid and athletic starting positions for pitching in the stretch. Because the feet provide the foundation for all of the movements that follow in a delivery, we'll begin there and work up the kinetic chain.

Starting Position for the Feet

Conflicting opinions still exist about where the pitcher should stand on the rubber. In the old days, it was common for the right-handed pitcher to stand on the right side of the rubber (toward third base) and the left-handed pitcher to be toward the left side (toward first base). Many people believe that this position creates an angle advantage for the pitcher (see figure 2.6). When facing a same-side hitter (i.e., right-handed pitcher facing a right-handed hitter), the pitcher would appear to be throwing the ball at or behind the hitter, possibly producing fear or at least making the hitter uncomfortable.

This is a solid theory, but only if the pitcher or coach takes into account a pitcher's arm slot. If the pitcher has a sidearm or even a low three-quarter delivery, then this approach would make sense, *assuming* that the pitcher could throw a strike from this point. However, if a pitcher throws from a high three-quarter arm slot or straight over the top, then the angle and thereby the deception may be slightly reduced, though it may still be effective. In the last 10 years or so, many pitchers have gone away from this traditional positioning and instead throw from the opposite side of the rubber. This means that the right-handed pitcher will throw from the left side and a left-handed pitcher will throw from the right side, as shown in figure 2.7. This position can be beneficial for the pitcher who has good movement on the ball, and it can create a slight angle advantage when facing an opposite-side hitter (right-handed pitcher versus left-handed hitter).

By now, you might be thinking that I am talking out of both sides of my mouth. You might be right, but the starting point on the rubber should accommodate the pitcher's movement, arm slot, and alignment to the plate and should aid in deception of the hitter (rather than just fit a preconceived notion that pitchers should start on the same side of the rubber as their throwing arm).

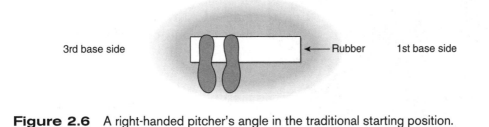

Figure 2.6   A right-handed pitcher's angle in the traditional starting position.

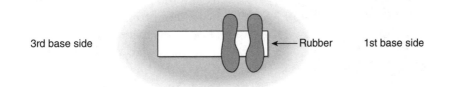

Figure 2.7   A right-handed pitcher's angle in the starting position when throwing from the opposite side of the rubber.

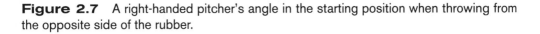

Another interesting strategy that has become popular recently is using the drag mark of the pitcher's back foot as a "tell" or signal for where the pitcher should start on the rubber. In this strategy, if the drag mark goes to the middle of the plate, the pitcher is on the correct side of the rubber because the drag line is a remnant of the pitcher's line to the plate. If the drag line goes away from home plate, the pitcher should move until his mark lines up properly. I have used this method with pitchers for the past year or two and believe it is a good starting point; however, other questions about ball movement and command of the pitcher still need to be answered. In other words, it is a great place to start, but not necessarily an absolute!

QUICK PITCH

I usually observe what side of the rubber a pitcher starts from for a few pens to get a general idea of how his ball moves to certain areas of the plate, as well as to gain a better understanding of his delivery. I will then ask the pitcher why he is on a certain side of the rubber to find out the history behind his reasoning. In time, the pitcher and I will discuss making a switch to another part of the rubber if necessary, or I will leave well enough alone. One size hardly ever fits all.

After a pitcher has taken a sign from the catcher and moves into the set position by taking an initial step with his stride foot and bringing his hands together, the feet should be no wider than armpit-width apart; the toe of the back foot should be lined up with the arch of the front foot (see figure 2.8). This setup will aid the pitcher's ability to lift the front leg (as opposed to swinging), and it also promotes loading the hips, which will be discussed further in chapter 5. Perhaps the greatest function of a narrow base is that it enables the pitcher to start in an athletic position. For most movement in athletics of any kind, athletes should start with a shoulder-width base and with knees bent. A wider stance may limit the pitcher's ability to lift the leg with balance, causing a swinging of the leg to start the delivery, which may limit the pitcher's ability to properly use momentum. Swinging the stride leg instead of lifting it can introduce unbalanced movements that contribute to poor posture. It may also lead to an overrotation of the hips, resulting in a fly-out or spinning movement on landing. Starting with a narrow base decreases these possibilities. Note that I am describing

Figure 2.8 Left-handed pitcher's toe–arch relationship.

optimal positions—not absolutes—and, like everything else, stance and positioning should be evaluated on a case-by-case, pitcher-by-pitcher basis! Look for efficiency first and aesthetics last.

QUICK PITCH

I will often have pitchers implement a component to the delivery known as front loading. Front loading means that the pitcher will place approximately 60 percent of his weight on the stride foot. As he makes his initial move, the weight distribution will cause him to load the back side, because the pitcher will go back before going forward. I have found this little trick to be very useful for pitchers who cannot create momentum out of the stretch position, and it will also help many pitchers learn the flex step, which we will discuss later in the book.

Foot Placement Next to the Rubber

Once the pitcher has determined which side of the rubber to start from and how to properly align his feet, the next thing to determine is how to place the foot on the rubber. Too often, this is overlooked by coaches and pitchers. I was told by my Little League coach that instead of throwing with my back foot resting on top of the rubber, I should start with my back foot just in front of the rubber. That was the very last piece of instruction I ever received about my back foot!

For pitchers to synchronize their pitching motion successfully, they need to understand the role foot placement has in the delivery. Fred Corral, a respected pitching coach, put it best when he told me, "The back foot acts as a rudder used to steer a boat. If the heel of the back foot 'sweeps' and leads the toe [as shown in figure 2.9], alignment issues occur, and the rudder (pivot foot) steers the boat (pitcher) in a poor direction." In many cases, the heel sweep is caused by swinging the stride leg violently instead of simply lifting it with the knee. A pitcher who sweeps the heel has the propensity to throw across his body because of the poor alignment created by the direction of the back foot (see figure 2.10). If that happens, the pitcher might struggle with command or may only command the side of the plate that he is directed toward. In extreme cases, that pitcher can create such a severe angle that his arm will not completely finish its correct path. When the path of the arm is cut off, proper deceleration of the arm is not possible. Over time, this could also injure the arm or shoulder.

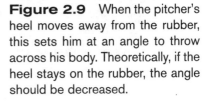

Figure 2.9 When the pitcher's heel moves away from the rubber, this sets him at an angle to throw across his body. Theoretically, if the heel stays on the rubber, the angle should be decreased.

Figure 2.10 Pitcher throwing across his body because of the sweep of the back foot.

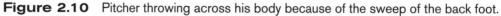

Sandy Koufax Exercise

This exercise helps prevent heel sweeping and promotes front-side loading in the pelvic region. It was taught throughout the Dodgers' system for many years and has been implemented by many successful players, including pitching great Pedro Martinez.

Setup

The exercise should be performed in the bullpen on a pitching rubber while working with a catcher.

Procedure

1. The pitcher stands in the stretch position with his back foot parallel to the pitching rubber.
2. From this position, while still maintaining contact with the rubber, the pitcher slides the toes of the back foot slightly forward so that they are closer to home plate.
3. The pitcher then lifts the outside of the heel (the side nearest to the rubber) so that it is on top of the rubber.
4. The pitcher begins the pitching motion and throws a pitch.

Pitching Point

At first, this exercise may seem awkward to pitchers. Coaches should watch them carefully and encourage them to stay with it for a while to see if it improves direction to the plate and the potential for greater use of the lower half of the body.

Modifications

This exercise should probably not be used with younger pitchers. The pitching motion should be simplified for younger pitchers. Hooking the foot in this manner may be too extreme and may affect overall balance and timing, which are much more important considerations for youth. Coaches should pay close attention to what the back foot is doing when the pitcher lifts the leg; the coach should make sure that the foot is not leading the toe. If this is the case, the young pitcher is most likely in a good mechanical position. Remember, every pitcher's goal should be to start on a solid back foot and land on a solid front foot.

Knee Positioning, Weight Distribution, and Hip Positioning

Once the feet are set and the pitcher has hooked the heel into place, the next area that the coach should observe and evaluate is the knees. I don't have a preference for how a pitcher stands in the set, whether it is completely upright or slightly bent over. However, the pitcher should refrain from extremes such as standing tall and rigid, standing too noticeably hunched over, or standing in a position where his knees do not align equally.

Regarding the knees, the main consideration is comfort and the pitcher's ability to maintain a posture that makes it easy to either attempt a pickoff to a base or make a pitch to the plate. Posture and the overall athleticism of the pitcher are crucial, and both of these can be compromised because of a bad starting point with the knees. If the knees align evenly at the start of the delivery and the weight of the pitcher is spread fairly even between his front side and back side, no further mention of the knees is necessary.

Along with misaligned knees, I have also seen pitchers use many odd setups for the starting position of the hips. Obviously, the starting position for the hips is directly related to the position of the feet, so if the pitcher maintains the back-foot toe to front-foot arch relationship mentioned earlier, the hips will align themselves properly. The pitcher's hips should be completely perpendicular to the rubber and the plate (see figure 2.11*a*). An inward turned hip or one that is severely closed off because of the foot placement can create a disadvantage for the pitcher when he begins to load his hip during the leg lift (see figure 2.11*b*). The loading and unloading of the hips will be addressed in greater detail later in this book.

A moderately to severely open hip, as shown in figure 2.11*c*, can also cause problems. Often, the pitcher who starts with a noticeably open hip is trying to compensate so that he can see a runner. Then, when he wants to throw the ball to the plate, he closes off with an inward turn of the shoulder. Loading problems (as with the closed-hip setup) and alignment issues such as drifting to the open side, which can lead to stepping across the body, can happen with this type of setup and should be avoided if possible. This type of setup can also lead to swinging the stride leg instead of lifting it, which often creates postural disconnects at the beginning of the delivery. In other words, the pitcher is either doomed from the beginning of the delivery or he must compensate in other movements of his delivery to get back on the right track.

So, in conclusion, a suitable and athletic starting position for the stretch is to have a toe–arch relationship of the feet, with the knees bent evenly about shoulder-width or armpit-width apart from one another. From this starting point, the pitcher will be able to stay balanced and aligned properly to the plate, and his subsequent movements will not be hindered.

Figure 2.11   *(a)* Pitcher's proper hip alignment in comparison to hips that are *(b)* closed or *(c)* open.

Leg Lift

The leg lift has already been mentioned several times in this chapter because of its role in creating postural, balance, and alignment issues. Now we'll look more closely at the proper action of the lead leg and its role in other features of the delivery. The primary function of the leg lift is to provide momentum for the delivery itself. The pitcher has to start from a standstill and then create momentum by gaining speed and power through synchronized body movements until ball release. The leg lift is the first movement in creating momentum. It is actually a counterrotation away from where the pitcher will be moving (the plate) to deliver the ball. As a result, it is often thought of as "winding the spring" to throw the ball.

As the pitcher comes set with his hands, he should then lift his leg to a height that is unique and comfortable to him, always keeping the following point of emphasis in mind: The leg lift should take place on the home plate side of the rubber and not around or behind it. See figure 2.12 for an example of an efficient leg lift compared to a less efficient leg lift.

When the foot is directed outside of the knee, the weight of the pitcher is displaced to the heel of his back foot. If the weight goes to the heel, the pitcher's head can go behind his center of gravity (belly button), causing a possible postural inefficiency or flawed alignment to the plate. Some pitchers will take corrective measures in the subsequent movements of their delivery, and in those cases, having the foot outside the knee becomes moot; however, for most pitchers, it is a flaw that cannot be overcome. They are doomed before they make another move.

The same is true for the direction that the pitcher lifts the lead leg. If he overrotates the stride leg and moves it around or behind the rubber, he may get very good torque from the leg lift, but not without consequences. First, when the pitcher overrotates, his back (post) foot often becomes unhooked from the rubber and spins, putting him in line with the batter's box instead of the middle of the plate. Remember the description of the heel sweep and the ensuing alignment issue that accompanies it? This is where it will show up. Besides this problem, overrotation will impede the back knee from angling itself into the plate, which will retard rotation of the lower half. If overrotation occurs, the pitcher's back knee will often stall, waiting to get

Figure 2.12 *(a)* An efficient leg lift creates a better chance for the delivery to be connected, whereas *(b)* a less efficient leg lift creates the chance for movement in the delivery, thus allowing it to become disconnected.

back to a position where the knee can invert and start the rotation to the plate (see figure 2.13). Overrotation leads to faulty alignment and poor rhythm.

Lastly, as we all learned in elementary physics class, for every action there is an equal and opposite reaction. In the case of overrotation during the leg lift, this often shows up as "spinning off" at ball release—the momentum that the pitcher created with overrotation at the beginning of the delivery cannot be harnessed at the end of the delivery. This can result in movement that is not functional, and it often leads to the pitcher having poor command.

A more functional approach to use with the leg lift is to lift the leg at the rubber (or in front of the rubber), as shown in figure 2.14, and then maximize momentum by loading the pelvis, a movement that will be discussed in the upcoming chapters. This technique will allow the pitcher to keep his line to the plate and direct his energy and power straight toward his target. As mentioned, exceptions to the rule can be found in many pitchers; the trick for the coach and player is to know what to change and what to leave alone.

Figure 2.13 Pitcher overrotating the lead leg, which can cause the back knee to stall.

Figure 2.14 Proper leg lift: The pitcher lifts his leg at the rubber.

Hand Positioning and Action

Moving up the kinetic chain, the next area to focus on is the function and movements of the hands in the set position. The hand set is like central command—a point where the glove side and throwing side meet and then go their separate ways to do a job. The throwing side throws the ball, and the glove side provides leverage and direction for the throw. A perfect tandem.

The hand set must be in a starting position that makes it possible for the pitcher to be on time with his delivery, and the action of the hand set provides a rhythm marker for this to occur consistently. Optimally, the pitcher should start with his hands together anywhere from his belt to his chest in what we call a prayer position, as you can see in figure 2.14.

QUICK PITCH

The hands should be in a comfortable position for the individual pitcher. There is nothing worse for a pitcher than to start in a position that isn't natural or comfortable for him. The only questions that need to be addressed are these: Is the position comfortable? Does the position enable the pitcher to conceal the pitch that he is about to throw?

The throwing hand and ball should be securely covered by the glove so that "pitch thieves" cannot see the pitcher's grip and identify what pitch is coming. At leg lift, the hands should travel upward about 2 to 6 inches (5.1 to 15.2 cm) and then break apart as the leg begins descending downward and toward the plate (see figure 2.15). This action is known as a hand bump. The primary function of the hand bump is to create rhythm and timing in the delivery, as well as to serve as a momentum builder for the arm action that occurs shortly after. If the hand bump is greater than 2 to 6

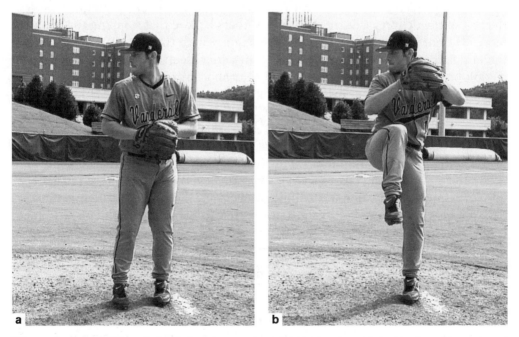

Figure 2.15   The pitcher's hands travel up (an action known as the hand bump) and break apart, giving the pitcher the opportunity to stay on time.

inches, the pitcher runs the risk of making the arm come through late, which works against his chances of getting to a consistent release point. The hand bump will happen primarily in the midline of the pitcher's body, though some pitchers' arm paths may take it closer to the throwing side. As long as it appears to work for the pitcher and the pitcher is consistently on time, hand action will be very individualistic.

 ## Windup Mechanics

Although it has many mechanical similarities to the stretch, the windup features other movements that a coach or pitcher needs to address. Too often, when pitchers move from the windup to the stretch, they use different leg lifts, different hand positions, and in some cases, entirely different movement patterns. Basically, this suggests different mechanics, and that certainly can't help in the pitcher's quest to have a consistent and repeatable delivery. Coach and pitcher must both be responsible for making sure that outside of the first part of the windup, the two deliveries morph into identical replicas of one another.

The Rocker Step

In the windup, the initial movement is the rocker step. The right-handed pitcher will start his windup by moving the left foot straight behind, to the side, or in front of the rubber. The left-handed pitcher will start by moving the right foot. A good amount of wavering back and forth has taken place in baseball circles regarding which direction the foot should move. Some believe that stepping straight behind the rubber provides the pitcher with the best chance to transfer momentum into the rest of the delivery (see figure 2.16*a*). Others believe that stepping to the side is more efficient because the hips will open slightly with the side-to-side movement, thereby making the transfer of momentum easier (see figure 2.16*b*). Yet another faction believes that stepping in front of the rubber is more efficient and effective because the momentum transfer happens in front of the rubber and thus happens closer to the intended target, or the plate (see figure 2.16*c*).

Personally, I do not have a preference as long as the rocker step is relatively short and does not inhibit the pitcher's balance or rhythm—and as long as it helps in transitioning momentum into the delivery and to the plate. Occasionally, I will encounter a pitcher who takes a large rocker step and then fights himself to get back into a rhythmical transition in the lifting portion of the delivery. If that is the case, I simply instruct the pitcher to shorten the step so that a more athletic movement results. I've also seen pitchers who start more facing the side and then overrotate on their leg lift. If this happens, the simple fix is to square the pitcher off and have him step behind or in front of the rubber, giving him less opportunity to overrotate. Other times, I've had pitchers get stuck in their transition with a behind-the-rubber rocker step. The step looked choppy and unathletic, so my fix was to have the pitcher move more to the side or in front of the rubber. I see value in all three methods because this motion is usually a matter of comfort for the pitcher, and what happens in the subsequent movements is probably of greater importance.

Figure 2.16   Rocker steps: *(a)* front, *(b)* side, and *(c)* forward steps. Any of these three types will work for the pitcher. It is a matter of comfort and then making sure that the movement doesn't adversely affect the delivery at a later time.

QUICK PITCH

The rocker step is designed to help the pitcher gain momentum as he goes into his delivery. If you think that more momentum can be gained by either adding or subtracting length to the rocker step or by changing the direction of the step, a change might be quite useful. Like most things, playing around with the rocker step can be helpful.

Hands

In the old days of baseball, pitchers would swing their arms virtually everywhere before making the pitch. Hands swinging overhead and double pumping of the arms before going overhead were fashionable techniques for those times. Then, in the early 1980s, the hand movements gradually stopped, and pitchers took a more functional approach with less movement at the start of the delivery. Coaches and pitchers figured that this would lead to fewer things going wrong at the end of the delivery—almost a "less is more" theory. Pitchers stopped going over their head in the windup, and they were taught to become quicker to the plate in the stretch in order to give the catcher a chance to throw out a would-be base stealer. Thus, the slide step was invented. Today, it is not uncommon to see even very young pitchers using a "no windup" approach—where there is no hand bump or hands overhead in the windup—and also employing a slide step to be more proficient at holding runners on base. Although the slide step has its place in every pitcher's arsenal, the 1980s paradigm of "less is more" is often more damaging to the pitcher than it is useful. Again, as explained in the stretch portion of this chapter, hand momentum is a force multiplier; it starts the arm and promotes a rhythmical quality that can aid the pitcher in being on time and consistent.

Modified Hand Bump Exercise

An easy way to learn the modified hand bump is to start with hands together in the stretch position. When the front leg is lifted, the hands will jump-start themselves by moving upward with the leg; then, as the leg goes down and the pitcher starts his descent to the plate, the arms move back down and separate. The same can be said for the windup—hands move up with the front leg and back down with the front leg. A good way to help the pitcher learn the movement is to tie a string or elastic tubing to the wrist of the glove (note that the pitcher should not throw a ball in this drill) and the front knee and then have the pitcher practice the movement. This is a quick and easy activity to promote the union and rhythm of the front leg and hands before separation.

QUICK PITCH

A mistake that many pitchers make is "cutting off" the throw instead of allowing the arm to complete its throwing path. This can generally be recognized in two distinct ways. The first is a head snap—the head will abruptly jar because the body does not allow the arm to finish the path of deceleration. The second indicator is that the arm will recoil after ball release; instead of the arm staying down during the rotation of the body, it will pop up after abruptly stopping. Neither scenario is functional, and the pitcher should be trained to finish the path of his arm. A good place to start is to remind the pitcher of this deficiency as he plays catch. As with all skills, the tendency for change and transition is greater with daily doses of purposeful practice—another good example of how throwing precedes pitching.

The starting position for the hands in relation to the pitcher's body is also important. When watching major-league pitchers, you will see many starting positions for the hands. Some pitchers start with their hands even with their neck and then move them down as they start their movement toward home plate, while others start with hands at the belt and move them up before throwing. The key for a pitcher is to find something that is comfortable as well as a movement that gives him the ability to use the hand bump to jump-start the arm action. A good place for most to start would be at midchest in the midline of the body. From this position, the hands can easily go up with the lift knee and then go back down, creating the momentum needed to start the arm action.

Other Considerations

In baseball, there are always other considerations because the game involves complex motor skills and individual differences. Once again, the first two considerations described here may seem foreign and unorthodox in this chapter about mechanics, but they are important parts of the fabric that make up the pre-mechanical model.

Small Movements and Gap Movements

When watching a baseball game, you will notice the idiosyncrasies of a hitter preparing to hit or a pitcher preparing to pitch. Adjustments of equipment and practice swings by the hitter are common. Pitchers make similar individualistic movements, some of which are simply the result of nervous energy, but perhaps some have a meaning that the pitcher can use to aid him in making the next pitch. We call these movements that have meaning "small movements" and "gap movements."

Small movements can help cue the pitcher to mimic movements that he wants to make during the delivery. For example, let's say that a pitcher has trouble keeping his eye on the catcher's mitt during the delivery. At the start of his delivery, the pitcher may lift his chin as a subtle reminder to keep his head up and keep his eye on the target. Another example may be a subtle flinch of the front shoulder as a reminder to stay closed when delivering the ball. Whatever the hint is, it should be something that the pitcher uses to aid him in being consistent with his delivery or his pitches. Small movements can range from being extremely subtle to being easily visible or quirky. These movements can pay large dividends if executed consistently.

QUICK PITCH

I instruct my pitchers to use small movements wisely. A pitcher does not need five of these movements just because he has five issues with his delivery. The pitcher should pick out the most important issue or the one that gives him the most trouble and should come up with something that will serve as a reminder for him as he starts his delivery. Hitters do it all the time in their practice swings as they approach an at-bat, so why can't a pitcher?

Gap movements are movements that the pitcher makes in between pitches, or in the gaps of time between pitches. This is where body language, both good and bad, can be seen emanating from the pitcher. The gaps are also spots where the pitcher has the most time to think and talk to himself, both positively and negatively, and this is usually when the game speeds up. For these reasons, it makes sense to have a plan to dismiss poor thoughts and to master gap movements so that they will help the pitcher rather than hurt him. For example, a great gap movement that a pitcher can use after a poorly executed pitch or after the opponent gets a hit or scores a run might be to take a deep breath and wipe away the dirt from the rubber with his spikes, signifying that he is "wiping away" what just happened.

Another aspect of gap movements for a pitcher to consider would be to literally slow his movements down when the game speeds up. Instead of hurrying into action, a pitcher may pretend to be in slow motion with each move that he makes until it is time to unleash the next pitch with a fury. The point of practicing gap movement is no different than practicing a fire drill in grade school—to prepare for a fire if there is one. And in baseball, there most certainly will be fires! The following points give the pitcher and coach an idea of what should be emphasized when working on gap movements:

1. Slow the movements down, especially when your mind is speeding up.
2. Come up with a routine that helps you become "all in" for the next pitch.
3. Remember to breathe big.
4. Remember to think small—the next pitch!

Slide Step Versus Flex Step

Lately, there has been a heavy emphasis placed on controlling the running game by being quick to the plate when runners are on base; the goal is to give the catcher a chance to throw the runner who is trying to steal out. One way to achieve this quickness is the slide step. To initiate the slide step, the pitcher needs to widen the base of his feet in the set position and then barely lift the front foot off the ground to trigger the throw, all the while using his standard motion and arm action. See figure 2.17 for an example of the slide step.

Figure 2.17 Slide step.

When properly executed, the pitcher should take 1.25 to 1.30 seconds to deliver the ball to the plate. (Coaches can measure this with a stopwatch, starting on the pitcher's initial move and stopping when the ball arrives in the catcher's mitt.) After receiving a pitch, a catcher whose arm is considered average by college standards makes the throw from home to second base in approximately 2.00 to 2.05 seconds. All tallied, this provides a runner with less than 3.35 seconds to successfully steal a bag. Given that the traditional stretch delivery takes between 1.4 and 1.8 seconds—depending on the overall tempo of the delivery—it is clear why so many pitchers and coaches elect to go with a slide step when runners are on base. After all, baseball truly is a game of inches and time!

Without a doubt, a good slide step can reduce a runner's lead and make it very difficult for him to get a good jump. It's a valuable tool in the pitching arsenal and one that most coaches teach to players early on. However, the slide step has a downside as well. The quick delivery can keep base runners in check, but it can also introduce poor mechanics. And in some instances, the arm health of the pitcher can be affected.

I am in the camp that believes the slide step will take a toll on a pitcher's arm over a period of time because the pitcher is basically eliminating the use of the lower half of his body and is throwing with "all arm." This all-out exertion and attempt to be four- to five-tenths quicker to the plate can easily take the pitcher out of rhythm, force him to open up early (rushing, flying open), or make his arm come through late. Any one of these actions—or a combination of them—can cause arm issues.

Because of this, I recommend the flex step. The flex step is initiated by the front knee buckling inward toward the back knee as the front hip is pushed to the plate by the back hip. Engaging the hips will create tension in the core of the body, winding it like a spring and preparing it to couple with the upper torso and arm to complete the rotation and deliver the baseball. See figure 2.18 for an example of the flex step.

The flex step may be slightly slower than the slide step, but it is still very effective in controlling the running game. More important for the pitcher, the flex step provides him with the ability to execute good pitches without jeopardizing the health of his arm; it allows the pitcher to access more momentum and allows him to load and use the lower half of his body instead of relying solely on the upper body (and specifically the arm) to create power.

Figure 2.18 Flex step.

Solid starting positions can easily improve mechanics, sometimes without needing to change the delivery, which is reason enough to pay attention to them. Pitching is an activity of precision, and so too is the pitching delivery; the smallest flaw at the beginning of the delivery may factor into the flaws in the middle or at the end. Pitcher and coach must be well aware of this dynamic, and the pitcher must routinely practice starting positions to decrease the chance of developing these flaws, without making the pitcher overly robotic or choreographed. Good starting positions give the pitcher the best chance for developing a strong base for the delivery as well as health.

THREE

Upper-Body Mechanics

The act of throwing the baseball—from the early stages of separating the hands to the release of the ball—is easily the most important part of the pitching delivery. And this seemingly simple act is brimming with variables that make it anything but uncomplicated. First, the pitcher has to be as physically efficient as possible so that he may deliver the ball with maximum velocity, command, and movement while staying injury free. Then, he must conceal the spin, angle, or trajectory of the ball from the hitter as long as possible by using different pitch types and pitch locations, giving himself every opportunity to succeed in defeating the hitter. And lastly, the pitcher must have a certain trust, rooted in the concept of "me versus you" and fortified through deliberate and intentional repetition, that the ball will arrive at the plate rendering positive results. All of this to simply throw the ball and start the action of the game! Who said baseball was easy?

The Cycled Approach

Before proceeding into an explanation of the mechanics of the upper body, I want to point out that pitchers and coaches need to have a plan for how to attack these areas on a day-to-day basis. The goal of every coach should be development of players, and every player who is serious about the game seeks improvement. So how should coaches and players attack mechanics? The best way is to use a cycled approach where the pitcher goes through purposeful repetitions of a particular skill, improves (even if only the slightest bit), and then moves on to another set of skills. In most instances, mastery of certain skills may be required to move forward, but this approach will work if a foundation is set and eventually mastered. The following sections serve as a checklist of the development cycle that I adhere to and the content that is included in it. Coaches and pitchers should feel free to change the order of the skills if needed to make them fit into their own styles or circumstances.

Why exactly is the cycled approach better than others? The parts of the delivery are connected and are largely dependent on one another; therefore, it stands to reason that each time a player cycles through the different delivery components, change in movements can be influenced. When the pitcher is working on one area, other areas are being influenced indirectly. This helps snap the pieces of the puzzle together. This is connection.

Taking into account all of these factors, it would be easy for any discussion about pitching to become intricate and complicated, but one of my main goals in the next two chapters is to keep the science behind pitching mechanics as simple as possible. Pitching (i.e., throwing) is a terribly complex skill, and thoroughly understanding the mechanics that make throwing possible is a daunting task. I have tried to keep this as informal as I can by using as many images and drills as possible so that you don't need a kinesiology degree to understand and apply the concepts. Also note that it should be a goal for every player and coach to take what is complex about pitching and simplify it so that the player can stay clear and focused.

Rhythm and Tempo of the Upper Body

In this chapter, we'll discuss how the mechanics of the upper body work to propel the ball, as well as ways to make these movements more efficient. But first, let's consider the vital role that rhythm and tempo play within the delivery. Rhythm links movements together, and tempo can help fix issues within the delivery because the body learns how to be more precise and fluid when the speed of the delivery is accelerated at the right times. Rhythm is the sequential unlocking of body parts—snapping movements together to create a flow in the delivery. So why does this matter and how does it affect upper- and lower-body mechanics? It's significant because mechanics of a body part or series of body parts—no matter what is practiced or how the pitcher practices them—are inconsequential if rhythm and tempo are not inherently present. The pitcher could have superior arm action or an efficient glove side, but something will still be missing if rhythm and correct tempo are absent. The delivery may theoretically be right, but it won't feel or look quite right, as evidenced by the lack of consistency a pitcher shows with his pitches. Pitchers need to find the correct rhythm and tempo so that one movement meshes into the next, eliminating any pauses, stops, or gaps of time between movements.

QUICK PITCH

The correct rhythm and tempo will be unique for each individual pitcher based on athleticism, length of movements, and skill level. The pitcher should always strive to maximize his tempo so that he can better stay "connected" through the delivery. Bigger pitchers or pitchers who lack athleticism must sometimes stay slower in their tempo, especially at the beginning of the delivery, whereas smaller pitchers or those more athletic can sometimes move at a faster rate.

Hands-Knees Exercise

This is an easy exercise that helps pitchers gain an understanding of rhythm. To execute this exercise, the pitcher simply practices the movement in which the hands go up when the knees go up; the hands go down when the knees go down, and then the hands break. This exercise serves two purposes: One, it gives the pitcher a reference point for how to keep his lower body and upper body in sync with one another; and two, it helps the pitcher understand how the hands serve as a jump start. Instead of having the hands stay still and then pulling the ball out of the glove, the pitcher is creating timing for separation as well as building momentum for the arm swing that follows.

Posture

The setup portion of the stretch and windup deliveries was discussed in chapter 2. These starting positions could also be called postures. Postures can be thought of as the many positions of the body during movement. For instance, if I walk from one side of the room to the other, my posture will change each step. Like rhythm and tempo, posture cannot be categorized as a feature of upper- or lower-body mechanics alone; it is a component of both. For the pitcher, posture starts as he sets up in the windup or stretch. As the pitcher moves his body toward home, his movements create either efficiency or inefficiency based on earlier postures. Therefore, the pitcher must be sure to start in a posture that gives him the best chance to maintain efficiency through the delivery. Generally, poor posture in the pitcher causes a poor directional line to the plate, or it creates movements that aren't synchronized with prior movements. Examples of poor posture can be seen during the descent of the pitcher to the plate. The body may move to the open side (right-handed pitcher leans toward third base), causing the pitcher to stride across the body. Conversely, the body may lean back to the glove side (right-handed pitcher leans toward first base) prematurely or too forcefully, causing a flying out or spinning effect. Either way, the pitcher who displays this characteristic often has trouble locating to one side of the plate or the other, and he may also be extremely inconsistent with a certain pitch or pitches.

QUICK PITCH

An easy way for a pitcher to properly apply the center of gravity is to focus on keeping his chin over his belt. This positioning basically aligns the pelvis, spine, and head with one another. If the alignment stays intact through the linear portion of the delivery (lifting the leg and stepping toward home, as rotational forces work up the kinetic chain) with minimal change, the pitcher's chance of achieving balance as well as consistently delivering the ball in the same arm slot increases exponentially. Put another way, the head, spine, and pelvis carry the body out to the plate so that the arms can load and unload the ball.

To get a clear idea of posture, think of a partial skeleton delivering a pitch. Because lifting the leg initiates the move toward home plate, the pelvic region (we call it the center) is like the engine of the train heading toward home. Wherever the center goes, the spine and the head will follow, especially if the pitcher is to stay balanced. The spine connects the center and the head. The head starts in a position directly over the pitcher's center of gravity. For our purposes, the center of gravity is usually just above the belly button. Posture then, is an essential element in commanding the flight path of the ball – very important for the target-seeking pitcher.

T-Drill

Besides providing pitchers with feedback regarding posture, this drill teaches them how to use their center—the core—to guide them in a straight line to the target. This drill can be very effective when used between pitches in a bullpen session.

Setup

Use tape, chalk, or other material to create a "T" on a gym floor or flat field surface. The T should be at least 3 feet (91 cm) wide on the horizontal plane and 5 feet (152 cm) long on the vertical plane. Pair each pitcher with a partner whose job will be to increase the pitcher's awareness of his posture through the delivery. The pitcher performs the drill by simulating the throwing of a pitch, or with an actual thrown ball.

Procedure

1. The pitcher assumes the stretch position with his post-leg (pivot) foot placed so that it is centered at the junction of the horizontal and vertical lines of the T as if he was placing his foot on a pitching rubber.
2. As the pitcher lifts his stride leg and his hands to begin the pitching motion, the partner gently pushes him and tries to disrupt his posture.
3. The pitcher, in anticipation of the push from his partner, must tighten his core behind his belly button before starting his motion to help resist the loss of posture.
4. The pitcher simulates throwing a pitch by completing the pitching motion and striding toward his target in as straight a line as possible while resisting the attempt to disrupt his posture.

Pitching Points

Make sure the pitcher's chin is centered over his belt at the start of the motion. Also, instruct partners to push gently and to vary the direction of their push each time. Watch to see that the pitcher does not alter his delivery by opening his front knee and front foot just so that he can land on the horizontal line. In the traditional T drill, the pitcher is instructed to stride in the direction of the vertical plane of the T, but that is not necessary here. The T is merely a suggestion and guide for the pitcher.

Arm Action

High-level throwers usually have one thing in common: They possess a quick arm. Their arms may function differently in how they load and unload the ball, the route they take with the hand and arm, or the size and direction of the arm swing, but once they land and their body rotates fully to throw the ball, the arm becomes a lightning quick blur. Arm action, more than any other part of the delivery, is most noticed by opposing teams, fans, and scouts. A pitcher's arm action is rated as good or poor rather quickly. It is the piece that stands out most of all.

Arm action may be *the* most important piece of the delivery. It is directly influenced by the rest of the kinetic chain based on the amount of momentum that is sustained through the delivery to reach the arm and help propel the ball. The more momentum that can be kept from leaking away from the arm's efficiency—and the higher the rate of force development (speed) that the body and arm can generate—the greater chance the pitcher has of owning a lightning quick arm. It is also known that the shoulder internally rotates at 7000 degrees per second, which is the fastest motion in sport (Clearing Up the Rotator Cuff Controversy, www.ericcressey.com). This further emphasizes the value of rhythm, tempo, and intent when pitching a baseball. As mentioned earlier, my goal is to keep this discussion of the mechanics of the pitching motion as user friendly as possible, so let's get right to the root of arm action, how it works, and how the pitcher can improve his level of proficiency.

QUICK PITCH

Have you ever heard someone say that a pitcher has a great arm but doesn't use his body? This usually means that the pitcher doesn't use rhythm, tempo, posture, and alignment to properly load his body when making the pitch. He may move like a pitcher, but the movements don't have anything behind them—they are weak or uncoordinated, making the pitcher appear to throw with "all arm."

Arm Slot

Arm slot is the angle at which the pitcher throws from, and it is a function of the spine's angle that the pitcher has when he is releasing the ball. Many people might think that arm slot is a product of lowering or raising the arm before release; however, the arm slot is actually produced by the posture that the pitcher takes as he lowers his stride leg down to the plate. See figure 3.1 for several examples of arm slot based on the pitcher's spine angle at release.

For our purposes, the arm slot of the pitcher is unique to the individual and should only be changed when another angle would present more freedom, better leverage, or increased skill. In other words, the pitcher might look stiff from one arm angle, but he may appear free and easy from another. A good test for determining the proper arm slot for a pitcher is to have him throw from the shortstop position.

Figure 3.1   Arm slot based on the pitcher's spine angle at release: *(a)* high, *(b)* three-quarter, and *(c)* low.

Have the pitcher stand at shortstop, and then hit him a ground ball. Instruct him to throw the ball over to first base as if he was making a routine 6-3 play. Often, this action will uncover the natural arm slot of the thrower. This occurs because the shortstop throw is a natural throw, there is no mound to influence the way the ball is thrown, and when throwing from that position, the pitcher won't be thinking about his pitching mechanics. Once the slot has been determined by this drill, the pitcher should go to the bullpen and try to re-create this newfound arm slot on the mound. The arm slot can also affect the pitcher's mechanical leverage, as well as the arsenal of pitches that he might be capable of throwing; therefore, the slot is important in determining the pitcher's total package. At the collegiate level, arm slot adjustments are usually made because the pitcher is not fluid when he throws, because he throws without ball movement, experiences chronic pain, or because he has not experienced success. This lack of success has made many high or three-quarter arm slot pitchers into submarine pitchers!

Arm Action Types

The types of arm action used by pitchers can be placed in five main categories: the classic (long, hand-driven) arm action, the classic with climbing elbows, the horizontal W, the inverted W, and the inverted L. All of these arm actions have their strong points and limitations, and hybrids of the various types are common. This section simply provides a way to identify and categorize the types of arm action.

Classic Arm Action

The long, hand-driven arm action is the most common arm action, possibly because it is often taught at the youth level. That's why we classify this as the classic arm action. This arm action features a large backswing with a long arc after the hand break. As the ball is taken out of the glove, the arm is maneuvered, or steered, by the hand; the hand manipulates the path of the arm (see figure 3.2). The classic arm action involves a fluid, graceful movement that has some aesthetic value. However, these aesthetic qualities do not necessarily increase the efficiency of the arm action, and because the hand drives the arm, the classic arm action can limit the function of the scapula that may increase throwing capacity (velocity). A lot will depend on the individual pitcher, as it is with all the types of arm action.

Figure 3.2 Classic arm action.

Classic Arm Action With Elbow Climb

A direct descendent of the classic arm action is the classic with elbow climb (also known as EC). The classic EC differs from the traditional classic in that once the arm reaches full extension after the hand break, the hand drive is replaced by the climbing of the elbows upward en route to a scapular loading, followed by the traditional unloading of the baseball (see figure 3.3). This arm action can also contain properties of the horizontal W and the inverted W depending on how the pitcher breaks his hands and the route his arm takes behind him. I like this type of arm action because of its propensity to enhance rhythm and timing, to increase the probability of scapular loading, and to permit a sense of freedom and fluidness in the motion.

Figure 3.3 Classic arm action with elbow climb.

Horizontal W Arm Action

Another type of action, the horizontal W arm action, occurs when the hands break away from and in front of the body, and the arms are immediately driven with the elbows to form a W (see figure 3.4). This arm action can look very stiff if the arm loop is shorter, but it can also be quite powerful because of its loading capabilities. The elbows generally stay parallel to or just below the shoulders, which is the main difference that separates this arm action from the inverted W.

Figure 3.4 Horizontal W arm action.

Inverted W Arm Action

The inverted W arm action is a result of a pronounced climbing of the elbows past shoulder height, placing the forearm and hand directly underneath. The pitcher creates an M (inverted W) as the front foot lands (see figure 3.5). The inverted W can create sufficient power as well, but rhythm and timing issues are commonly seen. Many experts believe that this type of arm action can lead to injury because of the elbow height and the force it places on the elbow and shoulder during the throw.

Figure 3.5   Inverted W arm action.

Inverted L Arm Action

The last of the five arm actions is the inverted L. This arm action's main characteristic is that the arms become asymmetrical early after the hand break. As the hands move away from one another, the throwing arm remains in the inverted W position while the front arm lengthens or straightens, taking on an L-shaped appearance (see figure 3.6).

Figure 3.6   Inverted L arm action.

In straightening the arm, the pitcher is likely attempting to create more force in the throw; however, timing can be a major problem with this arm action, and many L arm action throwers have the propensity to "pull off" or spin off of their pitches.

Scapular Loading in the Arm Action

No matter what arm action the pitcher uses, at foot strike (when the front foot touches down) and into foot landing, the action will produce a scapular pinch or scapular loading. The scapulae are two flat, triangular bones found on the posterior aspect of the shoulder that connects the humerus and the clavicle. Eighteen muscles either originate from or insert into the scapula, which makes up the shoulder girdle; four of the muscles that originate from the scapula form the rotator cuff. Most of the movements that can be made by the shoulder directly affect the scapula.

Because the scapula is the epicenter of movement, stability, and mobility of the shoulder, pitchers need to have a general understanding of this area. Having knowledge of the scapula will help the pitcher maximize its use, power, and efficiency. To have a lightning quick arm, the pitcher must have intent, tempo, and no stoppages during the delivery. He must understand that the arm action redirects itself at a critical point in the delivery. The arm goes back behind the pitcher in some form or fashion, and then it reverses itself in order to propel the ball forward. This reversal is scapular loading, and the faster the action is reversed, the greater the potential for efficiency and power.

The movement of scapular loading is the rapid horizontal abduction of the arm—creating what some call the scapular pinch—followed by a rapid horizontal adduction, which is the action that creates the release of the ball. An easy way to think of these actions is "load and unload." This process has also been compared to a bird flapping its wings; the wings spread out and retract, and then flap forward to protract. Loading takes place as the initial arm action—the separation of hands and subsequent movement and direction of the arm—repositions to reverse itself (see figure 3.7a). This repositioning takes place as the front foot touches down (often referred to as foot strike) and then moves into full landing (often referred to as foot plant). The unloading takes place as the arm is reversed back into external rotation, the ball is released, and then the elbows close, causing a hunching (see figure 3.7b). This hunching and closing of the elbows at the release point is a major reason why the glove-side action, discussed in the next section, is an important piece in upper-body mechanics.

Every part of the arm action and the way both arms interact with one another during the delivery will directly affect the force generated to make the throw. Arm action and glove-side action must work together to create synergy, timing, and power. Scapular training—whether through throwing, throwing drills, work with light dumbbells, or resistance training—should be a central component of a pitcher's training.

Figure 3.7 (a) When the pitcher loads his arm to throw, he retracts and stabilizes the scapula; (b) as the pitcher unloads the ball, the scapula stabilizes and helps propel the arm forward.

Glove-Side Action

The proper action of the glove side has been debated for quite some time. Growing up, I saw many coaches teach pitchers to pull and tuck the glove side as the pitcher turned or rotated to release the ball. This seemed to make perfect sense because it applied force to the rotation that the pitcher needed in order to maximize the throw. Unfortunately, the pull and tuck also presented timing problems and caused misplaced energy. Once this action was emphasized, the pitcher would pull the glove side so hard that the throwing arm had no chance to catch up, making it late; in addition, the head would be pulled away (head snap) from the arm at the release point (see figure 3.8). This action caused great stress on the arm, especially on the elbow, and likely resulted in many injuries over time. This action is also known in some circles as "forearm fly-out" because of the arm snapping out and around just after the external rotation into release. The result of the head snapping away from

Figure 3.8 Pulling or tucking the glove too much causes a disconnection of rhythm and timing, resulting in misfired throws and a potential risk of injury.

Figure 3.9 Pinch and swivel.

the arm is excess repeated force on the elbow, causing trauma to the medial side of the elbow. This type of movement is often responsible for damage to the ulnar collateral ligament—in baseball terms, the Tommy John ligament.

Sometime in the early 2000s, Tom House introduced the "pinch and swivel" concept for the glove-side action of a pitcher. This action was intended to eliminate tucking the glove by prompting the pitcher to hold the glove side out in front of the body, as shown in figure 3.9, and let the body carry itself to the glove. The "pinch" was closing the glove, a movement that had a firm, blocking type of feel to it. The "swivel" was a timing mechanism; the glove would swivel from its original position of thumb down, pocket down to thumb up, pocket up. This addressed the problems that the tuck and pull method caused, but it also presented its own challenges if the pitcher took the method too literally. The pinch and swivel technique often took the rhythm and, more important, the freedom out of the glove side and the delivery. The pitcher started to look "blocky" and "choppy," and the freedom and whip seemed to be gone from the delivery. The pitcher looked robotic and stiff.

As with most things in baseball, the best glove-side action is probably somewhere in between the old-school traditional methods (pull and tuck) and the new-school version (pinch and swivel) that is currently in vogue. Teaching the proper use of the glove side is difficult because a lot of movements are happening simultaneously in the pitching motion, and explaining them can be challenging, to say the least.

One pitcher may understand and implement a certain cue, while another pitcher may completely misunderstand and misuse it. House's pinch and swivel method was often perceived and implemented incorrectly. This is what my friend Brent Strom, a former big-league pitching coach and now a minor-league pitching coordinator, refers to as "verbal terrorism." As explained in the next section, the throwing side and glove side should load the arm for throwing by mirroring and counterbalancing each other out of the hand break and then move into a scapular pinch at foot strike and foot plant (see figure 3.10). The action should happen with great freedom, range of motion, quickness, and power all rolled into one movement. This does not occur with the pull-down (which is out of control, overly forceful, and out of synchronization) or the pinch (which is choreographed, stiff, too firm, and robotic). Instead, I recommend using a tempered hybrid of the two so that the action is active and free, yet firm and leveraged at the same time.

Figure 3.10 Efficient glove-side foot plant.

Once the pitcher starts to rotate his upper body toward the plate, the unloading process begins. As the pitcher begins to rotate, the glove-side hand closes to keep the desired drive line to the plate (pinch and swivel), but the spacing between the glove and the chest will narrow as the pitcher arrives at his release point and then beyond (see figure 3.11). Again, this is not a forceful tuck, but it's not a robotic "take the body to the glove" either. A good analogy is wrapping your hand around a pole and then pulling yourself toward it. At the end of the delivery, the glove-side hand will finish somewhere in between the armpit and the midline of the chest from the belly button to the waist (see figure 3.12). We refer to this area as the box.

Figure 3.11 Closing of the glove-side hand where spacing between the glove and chest narrows.

Figure 3.12 Glove-side hand finishes in the box, which is an area between the armpit and midline of the chest from the belly button to the waist.

Glove-Side Action Drill

This is an excellent drill that allows the pitcher to work on maintaining a feeling of stability throughout the pitching motion. It forces the pitcher to direct energy appropriately.

Setup

For this drill, you need Thera-Band or similar tubing, heavy baseballs, and two partners for every pitcher. Use flat ground or a pitching mound. The pitcher may throw to a catcher or a net.

Procedure

1. The pitcher starts in a "matched" stance whereby the arms are symmetrically equal and opposite of each other when the front foot lands the feet are spread apart as if landing after the stride, and the hands are separated as they would be shortly after the hand break. A length of tubing is attached to each hand. One of the partners stands directly behind the pitcher in a line to home plate and holds the tubing attached to the throwing hand; the other partner stands to the pitcher's back side holding the tubing attached to the pitcher's glove hand.

2. To initiate the drill, the pitcher rocks back on his pivot foot to create momentum and shift his weight. As this happens, the partner holding the glove-side tubing should apply pressure to force the pitcher to maintain stability.

3. The pitcher rotates his body and moves his throwing arm to simulate a pitch. As the pitcher does this, the partner holding the glove-side tubing will exert pressure and pull the tubing downward. The pitcher must try to resist this attempt to pull his glove arm backward and must try to maintain his glove "in the box" in front of his body.

4. The pitcher follows through with the simulated pitch. The partner holding the tubing on the throwing arm should allow the arm to move freely through the pitching motion with limited pressure.

Pitching Points

The glove-side partner should not pull too much and inhibit the pitcher from moving the glove side freely. Check for athleticism throughout the movement. Make sure that the front-side loop is not overly firm or rigid. Also check other key areas as in any drill: head stability and direction, chin over belt, and so on. This drill is especially effective when the pitcher is unaware that he has a poor glove side.

Modifications

To enhance the drill, add a heavy ball to the pitcher's glove. This will provide further resistance and awareness of the use of the front side. Follow the same steps as described. Next, eliminate the partner holding the tubing on the throwing arm and allow the pitcher to throw a baseball to a catcher or into a net. Finally, eliminate both partners, follow the same procedures, and let the pitcher throw unimpeded.

PEN SESSION   Training the Arm Action

The most effective way to train arm action is to eliminate all pauses or stops from the arm action once the hands are separated and the arm begins its arc or swing. This alone will smooth out the arm path and allow for greater transfer of momentum and force. This coincides with the idea stated earlier that throwing precedes pitching. If a pitcher becomes more skilled with his arm action on a daily basis through playing catch, a transfer of these arm action skills to the mound will be more possible if not inevitable.

To train the arm to move faster, the pitcher must have the intention (purpose) of moving his arm . . . drum roll please, FASTER! He does this through daily throwing, plyometric upper-body exercises (e.g., medicine ball), drill work emphasizing arm action (e.g., backward chaining), and overload-underload throwing. These exercises can be found in chapter 10 as well as on the companion DVD. It may sound too easy, but with proper planning, deliberate repetition, and the correct intention, pitchers can certainly acquire an increased efficiency in their arm action.

 # Arm and Glove Synchronization

Now that arm action and glove-side action have been addressed, it is time to mesh the two and fully understand what the upper body does during the delivery. The importance of rhythm in the delivery has been mentioned several times already, and the harmony between the throwing arm and glove arm will contribute to this rhythm. The human body is bilateral; that is, if you sliced it down the middle from head to toe, each side would be a mirror image of the other side. With that said, and because the shoulders are attached to the "coat hanger" we refer to as the shoulder girdle, it makes sense that when one side performs a movement, the other will respond similarly.

Creating symmetry between front (glove) and back (throwing) side is a matter of the pitcher understanding where the arm goes after the hands break at the midline of the body. Wherever the throwing arm goes and whatever distance it travels, the glove side should create a mirror image and a counterbalance by going in the exact opposite direction (see figure 3.13). If the glove side mimics the throwing side in length and angle, the pitcher will have a very good chance to be on time at the moment of truth: the release point. Consistently being on time at the release point gives the pitcher the ability to throw the ball where he wants and also gives him the best opportunity for making consistent secondary pitches. House referred to this as "equal and opposite." We refer to it as matching. Both mean the same thing, but the term *matching* creates a more visual image that the pitcher can perceive faster. We have been matching things our whole lives.

Using both sides of the upper body in tandem should also increase power output in the delivery. It is obvious to any pitcher that he must produce great effort on his throwing side, specifically his arm, to make a throw with any velocity. It should be equally obvious that if the pitcher uses the glove side to gain more leverage and produce more power, greater velocity or power can result. I use the terms *load and unload* when describing the role of the two sides of the upper body, a phrase coined by Paul Nyman of SetPro, whom I have referred to earlier. Loading of the upper body is accomplished when both sides are on time for the scapular load at foot plant. The chest is stretched, the upper thoracic spine arches without compromising posture (think of the head staying still and remaining over the belt), and the elbows are pinching (getting closer) toward one another. If the "no pauses, stops, or gaps" rule of athleticism is adhered to, a strong stretch reflex occurs, and the shoulders begin their rotation toward the plate. The arm moves back into external rotation, and then unloading occurs. Unloading

Figure 3.13 Symmetry between the front and back side with the arms creating mirror images.

happens throughout the acceleration and release of the ball, as the elbows close the distance between each other during forward trunk flexion and as the arm decelerates.

Slow-Medium-Fast Arm Interaction Exercise

This exercise is designed to help the pitcher understand the idea of symmetry. It helps the pitcher develop awareness of where the throwing arm is going behind him so that he can work on matching the glove side with it. The slow and medium speeds allow the pitcher to make corrections to the glove-side action, attempting to maintain symmetry with the throwing side. Then the pitcher puts the skill together by making the fast or normal throw. In other words, the pitcher first goes through the delivery or the critical area of the delivery in slow motion, noting where his body is in space and noting the subsequent movements. Then he adds speed. He goes a little faster and then faster until he develops a "feel" at full speed. This exercise can also be done using a backward chaining method; the pitcher starts at the end of the delivery, making corrections on the way back and then proceeding forward through the delivery.

Upper-Body Finish

As mentioned, throwing a baseball is one of the fastest motions in all of sports. And with speed and power comes the potential for injury. Obviously, the pitcher has to finish a throw, but specific points need to be addressed in relation to decelerating the arm. The goal for any pitcher is to find a way to slow down the throwing arm for as

Figure 3.14   The pitcher stays on his throw and then clears his head out of the way to complete the axis of rotation.

Figure 3.15   The pitcher does not stay on his throw, and the head pulls away from the arm early. This delivery includes a potential risk. This is seen more decisively when watching slow-motion video. Coach and pitcher can decide whether the lead lean is a by-product of posture/arm slot or a disconnected movement.

long as possible. The head, spine, and throwing arm are the most important areas to concentrate on for properly finishing the throw and slowing the arm.

When a pitcher is decelerating the arm, the main function of the head is to simply get out of the way. This is known as head clearing (see figure 3.14). As mentioned earlier, the head snap (as shown in figure 3.15), which is caused by pulling and tucking the glove during release, is the culprit behind elbow injuries because of the force that it takes away from the elbow joint. A better method is for the pitcher to take his nose to the middle of the plate at the release point. After this occurs, the head will veer a bit to one side (right-handed pitcher toward first base and left-handed pitcher toward third) so that a full rotation can occur and the arm can finish. These two head movements are different in that the second one lets the shoulder girdle rotate around the spine's axis and doesn't create a deficiency; in contrast, the head snap is a movement that is forced and is the result of poor timing, which creates a deficiency. This is an important distinction!

The spine's main job is to establish the posture of the pitcher, and this varies according to arm slot. At the release, the upper body rotates in a catapulting fashion, the head clears, and the rotation continues until the arm stops decelerating. For the arm to finish its full arc, the pitcher will want to finish with his upper body and chest over his front knee; his arm should be going to his opposite (glove-side) hip, and this is done by the back hip pulling around the front hip after ball release.

This will ensure that he has given his arm ample time to slow down. The arm itself is the final piece to the deceleration puzzle. At release, the arm will finish the arc of the throwing-arm path. Think of a table saw; whatever direction the arm goes after the hand break, the arm will continue on that same circular path—like the blade of a saw—through the entire range of motion. This, along with spine angle, is what determines arm slot. The end of this arc, though, is where many deficiencies occur. The pitcher will often cut himself off, shortening the arc and the finish. He may completely stop the arm or recoil (pull up) because of his inability to keep his chest over his knee. Often, this is due to a mechanical flaw or a strength or flexibility issue, and it must be addressed immediately.

QUICK PITCH

The pivot (back) hip joint rotating around the stride-leg (front) hip joint is also highly responsible for deceleration of the arm. If a good rotation of the hip joint occurs, the arm will naturally finish the throwing arc. If this rotation is stifled or inhibited, the arm will snap across the body like a rubber band or will cause the pitcher to recoil the arm. If I have a pitcher who recoils or snaps his arm across his body at finish, the first place I look for possible clues is the hip region. Remember, it is all connected.

Pronation has also become a popular buzzword in pitching circles. As the pitch is released, the arm is equipped to decelerate by pronating—the thumb starts to move down, turning the hand inward (see figure 3.16). This is a natural event, though some pitchers do it more naturally than others, and some pitchers start the process earlier (at or just after ball release). Many coaches are starting to have their pitchers train the arm to pronate with greater strength and earlier. The idea is that the pitchers can strengthen this movement and avoid injury. I fully endorse trying to strengthen pronation; the muscles that are responsible for pronation are the same muscles in the upper arm and forearm that we are trying to make stronger anyway, so it makes sense to address this movement.

Figure 3.16 Pronation of the pitcher's hand at release.

Upper-Body Considerations for the Youth League Pitcher

When dealing with youth league pitchers, the coach does not need to cover all the previous points; however, a young pitcher should pay attention to certain points of emphasis in order to achieve short-term success and long-term improvement. Movement patterns establish themselves at a fairly early age, so deliberate and purposeful repetitions on correct fundamentals can set the foundation for a solid base. Here are some important points that youth pitchers should keep in mind:

Rhythm and Tempo

Work on a one-piece delivery with no pauses, stops, or gaps. Understand that the hands work with the knees for timing and that speed can create precision in the delivery if momentum is building. Remember that a car can't go directly from first to fifth gear—build speed throughout the delivery. Also, understand that balance happens throughout the delivery, not simply at one point in the delivery.

Posture

Remember to keep the chin over the belt, tightening the belly button on the lift. Also remember that the center, especially the front hip, can take the pitcher EXACTLY where he wants to go.

Arm Slot

Correct arm slot may take some time to find, but understand what feels the best or what gives you the best opportunity for freedom and rhythm as well as velocity. As mentioned, a good test is to make a long throw from the outfield or from shortstop; a longer throw will generally give you an idea of what slot to throw from.

Arm Action

Eliminate pauses or stops in the arm action. Work to have a smooth and efficient arm action. Train the loading portion of the arm (scapular loading) through upper-body plyometric exercises such as Crossover Symmetry or medicine ball training. Above all, become very skilled in throwing—and throw a lot! There is no substitute for purposeful repetitions.

Glove Side

Understand "matching" and practice accordingly. Be aware that the glove side must provide direction and stability to promote using both sides of the body. Once the arm action is mastered, go to work on the glove side. Practice keeping the glove in the box, or thereabouts, to promote staying on line and to enhance the unloading process.

The pitcher and coach must first understand that the delivery is about connecting body parts together to make efficient movements that are coordinated and timed correctly. Once they understand this, they can begin to realize where to start and what actions to take to correct the pitcher's flaws. After identifying what needs to be corrected, the next step is to simplify the process as much as possible. They should isolate the critical area and focus on why the movement is happening. Is the root cause a movement that is happening before the flaw? Is it a physical constraint, such as joint instability or a lack of flexibility, that might be causing the problem? Is the flaw rooted in the history of the pitcher? Did he need to make this movement when he was younger or weaker to compensate so that he could compete? The flaw is not always as cut-and-dry as one might think. Find the root and reason first, simplify, and then execute a clear and concise plan of action.

Lower-Body Mechanics and Finish

When I was a youth player, one of the first pieces of pitching advice I received from a baseball coach was to use my legs more during my delivery. I was only eight or nine at the time, and although I understood the concept, I couldn't quite put my finger on how to approach doing it. There was no more mention of this for a few more years, and then I was approached by another coach with the same advice: I needed to use my legs more. When I asked the coach how to do this, he gave me that look that coaches sometimes give. You know, they tilt their head and act as if they can't believe that you don't know how, or they look at you as though you must have been absent for the two months that they covered lower-body mechanics earlier in the season. After scratching his head a couple of times and tilting his head back and forth, this coach peered down at me and offered, "You *do* understand that your legs are the strongest part of your body, and that in order for you to throw harder, you must be able to use them more in your delivery, right?" I replied that this made perfect sense, and he continued. "You just have to find a way to push off the rubber with greater force. You will simply have to find a way to do that, okay?" And that was my first and last lesson on how to use my legs—the strongest muscles in my body—to become a more powerful and efficient pitcher.

Lower-body mechanics are probably the least understood part of the delivery. Pitchers who use their legs efficiently often do so naturally and without any provocation from a coach. They have simply learned how to use them through trial and error or by mimicking a favorite pitcher whom they have watched on television or at the ballpark. For others, the "intent" that they put behind their pitch recruits more musculature to fire within their core and legs. In essence, the pitcher uses his legs without trying to use them or through pure aggression.

What makes the lower half of the body even more misunderstood is that the inner workings of the core and legs cannot easily be seen with the naked eye or even a video camera, thereby presenting problems for a coach who needs to teach or a player who needs to learn. Bones are surrounded by muscles, ligaments, and tendons, which are then wrapped in skin, all making it difficult to see how the body works. The good news is that the pitcher can focus on two or three areas of his lower body that will help him in becoming more efficient and perhaps more powerful without the need for 3-D imaging or technology. The way his pitches react and the way it makes his arm feel will be enough to teach him.

Rhythm and Tempo of the Lower Body

Not to beat a dead horse here, but rhythm and tempo must be given their proper due when it comes to understanding how the lower body functions. The kinetic chain of pitching starts at the feet and finishes out through the fingertips to the finishing point of the delivery. Each movement made is largely determined by what happened (muscles firing), when it happened (rhythm and timing), and how much it happened (momentum) from start to finish of the delivery. Just as there was a relationship between loading and unloading in the upper body—with the scapular pinch just before release and then the closing of the elbows just after (see chapter 3)—the lower body has its own loading and unloading mechanism: The leg lifts and the pelvis loads, the center of the body is carried to the plate (sustaining the load), rotation occurs, the ball is released, and the back hip joint unloads and rotates around the front hip joint to produce the finish. Figure 4.1 identifies the various parts of the lower body and their role in the pitching delivery. As you read through them, keep in mind the idea of "connection." If the body parts move in sequence and on time, efficient movements occur. The energy created by each movement is either integrated into the next movement or lost. The pitcher's job is to integrate as much energy as possible into the next movement of the kinetic chain until the ball is released; therefore, timing (rhythm) is essential, and the speed of the delivery (tempo) can either hamper or enhance the synergy of the movements.

Balance and Momentum

Before we delve into the nuts and bolts of lower-body mechanics, be sure to note that the lower body—feet, legs, and hips—is directly responsible for the creation of momentum in the delivery. The pitcher starts the delivery by moving the feet and lifting the leg, which generates the force needed to propel the ball. This momentum builder is referred to as the tempo of the delivery. Along those same lines, the lower body is responsible for maintaining balance during these movements, allowing rhythm and timing to occur. The pitcher wants to gain momentum so that more force can be harnessed and applied; at the same time, he needs to remain balanced so that the rhythm and timing of his movements will allow him to apply these forces at the proper time. As mentioned in chapter 2, balance serves as one of the seven foundational principles of this book. It promotes athleticism in the delivery, and if the pitcher strives to balance all areas of pitching, he has a better chance of becoming a complete pitcher.

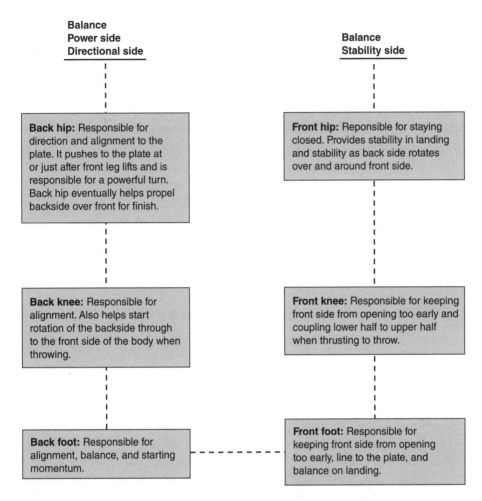

Figure 4.1   The various components of the lower body and their functions.

QUICK PITCH

The ability to move from one foot to another with power, precision, and balance is vital for the pitcher. These movements harness the pitcher's power so that he is able to apply maximum force to the baseball and control of the pitches that he throws. Every pitcher should practice developing a solid foundation on the back foot, as well as learning to land solidly on the front foot.

So how does a pitcher remain balanced and athletic with his lower body? As the lead foot and leg lift up to start counterrotation, the majority of the pitcher's weight should be distributed on the ball of his post-leg foot. As the delivery unfolds, the pitcher should be able to completely control the movements he is making, keeping his head in the middle of his body. And when landing, the pitcher should land flat with the majority of his weight distributed onto the ball of his stride foot as the ball is released. This is athleticism. This is balance! The pitcher moves his body where he wants and how fast he wants. He coordinates the upper and lower half of the body to create symmetry for the impending explosion at the end—the pitch.

Balance Drill

This drill uses an Airex pad, a foam pad designed to promote balance. The pitcher's main responsibility is to travel from one foot to the other while on the Airex pad, maintaining balance and posture. This drill can be completed with or without the use of a baseball.

Setup

The pitcher will execute this drill in sock feet so that he can feel the foam pad better. The drill will start with one foam pad and then an additional pad will be needed.

Procedure

1. The pitcher steps on the foam pad with his back foot and starts in the set position. He lifts his front leg multiple times trying to keep the back foot stable on the foam pad. An actual throw may or may not be used during this portion of the drill.

2. The pitcher starts in the set position with the foam pad directly in front of him at a distance that allows for a proper stride. He lifts his front leg one time and lands with his front foot as stable as possible on the foam pad. An actual throw may or may not be used during this portion of the drill.

3. The pitcher starts in the set position with the foam pad underneath his back foot and a second foam pad in front of him at a distance that allows for a proper stride. He lifts his front leg one time and lands with his front foot as stable as possible on the foam pad in front of him. An actual throw may or may not be used during this portion of the drill.

Pitching Points

It should be noted that pitcher should start slowly with his movements and build speed as he gets more comfortable with the foam pad underneath him.

Posture

As discussed in the previous chapter, posture is a series of movements that make up the delivery and help determine body alignment and direction to the plate. Subtle moves that the pelvis, spine, and head make during the delivery can cause inefficiencies and inconsistency of movements. Obviously, it then makes sense that posture can also affect what happens in lower-body mechanics. If the center (pelvis and core) isn't used as the engineer for movement, steering the body down the mound will be difficult, and poor direction can occur because, as noted, the legs and arms will always follow the center. A relatively common example of this is the lack of proper posture in a pitcher who strides across his body. This occurs because, as the pitcher lifts to the top of his delivery and starts his descent to the plate, the pitcher's head and spine work in front his center of gravity, causing a forward lean. As a result, the pitcher fails to initiate his core properly, and his body drifts toward the side, causing him to stride across his body (see figure 4.2). His legs did not necessarily lead him to striding across his body. It was poor posture and a poor "center" that led the way.

Figure 4.2   This pitcher doesn't initiate his core, and as a result, he throws across his body.

Another common postural deficiency that affects timing, alignment, and momentum is bending the back knee with too much flexion instead of angling the knee toward the plate (see figure 4.3). When the back knee is flexed, the posture of the pitcher

Figure 4.3   (a) Pitcher angling the back knee in toward the plate, which is more efficient; (b) the pitcher sits and stalls, which is less efficient.

changes dramatically (the pitcher sits, or lowers his profile and becomes smaller), and the hips are limited in their ability to move out toward the plate because they are stacked. This sitting action angles the knee toward the open-side base (right-handed pitcher toward third base and left-handed pitcher toward first) instead of keeping the knee under the hip and directing the back side toward home plate. This can create a stalling effect, or a starting and stopping and then restarting, which disrupts momentum to the plate. Stalling will often create rhythm and timing issues, and the pitcher's command and stuff can be compromised. The pitcher should instead attempt to get "down the hill," turning the back side and back knee into a closed-off front side, as shown in figure 4.3*a*. This will leverage the body and is known as riding the back leg down the hill.

The following list includes important features that can positively or negatively affect posture. A pitcher can work on these areas to improve posture naturally during training or bullpen sessions without changing large movement patterns—they are small details that create big changes.

- *Setup*—The feet should be hip-width apart in the stretch position; the front-foot arch should be in line with the back-foot toe so the pitcher is in a position that makes it easier to lift the front leg; the pitcher should be in an athletic starting position with knees bent and weight distributed evenly.
- *Ball of foot*—The weight of the back leg should be on the ball of the back foot and spread evenly along the foot; the pitcher wants to avoid letting weight go to the heel of the back foot, or too close to the toes.
- *Leg lift*—For a more compact delivery and for a greater chance of good posture and connection with other body movements, the leg should lift instead of swing; the front foot should be under the front knee the majority of the time through the lifting phase.
- *Chin over belt*—During the lifting phase, the chin should remain over the center of gravity; some flexibility can be allowed here as long as posture is not adversely affected. A still head early in the delivery is something the pitcher should strive for.
- *Tight belly button*—The pitcher should tighten the abdominal muscles directly behind the belly button when the front leg is lifted to start the delivery; this tightness can lead to proper alignment and posture.
- *Angled back knee*—As the pitcher lift and starts his decent, the back knee should start the chain reaction for rotation by angling itself toward the plate. If the back knee is angled properly, good alignment and proper rotation will occur.

Partner Push Drill

This drill emphasizes the importance of properly using the core to create posture and alignment of the body during the delivery.

Setup

The drill can be done on a flat surface or off of a regulation mound. All that is needed is a baseball and a partner.

Procedure

1. The pitcher starts in either the windup or the stretch position. The partner will apply subtle pressure to different areas of the pitcher's body such as the shoulders and, in particular, the chest and back. The partner's goal will be to push the throwing pitcher out of posture before he throws the ball.

2. As the pitcher lifts his leg for the delivery, the partner will gently apply pressure to the areas stated in step 1. The throwing pitcher will counter this pressure by tightening his core muscles and by using his back knee and back hip to steer his direction.

Pitching Points

- As the pitcher breaks his hands to throw the ball, the partner will get out of his way allowing for the throw.
- This drill has the most effect when throwing off of the mound and with a baseball.

Leverage Points

To throw the ball downhill, the pitcher must create leverage to fight the slope of the mound (staying balanced and having power), and he must use the slope of the mound to his advantage in terms of momentum and power. To create this leverage, as well as to create an angle to throw the baseball from, the pitcher should work on setting the hip, which in turn elevates the shoulders. Most hitters will tell you that it is very difficult to hit a ball that is coming at them from a steep angle. This is one reason why many believe that a taller pitcher is better; taller pitchers create a better angle. But no matter how short or tall a pitcher is, he can gain leverage and improve his angle if he sets the hips and shoulders. In figure 4.4, the pitcher is using the hips and shoulders for leverage and angle. He is using the slope of the mound for momentum, but at the same time, he is fighting the slope by staying back. In a sense, the pitcher that employs this technique is defying gravity—going forward, but staying back (more information on this concept to follow).

Figure 4.4 Pitcher using his hips and shoulders for leverage and angle.

Hooking the Foot

As mentioned in chapter 2, *hooking the foot* describes the way a pitcher places his foot next to the rubber. The spike on the outside of the cleat is wedged on top of the rubber, forcing the toe to be slightly in front of the heel as the pitcher lifts his leg going into his delivery (see figure 4.5). Here is where the usefulness of this technique comes into play. Hooking the foot can be functional in starting the loading process of the lower body. This technique is not an absolute necessity—some pitchers like the feel of the hook, while others do not—but it can provide certain advantages to those who use it. For one, the wedged foot creates great stability and a firm base for the pitcher to throw from. Because the toe is slightly ahead of the heel, the pitcher feels tension on his back leg as he lifts his leg for counterrotation; creating this tension is referred to as "winding the spring." Figure 4.6 shows how the pitcher's toes lead his heel, putting him in a better position to stay in line and potentially leveraging his body better. Wedging the foot can also eliminate the chance for the pitcher to sweep his heel, another fault that places him in danger of creating poor alignment (as discussed in chapter 2).

Figure 4.5   Hooking the foot.

Figure 4.6   When the pitcher lifts his lead leg, he is counterrotating. If the heel is hooked, a greater tension is felt on the inside of the back leg; this is called winding the spring.

Lifting the Knee

One of the main reasons why the pitcher should maintain the position of his chin over his belt (center of gravity) is because of its effect on the lower body. As the pitcher lifts his leg to start a counterrotation, the chin should stay in the same position. This will ensure that balance can be maintained throughout the delivery and that athleticism, alignment, and momentum can be directed squarely to the target.

Figure 4.7   A pitcher stays connected when he keeps the foot directly under the knee as counterrotation occurs.

As the knee is lifted, the pitcher should feel the bulk of his weight on the ball of the pivot foot and not the heel; weight on the heel might lead to a posture change and allow the chin to move behind or in front of the center of gravity. The leg lift itself is just that—a lift. Many pitchers make the mistake of swinging the foot up, which often leads to posture and balance issues. The pitcher should lift the leg by using the quadriceps muscle only, with the lower leg (calf and foot) just going along for the ride. Ideally, the foot is kept directly under the knee as counterrotation occurs (see figure 4.7). If the leg lift is performed properly, there is a greater chance for optimal hip loading to occur. Variations of the lift, such as swinging the leg or lifting with the foot outside the knee (see figure 4.8), present greater challenges for the pitcher when it is time to load the pelvis. The lift is extremely important for the rest of the delivery in terms of connection—snapping the parts of the delivery together for rhythm, timing, and power. If the initial lift of the stride leg is wide or swinging instead of compact and lifting, the pitcher runs the risk of early posture changes and

Figure 4.8   A pitcher's movements may become disconnected, for example, if the foot goes outside the knee.

balance issues. What happens early in the delivery affects what happens late in the delivery. The pitcher wants to lift the stride leg strong and compact, keeping the foot underneath the knee, so that connection can occur. A strong first move can lead to a strong delivery.

Double Lift and Throw Drill

The double lift and throw drill emphasizes proper leg lift, which can aid in better posture and alignment for the delivery.

Setup

This drill can be done on a flat surface or off of the mound. No special equipment is needed.

Procedure

1. The pitcher starts in the stretch position. It is possible to start out of the windup although the windup position is too awkward for some pitchers.
2. The pitcher lifts his leg twice, making sure that the foot is under the knee. It is common for corrections to be made during the second lift.
3. After the second leg lift, the pitcher will make a throw to his target.

Pitching Point

Always be aware of the weight distribution on the back foot and how the leg lift may affect it.

Setting the Hip

Pelvic loading occurs either just before the apex of the leg lift or just after it, depending on the overall rhythm and timing of the pitcher's delivery. Much like the upper-body loading where the scapula pinches together and then unfolds to create the arm whip, the lower body will also load—to what degree is largely dependent on how well the pitcher leverages his body. Again, the goal here is for the pitcher to maximize his movements in the hopes of becoming more powerful and more efficient, as well as reducing stress on the arm.

As the pitcher nears the apex of his leg lift, he will make a move that will essentially defy gravity. At this point—as the leg is lifted—the back knee and back hip will push forward, causing the hip joint to be tilted toward home plate so that the front hip joint is leading the rest of the body. This tilting action "sets" the hip in place, and the movement defies gravity by pushing the pitcher forward with added momentum while at the same time keeping the pitcher's head over his back foot (and the rubber). Leading with the hip creates leverage by setting a small uphill angle of the shoulders on the way down the hill. Some coaches believe that a pitcher's shoulders should be level, but very few high-level pitchers, especially those who throw with power, display level shoulders from start to finish. They instead let the hips set the shoulder angle; then, at landing and through rotation to release point, everything snaps together, creating the downhill plane and flight of the ball. Note, however, that there is a difference between setting the hip and setting the angle of the shoulders (see figure 4.9) versus trying to tilt the shoulders without the aid of the hips (see figure 4.10). Though these methods look similar, tilting the shoulders without first tilting the hips can promote "uphill throwing" where the pitcher is not on time to throw the ball and misses high in the strike zone or misses the zone completely.

Figure 4.9 The pitcher uses his hips and sets a leveraged angle with his shoulders, giving him a good chance to throw downhill.

Figure 4.10 The pitcher tilts the shoulders without setting the hips, thus finding it difficult to get the ball down in the strike zone.

Setting the Hip Drill

This drill sequence promotes awareness of what the back leg and the hips are doing during the delivery. Again the beauty of this drill is that all that is needed is a baseball and a target to throw to.

Setup

This drill can be done on a flat surface or off of the mound. No special equipment is needed.

Procedure

1. The pitcher begins by crossing his feet in the stretch position. The right-handed pitcher's left foot will cross over and then behind his right foot. The pitcher will initiate the throw by lifting his left leg up and over the right foot much like his normal delivery. He will then throw the ball.

2. After gaining a feel for the cross-foot pitch, the right-handed pitcher will then cross his left foot over his right knee. He will start his movement to the plate by simply pushing his back knee and back hip toward his target, keeping the left foot over his right knee. Just before he lands, the left foot will be unhooked and the throw can occur.

3. In this step, the right-handed pitcher's left foot is hooked behind the right knee. He starts his movement to the plate by simply pushing his back knee and back hip toward his target, keeping the left foot behind his right knee. Just before he lands, the left foot is unhooked and the throw occurs.

Setting the Shin Angle

As mentioned earlier, as the pitcher loads the hips and starts his descent to the plate, the back knee can either enhance the movement (by making an inward turn toward the plate) or hinder it (by increasing flexion and collapsing). If the latter occurs, the back knee creates a stall of the intended rotation on top of the rubber. One way to prevent the stall from occurring is to set the shin angle of the post leg. As the front leg is lifted and the pitcher sets the hip, he will simultaneously set the shin angle by directing the back knee toward home (see figure 4.11). When this is performed correctly, the pitcher creates a tension in the lower body that feels as if the legs are being spring-loaded.

Figure 4.11 The back knee turns in just when or just after the hip is set, helping the pitcher stay in line and promoting strength and momentum at the beginning of the delivery.

Riding the Back Leg Down

After the hip and shin angle are set in the post leg (a technique known as pelvic loading), the pitcher's objective becomes to deliver the ball as powerfully as possible. From a lower-body perspective, this is done by carrying the load that was created (through counterrotation and setting the hip and shin angle), keeping the front leg from opening too early, planting the front foot firmly, and then explosively rotating the hips and shoulders to make the throw. "Riding the back leg down" is the phrase used to explain these intricate movements. As the pitcher rotates the throwing side of his body into the closed and leveraged front side, he will feel as if the majority of his weight is riding down along with his back leg (see figure 4.12). This feeling will ensure that he is not leaking energy to the front leg and that he is maintaining the momentum he has created with his lower-body movements. Leaking movements, as shown in figure 4.13, would include unloading or opening the front hip early, opening the front foot or front knee, or leaning with a low front shoulder.

Figure 4.12 Pitcher keeps the weight on his back leg as he strides to the plate, thus keeping his leverage intact. When he touches down, the pitcher can then forcefully turn and thrust.

Figure 4.13 Leaking movements.

Front-Leg Action, or Stride

The function of the front leg is to help steer the body toward the intended direction. The front leg also keeps the lower body from opening up prematurely, which would cause the pitcher to lose the rotational power that is being created by hip and core rotation. After the hip is set, the front leg begins its descent down the mound. The action or movement of the front leg varies from pitcher to pitcher, but the function must remain the same; the front foot and front knee should travel "closed off" to the

Figure 4.14 The pitcher's back hip starts to rotate first, but the knee and foot remain closed off so that the front side works against the back-side rotation. This keeps the pitcher from spinning too early, allowing him to stay closed off and on time.

hitter for as long as possible. Some coaches teach a traditional method of "up, down, and out," where the pitcher goes up into counterrotation and then drops the leg straight down and into a linear path straight out to landing. This method is often used to help keep the pitcher from opening up his front side prematurely; however, the method may be flawed because its linear nature curtails rotational properties of the hip and core. Instead, a coach should search for ways to keep his pitcher's front side closed off, as shown in figure 4.14, while still promoting rotation on the back side. The most important thing might be that the front side works against the back side to keep it from opening up too early.

The length of the stride is also a much debated topic in pitching circles. Many believe that the stride should be a natural thing, while some pitching coaches with science backgrounds have concluded that the stride length should be approximately 85 percent of the pitcher's height. In my experience, I have found that stride length is usually the result of physical limitations, or in some cases physical abilities, that the pitcher possesses. Many times, a short stride is a result of poor flexibility in the lower body—the body protects itself from injury by staying in a shorter range and within the ability of the pitcher. A long stride is not necessarily a bad thing either, as long as rotation of the lower body and the ability to finish the arc of the throwing arm are not impeded. If the pitcher has intent to throw the ball hard—and if there is balance, rhythm, and tempo in the delivery—an acceptable stride length usually just happens.

Landing

Before discussing the controversial issue of landing, let's again touch on the importance of taking care of the mound. Often, after only a few innings or after a few bullpens, the terrain of the landing area on any mound will be similar to the terrain of the moon—smooth in some areas, craterous in others, and at the very best, uneven. Because of this, the pitcher must remember to fix the areas just in front of the rubber and the landing areas. This will help him land as smoothly and as flat as possible.

People have many different theories about how the front foot should land and what the body should do as a result of that action. Some pitchers land on the ball of the foot, and some land on the heel and then shift the weight to the ball of the foot. However, most pitchers who land smoothly and transition well from the throw to the follow-through seem to simply land flat and then redistribute the weight to the ball of the foot (see figure 4.15). Pitchers who land on the heel (as shown in figure 4.16*a*) and, more important, stay on the heel as they release the ball seem to struggle to redistribute the weight (it's almost as if they get stuck). Pitchers who land on the ball of their feet (as shown in figure 4.16*b*) seem to lift on the toe, and they lack balance or may spin like a top after ball release. Also, the foot should land slightly closed or with the toe pointing directly at the target, as opposed to landing extremely open or extremely closed. Both extremes can create problems in the unloading process as well as create the potential for injury.

Figure 4.15 A pitcher who lands with a flat front foot can typically transition well from the throw to the follow-through.

Figure 4.16 Pitchers whose front foot lands on *(a)* the heel or *(b)* the ball of the foot tend to struggle in the unloading process.

QUICK PITCH

Remember to develop a solid base in the ground with the back foot and then land firmly on the front foot. This helps harness your power and control your pitches! Start flat and land flat.

Coupling and Finish

When the pitcher lands completely on his front foot, an explosive rotation erupts that passes through his hips and core, delivering the shoulders and then finally the arm and ball to home. Coupling refers to connecting the energy and rotation of the lower body to the energy and rotation of the upper body, and it happens in conjunction with the release of the ball. This is the point in time when the summation of forces can be maximized or compromised depending on the efficiency of the transfer and coupling. As the shoulders square up to release the ball, the lower back creates a backward C extension, as shown in figure 4.17, which is yet another loading mechanism that happens in conjunction with the scapula's retracting or pinching.

From this backward C position, the pitcher's arm then lies back into external rotation, and his chest is thrust out. As the arm moves forward, the chest is thrust out, and the front knee and leg begin to stabilize. The pitcher then releases the ball while his trunk moves from extension to flexion (think of a catapult launching a rock), delivering the back hip joint around the front hip joint. If the knee and leg are stable and no forward movement occurs from the knee (such as the knee leaking forward), then a successful coupling occurs. Problems stemming from coupling could include the front leg bracing too early or the knee entirely locking out. Some pitchers have the flexibility to shift their weight onto the ball of the lead foot and complete the rotation (see figure 4.18); others do not have this flexibility, and they "cut off" their throw. The by-product of this movement is a recoil of the arm—the pitcher stands up or bounces up because of the leg locking, and the arc of the arm does not fully decelerate. The recoil can affect the location and action of the pitch,

Figure 4.17   Backward C taking shape, thus creating the force to propel the trunk and arm to rotate and thrust forward.

and over time, it may serve as a factor for injury. The pitcher should strive to be firm on a stable and balanced front leg so that the full arc of the arm can be completed, allowing the back hip joint to fully rotate around the front hip joint. These movements create the final phase of the delivery. When done properly, these movements keep the pitcher behind the ball for as long as possible, maximizing location, velocity, and spin of the ball while reducing the chance for injury and wildness.

Figure 4.18 Pitcher in the coupling phase when finishing the pitch; his chest is over his knee, and the back hip joint is rotating around the front hip joint.

Lower-Body Considerations for the Youth League Pitcher

My mother told me that in most endeavors one must crawl before he walks. This rule should be applied to lower-body mechanics when it comes to teaching the youth pitcher. It would be great if an eight-year-old pitcher had the lower-body strength of a big-league pitcher, but the youth pitcher has certain limitations of strength, balance, and coordination that will inhibit him from mastering some of the movements that have been described. Because of these limitations, youth pitchers should start with balance and posture and only progress to other elements after mastering these. Simple tasks such as lifting the front leg instead of swinging it may prove challenging for the youngster. Solidifying starting positions (rocker step in the windup and set position in the stretch) can greatly enhance the pitcher's chance of achieving good balance and posture. The youth pitcher must also understand the difference between the heel and ball of the foot and how to apply pressure on this area for both the back foot (when lifting) and the stride foot (when landing). A simple cue of "chin over belt" may remind the young pitcher to keep his head still and his weight over his center of gravity as he is moving toward the plate. Once a baseline of balance and posture is established, the young pitcher may move onto more complex movements such as pelvic loading, rotation, and stride length.

The use of the lower half of the body is important, and coaches and pitchers must know how to manipulate lower-body mechanics to gain greater results. In many ways, the lower body is easier to adjust because coach and pitcher are dealing with bigger muscle groups and gross motor patterns—compared to the smaller, more intricate muscle groups and complex motor patterns of the upper body, especially the throwing arm. But even if the lower body is easier to fine-tune, there is still much more involved than the "use your legs" direction I was given in my youth. As you learned in this chapter, lower-body techniques are much more dynamic and complex.

PART II

The Art of Pitching

Developing an Arsenal

Every pitcher is infatuated with the grips of his pitches. Pitchers are constantly searching for the holy grail of pitching grips, trying to find the perfect fit for their hand or for the way they throw a particular pitch. By finding the perfect grip, they hope to add velocity, sharper movement, improved command, or better yet, all three in unison. Pitchers seek the perfect feel of the ball in their hand and the way it leaves their fingertips; they want the ball to feel just right and have the perfect spin as it leaves their hand so that the pitch will deceive the hitter completely or miss the barrel of the hitter's bat. The perfect fit of the ball will be dependent on many factors, so there is not a one-size-fits-all model when dealing with pitch grips. However, there are a few tried-and-true methods for finding the grip that works best for the individual, and that is what we will be discussing in this chapter.

Considerations in Developing an Arsenal

Before we get into the details about the specific types of pitches that pitchers should have in their arsenal, let's review a few key concepts that every pitcher should be aware of: determining the type of pitch to throw, finding the correct arm slot, owning versus renting the pitch, and using the strike zone.

Determining the Type of Pitch to Throw

Every pitcher is constantly wanting to learn another pitch to supplement his arsenal. When I was a kid, I wanted to throw a Nolan Ryan fastball, a Bert Blyleven curveball, a Fernando Valenzuela screwball, a Steve Carlton slider, and a Tommy John changeup. Unfortunately—or maybe fortunately—our catcher didn't have enough fingers to put down to call all of my pitches. In addition, most of the pitches I borrowed from those superstars weren't as good as the ones their owners threw, so I saved them for the backyard games I played by myself throwing against a concrete stoop. As time and many trials and errors passed, I ultimately learned what worked for me and eliminated the pitches that I couldn't command or the pitches that simply didn't work.

This process of elimination is the starting point for every pitcher in developing the arsenal. Once a young pitcher starts to throw pitches other than the fastball, he should definitely experiment with different grips and pitches to find out what might work for him. Accordingly, the pitching coach should encourage him to discover such grips and pitch types. One major consideration for the pitcher to think about would be whether his physical size lends itself to throwing a particular pitch. An example of a bad fit would be a pitcher with very small hands trying to throw a split-finger fastball. Throwing the split-finger might not be impossible for the smaller pitcher, but because of his hand size, he may end up altering his arm action or delivery in order to execute the pitch. If this is the case, the pitcher increases his chance for injury, and the hitter will likely receive early clues regarding what pitch is coming. Neither scenario benefits the pitcher.

Finding the Correct Arm Slot

Another consideration to take into account before a pitcher develops his arsenal is the pitcher's arm slot. I watch a good number of high school pitchers each spring and summer as part of my recruiting duties, and many of these pitchers throw pitches that their arm slots simply do not complement or support. An example of this might be a pitcher with a low to mid three-quarter arm slot attempting to throw an overhand curveball, also known as a 12-6 curveball because of the rotation of the pitch spinning straight over the top from 12 o'clock to 6 o'clock. A pitcher with a low arm slot must obviously change something in his delivery to create the correct spin, and the only reasonable strategy would be to elevate his arm slot to promote the desired rotation.

At a younger level, this arm slot change may work quite well, and the pitcher may have success. However, as the pitcher advances to higher levels, the hitters will find it easier to recognize that something other than a fastball is coming. In addition, the hitters will be able to recognize this earlier in the pitch, giving them time to readjust or redirect their swing. What were relatively easy outs for the pitcher in Pony League or high school will become "easy pickings" for the more seasoned hitter in college or professional baseball. Therefore, after tinkering with different grips and pitches, the pitcher needs to make prudent decisions on the pitches that he will throw based on his arm slot and whether or not the pitch provides early visual clues for the hitter. If these two elements are satisfactory, then it is time to move on to the next step.

Table 5.1 lists the various pitch types and gives suggestions that the younger pitcher might follow when choosing an arsenal. As with most things in baseball, there may be exceptions to these rules, but nonetheless, this chart presents guidelines for distinguishing which types of pitches might be appropriate for the pitcher.

Owning Versus Renting the Pitch

Pitchers need to understand the concept of "owning versus renting" the various pitches in their arsenal. As mentioned before, it is common for young pitchers to

Table 5.1   Arm Slot and Pitch Type Integration

Pitch Type	Arm Slot	Limiting Factors
Fastball (4 seam and 2 seam)	All	None; power pitchers often stay with the 4-seam fastball; the 2-seam fastball will often be used for fastballs thrown on the arm side of the plate, and the 4-seam is used for fastballs thrown on the glove side.
Sinker (fastball)	All	Pitchers with a lower arm slot have a tendency to use the sinker more, but it can be thrown with most slots.
Cutter (fastball)	Three quarter to over the top	Some pitchers naturally come around the ball (supinate) and cut the ball. Force must be applied to the outside of the ball. The lower the arm slot, the greater risk of coming around the ball and creating an undesirable action.
Changeup	All	Usually none. Pitchers use varying degrees of movement and various grips.
Curveball	Three quarter to over the top	Pitchers with lower arm slots have trouble getting on top of the ball, which inhibits them from getting correct spin on a curveball. Spin is usually between a curveball and slider (slurve).
Spike curveball	Three quarter to over the top	Finger on top produces a firmer wrist so that consistent spin and force can be applied. This is often taught to a pitcher with a "sloppy" or loose wrist.
Slider	Sidearm to over the top	Much like throwing the cutter, the pitcher applies force to the middle outside of the ball, creating a sidespin. Pitchers should use the fingers to manipulate the ball rather than use a forceful turn of the wrist.

adopt the various types of pitches that their favorite big leaguers throw, and they sometimes end up throwing four or five different pitches.

Unfortunately, the young pitcher can rarely master and command his full repertoire. Though he is capable of throwing a certain pitch, he may not be able to throw it for a strike very often, and the pitch presents no real threat to the accomplished hitter. This condition is called renting the pitch. The pitcher has the ability to throw the pitch, but his inconsistency and lack of command with it make it a low-percentage strike pitch. In other words, the pitcher can't rely on the pitch in a crucial situation; it is not a sure thing, and he is therefore renting the pitch. Owning the pitch means that the pitcher is sure-minded when throwing it. He is able to throw it in any count or situation, and he places full trust in its action and his command. An owned pitch is one that is thrown in the strike zone more often than not (high strike percentage) and one that will force the hitter to make a decision to swing or not. This is an important distinction for the pitcher to make as he is preparing the tools for his arsenal.

QUICK PITCH

Before any pitch can be owned and then used in any situation or count, the pitcher must first place trust in his ability to execute the pitch consistently. Trust in a pitch comes through purposeful and focused practice—or intention. When practicing a new pitch or a pitch that the pitcher currently rents, the pitcher should remember that consistent, powerful, and focused intention must be present in order to develop trust in the pitch. The core concept "Training vs. Trusting" can be applied here too; the more the pitcher trains with a certain pitch, the more he will trust it.

Using the Strike Zone

As part of a pitcher's foundation and arsenal, a major goal should be to have the ability to pitch to specific lanes and levels within the strike zone. This will be discussed more fully in the next chapter, but all pitchers need to understand that the fastball can be thrown to almost any area within the strike zone, while other pitches may be limited to being thrown in a specific area. An example of the latter would be the use of the slider. If a right-handed pitcher created sidespin on the ball (slider), the most advantageous spot for him to throw the pitch would be down and away to the right-handed batter. If the pitcher threw the same pitch inside to a right-handed batter, the pitcher most likely made a mistake, and the pitch was not properly executed. Thus, the pitcher should strive to command his fastball in all areas of the strike zone, but he should confine his off-speed pitches to an area of the zone that will yield the greatest movement, speed, or action on the pitch in order to give the pitcher the greatest chance for success. Figure 5.1 shows home plate and the corresponding strike zones that a pitcher can throw his pitches to. The zones are broken into three mastery levels that correspond to age or skill (basic, intermediate, and advanced). Essentially, the older the pitcher, the more zones he should be able to throw to, as shown in the progression through these three illustrations. Pitchers must determine what skill level they are currently at, and they should not move to the more challenging zones until their accuracy and skill improve.

In the basic strike zone, as shown in figure 5.1a, the catcher sets up in the middle of the strike zone, and the pitcher throws to a large area with all of his pitches. When the pitcher gets way ahead, he will expand the zone either by throwing the ball in the dirt (fastball, breaking ball, or changeup) or by elevating the ball above the strike zone. In the intermediate strike zone, as shown in figure 5.1b, the catcher splits the plate in half, and the pitcher will throw his pitches to the outer half of the plate. When the pitcher gets ahead, he will expand the zone by throwing the ball low, outside low, or inside low with a fastball, breaking ball, or changeup. The pitcher may also elevate his fastball up by the letters of the hitter and in the middle of the plate. In the advanced strike zone, as shown in figure 5.1c, the catcher splits the plate into thirds, and the pitcher throws to zones 3, 4, and 5 to get ahead in the count. Once ahead, the pitcher can then expand to zones 7, 6, or 1 and may also use the dirt to make the hitter chase the ball. Until certain levels of competency and command are reached, the pitcher should stay in the appropriate level of the various strike zones.

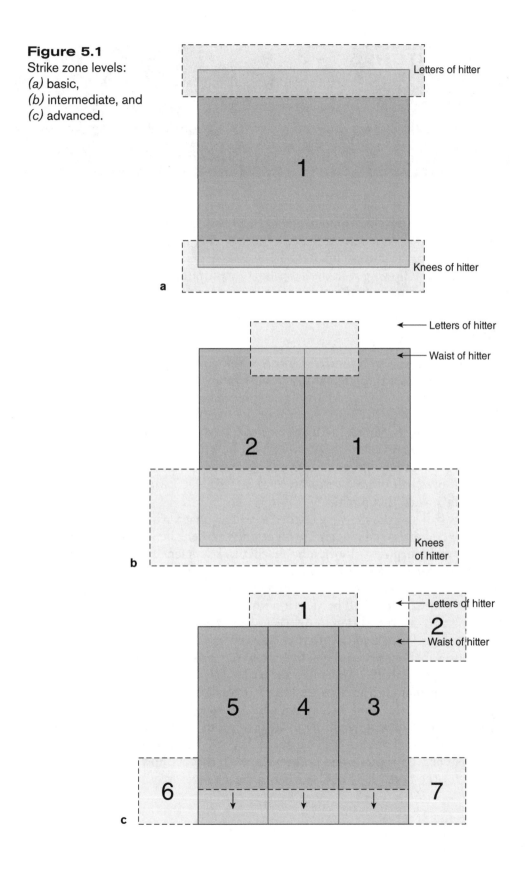

Figure 5.1
Strike zone levels:
(a) basic,
(b) intermediate, and
(c) advanced.

QUICK PITCH

Even at the higher levels of baseball, the middle and down pitch can be an effective pitch. For most pitchers, their ball moves to one side or the other, so if the pitcher is aggressive in the strike zone and throws the ball at the knees and toward the middle of the plate, chances are the ball will arrive just to the left or right of center, making it a quality pitch.

The pitcher must gain an understanding of what types of pitches fit his arm slot. He then needs to develop competency in a few basic pitches and learn where in the zone these pitches work best. At that point, the pitcher may go on to another pitch or perhaps enhance the current pitches he possesses with more movement or improved command. The following sections describe the basic pitches along with a few "twists" that may help a pitcher find the correct niche for his pitches.

Fastball

For many reasons, a well-located fastball is the most important pitch in baseball. First, the fastball is the pitch thrown most often, so it must be a pitch that the pitcher can truly command. Many big-league pitchers and coaches subscribe to the ratio of 65 percent fastballs, 20 percent of the second best pitch, and 15 percent of the third best pitch. Simple mathematics would tell us that if a pitcher threw 100 pitches in a game and subscribed to this ratio, he would perhaps mix 65 fastballs, 20 curveballs, and 15 changeups to arrive at his total of 100. I am not a brain surgeon, but if well over half of my pitches were to be fastballs, I would want to make sure that I truly owned that pitch!

The fastball and the delivery of the fastball also factor into the pitcher's ability to throw good off-speed pitches. As mentioned earlier, the intent to throw the ball hard and with purpose will often fix mechanical deficiencies. This is also true for the way off-speed pitches are thrown. Many times, pitchers throw off-speed pitches with significantly less velocity and less efficiency than they could if they placed more intent on throwing the ball harder or with better tempo. As a result, pitchers end up having two or three different deliveries based on what they are throwing—one delivery for the fastball and a different delivery for the changeup and breaking ball. This creates inefficiency in the delivery and inconsistency in pitch location.

Finally, the fastball is the most versatile pitch in a pitcher's arsenal. It can be thrown at many different speeds and to various locations. The pitcher usually doesn't have the same luxury with his off-speed pitches because the spin he imparts on the ball will generally make it move in a certain direction. Changing speeds on off-speed pitches is also difficult because it requires a great deal of "feel" by the pitcher. As the chapter progresses, we'll discuss how to add and subtract velocity for the fastball, as well as when speed changes may be used for particular pitches.

Four-Seam Fastball

The four-seam fastball is probably the most common fastball used today, and because many young pitchers are also position players, it makes sense to start with this pitch. The four-seam is aptly named because the four seams of the ball spin in the same direction that the pitcher throws the ball. The "horseshoe" of the ball can be placed either on the outside of the middle finger (see figure 5.2*a*) or on the inside of the first finger (see figure 5.2*b*), whatever is most comfortable for the pitcher. The four-seam grip with the horseshoe on the outside of the middle finger will sometimes create a cutting action on the ball, a consideration for the pitcher looking for movement on a pitch. Again, comfort will dictate which four-seam grip will be used.

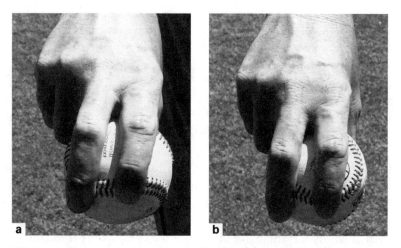

Figure 5.2   Four-seam fastball grip: *(a)* horseshoe outside the middle finger and *(b)* horseshoe inside the first finger.

Finger and thumb placement as well as spacing of the fingers on the ball are possibly the most important considerations when throwing a fastball. Anyone who's been around baseball long enough has heard the phrase "staying behind the ball." Staying behind the ball refers to applying force to the middle of the ball by keeping the fingers behind it during the throw. An easy way to do this is to hold the ball so that the middle finger and thumb bisect the middle of the ball (see figure 5.3). If the thumb and middle finger are in the middle of the ball at release, proper force can be applied, and the pitcher will stay behind the ball. This would also mean that the first finger (pointer finger) needs to rest on the ball close to the middle finger.

Figure 5.3   Proper finger and thumb spacing for the four-seam fastball grip.

I generally tell our pitchers that spacing between the first and middle finger should be approximately a pinky-width distance apart. The fingertips of the first two fingers should rest directly on the seams so that when the pitcher is releasing the ball, the fingertips rip or pull down and across the laces, producing more spin. Producing greater spin will often create more velocity and action on the pitch. Remember, speed and movement are a pitcher's friend.

Two-Seam Fastball

Although there are many versions of the two-seam fastball, we'll cover three main versions here. Most of the other versions have likely been spawned from one of these three versions. After all, there aren't too many different ways to grip two seams and make the ball move. Doing different things or making the ball move is precisely why the two-seam fastball is thrown. While its brethren, the four-seam fastball, is designed to fly true and straight with maximum velocity, the two-seamer's function is to create late movement with a slight decrease in velocity.

For the two-seam fastball, some procedures are the same as for the four-seam fastball, including the spacing of the fingers (pinky-width apart), fingertips on the seams, and thumb in the middle of the ball. The place the ball is gripped—on the seams—will be the only difference. The first grip, which may be the most common, is holding the ball with the first two fingers placed on top of the narrow seams (see figure 5.4a). This is known as throwing the ball "with the seams." This type of pitch often has a running action, or fade, toward the batter who stands facing the arm side of the pitcher. The two-seamer is usually 1 or 2 miles per hour slower than the four-seam fastball, and it is used to change zones in the strike zone. For example, a two-seamer thrown by a right-handed pitcher will often start toward the middle of the plate and end up inside to a right-handed batter. Why is this important? The hitter has about .40 seconds to decide whether to swing the bat or not, so if a pitch starts in one place but ends up elsewhere, the hitter will have already committed to his swing. The hitter may indeed still hit the pitch that was thrown, but the late movement created by the two-seamer often makes the hitter hit the ball on a dead part of the bat or improperly adjust the club head so that he makes weak contact. "Missing the barrel" is what attracts pitchers and pitching coaches to the two-seam fastball—now you see it, now you don't!

Another two-seam grip that can be used is to hold the ball across the narrow seams (see figure 5.4b). This type of two-seamer will sometimes have both run and sinking action on the ball. Thumb and finger placement are the same as for the "with the seams" two-seamer, and the pitcher must make sure that the fingertips are on the seams and not on the smooth part of the ball for command purposes. This grip sometimes creates two-plane movement of the fastball; that is, not only does the ball move within the strike zone, but it may also change height, or level, as explained in chapter 7. The pitcher wants the pitch to make the hitter have the same reaction as the other two-seamer—the hitter commits to his swing, and the ball moves from one part of the zone to another, forcing the hitter to change his intended swing path or completely miss the ball. Either way, if the ball misses the barrel of the bat, the pitcher has executed the pitch properly.

The third and final type of two-seam grip we will be discussing is the X grip. The X grip is a "with the seams" two-seamer that is turned slightly in the hand, creating an X shape of the seams (see figure 5.4c). Grip and spacing of the X grip are the same as the other two-seam grips, with the exception that only the middle finger will be placed on a seam and the first finger will rest beside on the smooth part of the ball. Essentially, this pitch is a hybrid of the "with the seams" and "across the seams" two-seam fastballs. Because of that, the action of this pitch will vary from pitcher to pitcher. This grip is particularly useful for pitchers who cannot produce movement with the other two-seam grips and for pitchers who have a high arm slot.

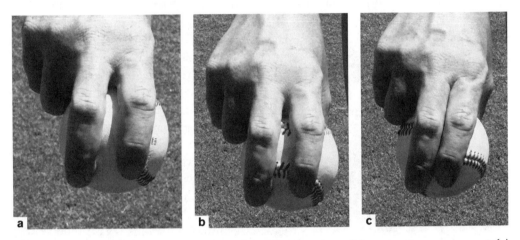

Figure 5.4   Two-seam fastball grips: *(a)* with the seams, *(b)* across the seams, and *(c)* X grip.

QUICK PITCH

Most pitchers are unique in the way they release the ball. This is largely because of arm slot and the timing within the delivery, so it is vital for the pitcher to experiment with different types of two-seam grips to find which one may suit him best. Older pitchers might also try experimenting with strengthening pronation at the release of the pitch. Pronation of the throwing arm happens naturally to all pitchers when throwing a baseball, but it happens earlier and more pronounced for some pitchers. Pronation is generally thought to be a protective movement that the arm makes as it begins to decelerate. Usually, the more pronation of the arm at release, the more action or movement the ball has on its path to the plate. Therefore, training the arm to pronate more efficiently has the tangible benefits of both maintaining arm health and creating movement for the pitcher.

Split-Finger Fastball

I chose to categorize the split-finger in with the other types of fastballs for one simple reason: The split-finger is simply a fastball that moves a bit more and a bit later than a typical fastball. The grip of the split-finger fastball is quite simple in that the first two fingers are placed just outside the seams (see figure 5.5). The thumb is placed in the middle of the ball, but thumb placement can change as pitchers adjust to throwing the pitch. A common mistake when implementing the split-finger is placing the fingers too far away from one another. This does two things: It forces the wrist to tighten, thus causing a knuckling action of the pitch, and it slows the speed of the pitch considerably. The resulting pitch is known as a forkball, and although a forkball has merit by the way it moves, it can be a dangerous pitch because of the strain it puts on the forearm and elbow. The forkball is also a very difficult pitch to command.

Figure 5.5 Split-finger fastball grip.

Beyond the differences in the grip, there is no magic formula in throwing the split-finger. A split can be easily learned by keeping the wrist loose and keeping the arm speed and arm action the same as the normal fastball. When thrown correctly, the split-finger acts like a "power sinker" and can create a large amount of late movement down and to the arm side of the plate.

Note that an advanced move for the split-finger is pronating the wrist at release. In this move, the pitcher rolls his first two fingers over the ball while rolling the thumb under as he releases the ball (see figure 5.6). This is a difficult skill to master, but it will aid in ball movement and the nastiness of the pitch.

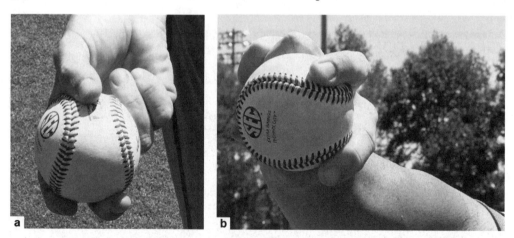

Figure 5.6 The split-finger gets its tumbling sinking action from the pronation of the wrist and fingers. The fingers roll over the inside of the ball, and the thumb cuts underneath the ball, making the pitch tumble.

Cutter and Sinker

The cut fastball (cutter) and sinking fastball (sinker) have become much more popular in the last 10 years at the major-league and amateur level. One reason why these pitches have evolved may be that the hitters are stronger and faster than before, which might require a pitcher to have more weapons (other than just velocity and location) in his bag of tricks. Pitches thrown at higher velocity are now much more common in high school and college baseball, and today's hitter is used to seeing high velocity—some hitters even welcome it. Another reason for the popularity of these pitches is that the strike zone continues to get smaller; more and more umpires are eliminating calling the high strike. If the high strike is consistently called a ball, it makes sense for the pitcher to look for options that fit the parameters of the strike zone using the width of the plate and beyond. Enter the cutter and sinker. In my mind, the cutter and sinker are essentially the same pitch, but they move in different directions because of subtle grip differences. Making this distinction is important when learning or teaching the pitch simply because it is easy to forget that these pitches are still fastballs and should be thrown accordingly.

Cutter

The cutter is a fastball with the force applied to the outer part of the ball as opposed to the middle of the ball, as in a normal fastball. In all of the previous fastball examples, the middle finger and thumb were placed in the middle of the ball with the idea of staying behind the ball, or applying force to the middle of the baseball. With the cutter, the middle finger will still be on a seam, but the seams should be placed in such a manner that the middle finger will rest just outside the middle of the ball (see figure 5.7). Generally, a two-seam grip of some variety will be used, although a four-seam fastball with the horseshoe on the outside of the middle finger can also sometimes create a cutting action of the ball (as described earlier). Finger spacing should mimic that of a normal fastball;

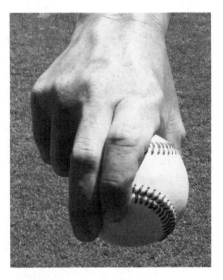

Figure 5.7   Cutter grip.

the first finger and middle finger should be a pinky-width distance apart from one another, though some pitchers may opt to keep the fingers together—it's all about feel and preference. The thumb should sit in approximately the same place as on a normal fastball. Variances of the finger spacing can be experimented with to find the best fit and feel for each pitcher.

When throwing the cutter, the pitcher must be sure not to alter the intent or effort that he would normally show with his fastball. By offsetting the grip and applying force just outside the middle of the ball, the pitcher creates sidespin, and the ball veers or cuts away from the arm side of home plate. The harder the pitcher can throw this pitch, the later and shorter the break will be on the ball; as discussed for the two-seam fastball, late break will serve the pitcher positively. The cutter can be a phenomenal pitch to throw to opposite-handed hitters, as Yankee closer Mariano Rivera has shown throughout his brilliant career. A right-handed pitcher should start the cutter in the middle of the plate to the left-handed hitter. The hitter reads location and starts his swing just as the ball cuts into his hands. The hitter does not have time to alter his swing to get the barrel to the ball, and this hopefully results in weak contact or a swing and miss.

PEN SESSION   Employing a Cutter

When learning the cutter, the pitcher first needs to identify the grip. He should then practice by first playing catch and then moving to a more pitching-oriented situation such as a flat-ground or bullpen session. Many pitchers have a natural tendency to "come around" the ball at first (by deliberately turning their wrist), making the ball react like a slider. When a pitcher first starts throwing this pitch, he should throw the ball exactly as he would if he was throwing a fastball with an odd grip (middle finger just outside the middle of the ball). At first, this may produce many straight cutters that will perhaps surprise the catcher, but over time, the pitcher will generally find the correct feel of the pitch. Pitchers may also want to start working on the cutter by throwing on two knees; they can then progress to standing, stepping and throwing, flat-ground throwing, and finally throwing the cutter off the mound. If done this way, the pitcher eliminates parts of his body and can isolate the arm and then eventually connect the rest of the body with his arm and the act of throwing a cutter. Another resource that might aid in developing the cutter is the use of a radar gun. Though there is no perfect speed differential between a cutter and a normal fastball, the radar gun can provide immediate feedback on how close the cutter's speed comes to the pitcher's fastball speed.

Cutter Drill

This drill helps pitchers learn the correct way to throw the cut fastball.

Setup

The drill can be performed on flat ground or on a bullpen mound; a catcher and baseballs are needed.

Procedure

1. The pitcher grips the baseball the same way as he holds his normal fastball except that instead of placing his middle finger in the center of the ball, he moves the finger slightly toward the outside portion of the ball.

2. The pitcher assumes the windup or stretch position on the rubber or marked area of flat ground.

3. The pitcher initiates the pitching motion and throws the ball exactly as he would if throwing an oddly gripped fastball to his catcher.

Pitching Points

At first, the ball will probably only spin and create what is called a "straight cutter," a pitch that may veer slightly off the straight line but with no downward movement. Encourage pitchers to stay with the grip. Over time, they will find the correct feel for the pitch, and the ball will start to move down as well as out. A common problem with the grip being slightly off center is that pitchers will have a tendency to want to come around the ball by turning their wrist when they release it. This will actually make the pitch less effective and could cause some arm problems if continued. Coaches should remind pitchers not to deliberately rotate their wrists as if throwing a slider.

Sinker

The sinking fastball is becoming one of the more prevalent pitches in the game. The function of the sinker is generally to run or tail and sink toward the arm side of the pitcher. Like the cutter, the sinking fastball will promote weaker contact and more swings and misses by the hitter because of the late action on the pitch. The sinker is usually a bit easier to master than the cutter because the pitcher uses the natural pronation of his arm to create the spin on the ball. With the cutter, the pitcher applies force to the area just outside the middle of the ball to create sidespin. In the case of the sinker, however, the pitcher will apply the force to just inside the middle of the ball, creating the opposite spin. Some pitchers, because of

Figure 5.8   Sinker grip: first two fingers closer together.

arm slot and timing of the delivery, naturally create run and sink on the ball, as evidenced in many throwers with low three-quarter slots. Also note that a two-seam fastball will often create the desired effect of a sinker without any further effort by the pitcher.

For our purposes, the sinker will be thrown with one of the three two-seam grips that were discussed earlier. The pitcher should first experiment with the grip he finds comfortable to see if sinking action occurs by simply throwing the ball normally. If the ball does not sink, the pitcher should try placing his middle finger just inside the middle of the ball. The first two fingers may be moved closer together, and the thumb will again start in the middle of the ball (see figure 5.8). As coach and pitcher observe the shape of this pitch, they can determine any further adjustments that the pitcher needs to make. Again, the determining factor for any pitch in the pitcher's arsenal is what the hitter sees or does not see. If late-breaking action occurs on the sinker, interrupted or mistimed swings are bound to occur.

The first finger may be the most important element of the two-seam fastball, particularly for making the ball sink. The middle finger and thumb are most often placed in the middle of the ball so that the pitcher has a chance to stay behind the ball—that is, he gives himself the best chance to maximally produce force behind the ball. As the pitcher becomes more comfortable with throwing the two-seam fastball, he may start to experiment with putting a slight amount of pressure on the first finger, as well as sliding the first finger closer to the inside of the ball (see figure 5.9). The first-finger pressure can influence the action and spin of the ball, making it move more. Often, the first-finger pressure can produce later sinking action on the ball, forcing the hitter to react to something that is breaking later or sharper than before—both good attributes for the sinker to possess!

Figure 5.9 Pitcher sliding the first finger closer to the inside of ball in the sinker grip.

Sinker Drill

This drill helps pitchers learn the correct way to throw a sinking fastball.

Setup

The drill can be performed on flat ground or on a bullpen mound; a catcher and baseballs are needed.

Procedure

1. The pitcher grips the baseball the same way he would if he were going to throw a two-seam fastball.
2. The pitcher assumes the windup or stretch position on the rubber or marked area of flat ground.
3. The pitcher initiates the pitching motion and throws the ball to his catcher, concentrating on moving the fingers toward the inside of the ball while the thumb moves in the opposite direction. The motion is much like adjusting a radio knob to the left on a car stereo.
4. The pitcher follows through normally, maintaining stability and symmetry.

Pitching Points

The key to this pitch is the placement of the thumb and the action of the thumb at release. In effect, the rotating of the thumb and fingers results in extreme pronation of the throwing arm. If the pronation is radical enough, throwing this pitch is much like throwing a screwball. When thrown correctly, the pitch thrown by a right-handed pitcher will move down and in to a right-handed batter.

Modifications

Some pitchers have found it beneficial to move the thumb farther up the inside of the ball (directly under the pointer finger) when gripping this pitch instead of keeping the thumb in the center of the ball. Teaching this pitch to young pitchers should be done cautiously and with much supervision. The sinker should be reserved for older, stronger players whose bones and muscles are more developed.

Batting-Practice Fastball and Extra Fastball

The last two types of fastballs are the batting-practice fastball (BP fastball) and the extra fastball. As previously mentioned, it is usually easier for the pitcher to change speeds on the fastball than on a breaking ball or changeup, largely because of the "feel" aspect needed to throw good off-speed pitches for strikes and to maintain the intended movement pattern of each pitch. In addition, most pitchers throw the fastball more often than any other pitch and in more locations. With that in mind, it follows that pitchers should be able to vary the speed (BP and extra fastball) and movement (four-seam, two-seam, cutter, and sinker) of the fastball going in all locations within the strike zone. When the pitcher demonstrates these abilities, he makes the jump from being a thrower to becoming a pitcher, and this maximizes his chance to disrupt the hitter's timing.

The BP fastball is a fastball thrown at submaximal velocity (hence the name BP, which means "batting practice"), while the extra fastball is a pitch thrown at top-end velocity. Most pitchers have a comfort zone for throwing a fastball; in other words, when they throw the fastball at just the right speed, they achieve optimal command and movement. Anything over that speed, and the pitcher feels out of control and basically overthrows. If we were to align the fastball that the pitcher throws most often with an effort scale of 1 to 10—with 1 being the lowest effort and 10 being the highest—we would find that most pitchers are somewhere around a 9. This will be the starting point for arranging the BP and the extra. The BP will approach a 7 on the effort scale, and the extra will be a 9 1/2 or a 10. Grips for these pitches do not vary much, if at all, from the normal fastball grips unless a pitcher stumbles onto something that may work for him. For instance, I had a pitcher several years back who threw his BP fastball with his fingers spread a bit farther than the normal pinky-width distance that he used on his regular fastball. This slowed the ball down enough (7 on the effort scale) without requiring any further changes in his delivery or thought process.

The BP, much like the changeup, can be a great pitch to throw in a count where the hitter expects to see a fastball (e.g., a 2-0 or 3-1 count). The hitter expects fastball, sees fastball, and reacts to what he perceives to be the fastball only to be disappointed when the pitch arrives a little later than he expected. Many ground balls and weakly hit fly balls occur when this pitch is thrown properly. Note that the speed of the BP should be in the middle of the regular fastball and the changeup, so if the pitcher normally throws an 80 mph fastball and a 72 mph changeup, a 76 to 77 mph BP should be the goal.

PEN SESSION   Recognizing and Controlling Overthrowing

How can you tell when a pitcher is overthrowing? Late posture changes—such as a glove-side yank that causes the pitcher to veer off the target line before release—are very common in pitchers who try to "write checks that their body cannot cash." Another common occurrence, especially in games, is the pitcher's normal tempo becoming faster than usual. As he moves his body faster and faster in an attempt to gain more momentum and access more strength, his movements will appear to be out of rhythm, out of sync, and out of control. They probably are, and so is the pitcher. When this happens, it is a good time to instruct the pitcher to slow down, breathe deep, and practice the gap movements described in chapter 2. Use of the radar gun during bullpens to further define a 7, 8, 9, or 10 velocity may be helpful for the pitcher to gain a better understanding of his locus of control. For instance, if the pitcher throws his normal fastball at 85 mph, a 7 might be 80 or 81 mph or whatever speed you correlate with the number. The point of the exercise is to help the pitcher develop the feel of what it is like to throw below his threshold of velocity with varying speeds. When this happens, the pitcher gains two advantages. First, he will be able to slow the game and himself down as previously mentioned. Second, he will have the ability to change speeds on the fastball to keep the hitter off balance. Very beneficial if the pitcher has the skill level to execute, but also beneficial in building this skill if he currently cannot master speed change.

The extra fastball will be thrown when the pitcher is ahead in the count. Many major-league pitchers talk about leaving a "little bit in the tank" for when they most need it. This means that they will be pitching within their comfortable level of effort (a 9 fastball), but then they will use the reserve in their proverbial tank to blow a hitter away. Often, this is done with a high fastball or an expanded fastball just outside the zone that the hitter will chase. That's why it is appropriate to throw the extra when the pitcher is ahead in the count; the pitcher wants to expand the strike zone while the hitter is defensive. As with the BP, there is no special grip with the extra—just a good ol' "me versus you" mentality.

Changeup

A good changeup is one of the best pitches that a pitcher can have in his arsenal. Many people think the changeup is the best pitch in baseball because it creates the most deception for the hitter—the pitch appears to be a fastball, only to arrive at the plate a bit later than the regular fastball. Many young pitchers become enamored with learning to throw a breaking ball of some variety, and having a good breaking ball certainly merits attention because it can provide the pitcher with a pitch to get swings and misses or outs. But the breaking ball has a negative side too: A breaking ball is potentially easier for the high-level hitter to recognize earlier because of the spin and trajectory out of the hand. Within the first 40 feet of flight, the hitter will be able to read if the pitch is coming from a slightly varied trajectory (the curveball looks as if it comes up and over the hand, marking a trajectory change) and also read the spin of the ball (slider or curveball spin). The hitter then has the last 20 feet of flight to decide on whether to swing or not. This same scenario does not happen with the changeup; trajectory and spin of the changeup are virtually identical to the fastball, so no early clues are given to the hitter. This makes the changeup a much deadlier pitch if it is thrown well.

The changeup—or "slip" pitch, as it was known in baseball's early days—has been around for many years. Numerous grip variations are used for the changeup, and the most popular changeup these days is the circle change. The circle change is indeed a good pitch, but the pitcher must realize that it is not the only type of changeup to choose from. For our purposes, we will assume that the pitcher has never thrown a changeup, and we will start with the pitchfork grip. The pitchfork is a three-finger grip that should be thrown with the same seam orientation (four seam or two seam) and same arm action as a fastball (see figure 5.10). As with the normal fastball, the thumb and middle finger will bisect the middle of the ball. Using the same grip organization as the fastball will keep deception at a maximum. If the pitcher normally throws his fastball with a four-seam grip, he should do the same with the changeup so that it looks identical to the hitter. The changeup is usually a pitch that is thrown to an area from the middle to the arm side of the plate, so if the pitcher throws a two-seam fastball to this side of the plate, he would be wise to throw a two-seam changeup to the same side.

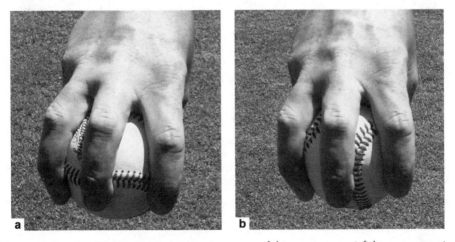

Figure 5.10 Pitchfork grip for the changeup: *(a)* four-seam and *(b)* two-seam grip.

Once the pitchfork change is mastered, the pitcher can move on to the circle change. This should be a fairly easy transition for the pitcher to make; it is simply a matter of slowly bringing the thumb and first finger closer together on the inside part of the ball (see figure 5.11). As the pitcher becomes more comfortable with the thumb and first finger on the side of the ball, he can then experiment with how loose or firm his grip should be, as well as the spacing of the fingers on the ball. Each pitcher will be a bit different in the way the ball feels, but the ultimate result still must be that the changeup looks like a fastball to the hitter.

If the pitcher would like to have more movement on the circle change, he can begin to experiment with sliding the ring finger toward the center of the ball (see figure 5.12). This puts his hand on the inside part of the ball, much like the sinker grip described earlier. Some pitchers have very good luck with this grip because it enables them to get late-breaking movement with the changeup and gives them the ability to take more speed off the ball, a common problem for many when first trying to throw a changeup. A good rule for the speed differential between the fastball and changeup is that the changeup should be 8 mph slower than the fastball. Some pitchers have been able to take even more speed off with good results, but again, each pitcher will be different, and the important thing is that tempo and arm speed remain relatively the same as the fastball.

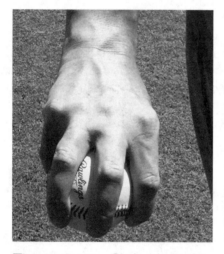
Figure 5.11 Circle grip for the changeup.

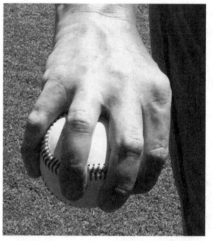
Figure 5.12 Circle change grip with the ring finger closer to the center of the ball.

Changeup Drill 1: Arm Movement

This drill enhances the pitcher's feel for the changeup and teaches him that the arm must move through the throwing zone quickly.

Setup

Perform this drill on a flat surface. The pitcher and catcher should be 75 to 90 feet (22.8 to 27.4 m) apart. Baseballs and a home plate are needed for this drill. Mark an area on the ground to replicate a pitching rubber.

Procedure

1. The pitcher holds the baseball in a changeup grip (a grip that he is comfortable with).

2. The pitcher assumes the windup or stretch position on the area marked as the rubber.

3. The pitcher initiates the pitching motion and throws the ball exactly as he would if throwing a fastball to his catcher.

4. The pitcher should gradually move back from 75 feet to 90 feet as he becomes comfortable with the grip and delivery.

Pitching Points

Coaches should encourage pitchers to throw the ball with the same arm velocity that they use for throwing a fastball. Watch to be certain that pitchers do not slow their body down in the process of throwing. A benefit of throwing the longer distance is that the pitcher will have to use more effort to get the ball to travel the required distance to the catcher. This means the arm will have to move quickly through the throwing zone.

Modifications

With younger players, shorten the distance to an age-appropriate length. Coaches should emphasize the importance of developing a changeup to young pitchers and convince them that as they progress up the ladder, their fastballs will not be enough to get batters out.

Changeup Drill 2: Ball Flip

This drill helps a pitcher develop a feel for the grip pressure of the changeup. It also gives a pitcher practice in setting the grip without looking at the ball (looking at the ball is sometimes a dead giveaway to a batter that an off-speed pitch is on the way) and helps take thinking out of the changeup equation.

Setup

This drill can be done on flat ground or on a pitching mound. Pair pitchers with a catcher. Baseballs are needed for each pair. If doing the drill on flat ground, mark an area on the ground to replicate a pitching rubber.

Procedure

1. The pitcher assumes the stretch position with the throwing and glove hand together in the center of his body.

2. As the pitcher lifts his leg to initiate the pitching motion, he tosses the ball into the air in front of him. This part of the drill should be performed deliberately and not too quickly.

3. With his leg still lifted, the pitcher catches the ball and grips it in a changeup grip.

4. Maintaining his balance and symmetry, the pitcher finishes his motion and throws the ball to his catcher.

(continued)

Changeup Drill 2 (continued)

Pitching Points

Remind pitchers to just catch the ball and feel the hand assuming the proper grip. When performed properly, this drill promotes the correct amount of firmness or looseness that each individual pitcher will need. Also, the emphasis here should be on feeling comfortable with the grip and the throwing motion, not necessarily throwing strikes.

Modifications

Because of its complexity, this drill is not recommended for younger pitchers.

Changeup Drill 3: Open Stride

Along with adding to the pitcher's comfort level for the feeling of the changeup grip and arm action, this drill forces the pitcher to stay "inside the ball" and release the ball off of the ring finger. This action aids in the arm pronation that is needed to properly throw a good changeup.

Setup

This drill can be done on flat ground or on a pitching mound. Pair pitchers with a catcher. Baseballs are needed for each pair. If doing the drill on flat ground, mark an area on the ground to replicate a pitching rubber.

Procedure

1. The pitcher holds the baseball in a changeup grip (a grip that he is comfortable with).
2. The pitcher assumes the stretch position with an exaggerated open stance. This means that the stride leg is placed to the open side of what is known as the T line between the pitching rubber and home plate rather than parallel to it.
3. Lifting the stride leg, the pitcher initiates the pitching motion and loads his pelvis.
4. As he rides his back leg forward toward home plate, the pitcher deliberately strides with his front leg toward the open side of the T, forcing his front hip to fly open.
5. Because the front hip will be open, the pitcher will have to work hard to pronate his throwing wrist to keep the changeup on line to the plate. This facilitates releasing the ball off of the ring finger, creating more movement on the ball.

Pitching Points

Because the open body position will make the pitcher fight to keep the pitch on line, the arm action will seem natural. Repetition of this drill will ingrain the proper arm action and release mechanics into the pitcher's delivery. It should be emphasized, though, that opening up in this manner should only be done when performing this drill. As always, remind pitchers to throw the ball with the same arm velocity that they use to throw a fastball. Watch to be certain that pitchers do not slow their body down in the process of throwing.

Modifications

This drill is not recommended for use with younger pitchers, because they need to replicate proper mechanics continually. Use this drill only with mature athletes who understand the throwing motion.

Breaking Balls

The last weapon that a pitcher needs to complete his arsenal is the breaking ball. This is probably the most mysterious pitch in the arsenal. Many a pitcher and pitching coach fawn over the idea of having devastating breaking stuff, and younger pitchers have a tendency to fall in love with their breaking ball at the expense of developing their other pitches, including the fastball. Please don't misunderstand; a well-executed breaking ball can be one of the best pitches that a pitcher may throw, and at the higher levels of the game, the breaking ball may yield more outs than any other pitch. But to be a complete pitcher, pitchers must understand that the breaking ball is only a portion of their arsenal and should be treated accordingly. Another issue is that some

Figure 5.13 Note that the ball is marked in sections—top, bottom, front, back, and sides. It is also marked with spots for corners. This is important for hand placement and how the ball should spin out of the hand.

pitchers will be inclined to develop two or three types of breaking balls rather than master a single breaking ball that will work consistently for them. This tendency goes back to "renting versus owning," and I cannot stress enough the importance of attempting to master each pitch before going to another. As my grandfather used to say, "Don't put the cart before the horse!"

Pitchers should also keep in mind, especially with breaking balls, the concept that the ball has sides and corners (see figure 5.13). Though the idea of the ball having sides and corners simply involves "feeling" images for the pitcher (the ball is still round), this concept can help the pitcher gain a better understanding of how to make the ball spin properly and with maximum revolutions—two keys for good breaking balls. This helps the pitcher understand what he is trying to do with the pitch (instead of just searching for the perfect grip).

Curveball

The curveball can be a great pitch for pitchers who have a straight over-the-top or high three-quarter arm slot. Generally, an arm slot lower than the high three-quarter slot will not support throwing an adequate curveball because the pitcher's fingers cannot stay on top of the baseball. Typically, the curveball is gripped by placing the middle finger on the long seam of the ball; the thumb offsets the middle finger on a seam directly across or resting directly below the seam across (see figure 5.14). This type of grip will create four-seam topspin on the ball. The spin of the curveball is created by supinating, or turning the hand in a "karate chop" manner, at release of the ball. As the pitcher supinates and turns the hand over, the fingers pass over the top of the ball, thus creating topspin. The faster the pitcher can move his fingers over the top side of the ball through to the front side of the ball, the greater spin he will impart.

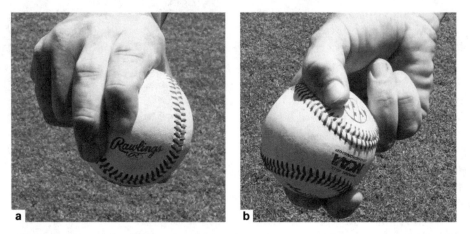

Figure 5.14   Curveball grip: *(a)* thumb directly across the seam and *(b)* thumb directly below the seam.

On paper, the curveball seems easy to throw, but that is hardly the case. Many pitchers change a number of things when delivering a curveball, most notably their intent (arm speed) and arm action, which in turn can alter tempo and rhythm of the delivery. If any of these actions are altered, the pitcher's consistency and ability to repeat this pitch are seriously compromised. This is likely one of the reasons why youth-level pitchers have a difficult time throwing the curveball properly and often injure themselves. Because most youngsters are not strong enough to support the movements necessary to throw a curveball, inconsistencies in the mechanics occur, and repeated stress is placed on the shoulder and elbow of the pitcher.

Curveball Pressure Drill

This drill is especially good for a pitcher who has trouble keeping his hand on top of the ball when throwing a curve. It also reinforces proper arm mechanics.

Setup

This drill can be done on flat ground or on a pitching mound from either the stretch or windup position. Pair pitchers with a catcher or other partner. Baseballs are needed for each pair. If doing the drill on flat ground, mark an area on the ground to replicate a pitching rubber.

Procedure

1. The pitcher assumes the stretch or windup position.
2. Before beginning his motion, the pitcher should firm up his grip on the ball by exerting more pressure with his middle finger on top of the ball.
3. The pitcher initiates his pitching motion and throws a curveball to his partner, making sure that he maintains pressure on the middle finger until release.
4. After releasing the pitch in front of his body, the pitcher follows through by turning his throwing hand over in a karate chop motion.

Pitching Points

Coaches should watch to see that pitchers maintain a firm wrist throughout the motion and that the wrist does not become loose or sloppy. This is often the reason why fingers do not stay in correct position on top of the ball. Also, pitchers should be reminded to keep their arm speed and arm motion as similar to their fastball motion as possible.

Pitchers need to remember four important things when throwing the curveball. First, this pitch's effectiveness relies on the amount of spin that can be imparted on the ball—more spin equals better (tighter and faster) spin. The proper way to impart more spin on the curveball is to tighten the grip. Second, the pitcher should draw the ring finger down to the side of the ball, creating pressure on the ball and forcing it to spin tighter (see figure 5.15). Third, when throwing breaking pitches, the pitcher should remember that the ball has sides and corners. In the case of the curveball, the pitcher wants to impart spin from the back side of the ball through the front side of the ball, thus imparting spin from back to front. And finally, the last crucial element of the curveball is that the pitcher must be able to finish the pitch with proper deceleration of the arm. The arm should finish its path, and the back hip should rotate around the front hip, forcing the chest over the front knee.

Figure 5.15 Pitcher drawing the ring finger down to the side of the ball for the curveball.

Slider

The slider became wildly popular in the 1980s, largely because it is easier to throw, can be thrown harder, and results in a higher percentage of strikes than a curveball. The grip of the slider is much like—if not exactly the same as—the curveball. The difference between the two pitches is that with the slider the hand and fingers stay behind the ball (see figure 5.16) versus coming around and over it as on the curveball. Staying behind the ball on the slider is the main reason why it can be thrown harder and probably why it is easier to throw for strikes than the curve. Middle-finger pressure should be applied to the outside third—to middle of the ball. This will create sidespin at release. When proper spin is imparted on the slider, the hitter sees a small red dot on the ball, and late two-plane depth will occur. Because topspin is imparted on a curveball, the pitch moves more straight up to straight down. The slider will move both from one side of the plate to the other and on a diagonal (see figure 5.17). Both pitches are intended to change the swing path of the hitter and create timing differences to keep the hitter off balance.

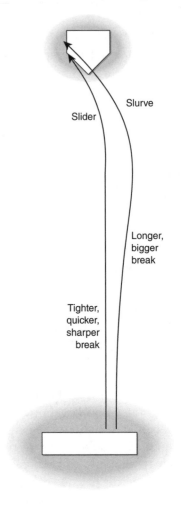

Figure 5.17   Diagonal action of the slider.

Figure 5.16   Slider grip.

Slider Exercise

When beginning to throw the slider, a pitcher must be sure to keep the fingers from coming around the ball too much, which makes the pitch slower and makes the break on the ball bigger or longer. A slower and bigger break on the slider will provide early clues for the hitter; this is something the pitcher definitely does not want. Middle-finger and first-finger pressure can help the pitcher stay behind the ball until release, and the pitcher can further accentuate this movement by manipulating his fingers up, over, and through the ball. We refer to the two-finger pressure as the fat-finger slider (see figure 5.18). Pitchers should think about turning a radio dial with the fingers versus turning a doorknob with the wrist. This "feel image" seems to help the pitcher stay behind the slider.

Figure 5.18 Fat-finger slider.

QUICK PITCH

As with the curveball, pitchers should keep a few points in mind when throwing the slider. First, the pitch requires one- or two-finger pressure to make it spin properly. Second, the pitcher can use the concept of the ball having corners to throw "up and over" the side of the ball, or he may use the radio tuner image to make the ball spin. Finally, the pitcher should keep the same arm action and same arm speed on the slider as he does on the fastball, and he must have a proper finish of the pitch and the arm.

As with all pitches, there are variations of both the curveball and slider. A pitcher who has a loose wrist may resort to the spike curveball. By spiking the finger on top of the ball, as shown in figure 5.19, the wrist automatically firms up so that a consistent delivery and consistent spin can occur. Some pitchers may be caught in between a curveball and slider spin, thus throwing what is known as a slurve. The slurve is a hybrid pitch that moves across the strike zone more than a curveball but breaks earlier and bigger than a slider. Nonetheless, it can still be an effective pitch if it is thrown regularly for strikes and keeps the hitter off balance. No matter which grip is ultimately chosen, the important considerations are the pitcher's ability to throw the breaking ball for a strike, movement in the strike zone, and a consistency of delivery.

Figure 5.19 Spike curveball grip.

Deceptive Pitching Qualities

I've often heard hitters coming back to the dugout after an at-bat mumbling about not being able to "see" or "pick up" what the pitcher just threw to them. I can remember that feeling too when I was a hitter. However, I usually had trouble seeing most of the pitches that any pitcher threw to me, so I concluded that the problem wasn't so much the deception of the pitcher but instead my inabilities as a hitter! What is it about some pitchers that make it difficult for the hitters to pick up the ball out of their hands? What makes them deceptive?

Some pitchers simply "will" the ball to the plate. They have so much conviction in what they are throwing—they are so competitive and have such complete trust in what the ball is doing and where it is going—that they somehow seem to make batters miss even when they throw a terrible pitch. This pitcher is deceptive because of his "me versus you" attitude. Some people might say this pitcher is lucky. Others will say that he pitches with "smoke and mirrors." I say he pitches with a great intent. With balls and strikes. With trust.

Some pitchers are deceptive because of their individual pitching style. Let's look at four disguises that a pitcher can use to hide the pitch.

Throwing Across the Body

The first deceptive quality that a pitcher can use is throwing across his body. You will see many relievers in the big leagues who throw across their body, possibly for the sole purpose of concealing their pitches (see figure 5.20). Although this may not be the most functional and efficient move toward the plate, throwing across one's body can create a disadvantage for the hitter because of the angle at which the pitch is thrown or because of the jerky motion the pitcher uses to rotate and throw the pitch. The pitcher must now determine whether the deception of stepping across his body outweighs the risk of injury or becomes a hindrance for creating more velocity. A general rule for me is that if the pitcher can throw the ball to his glove side and demonstrate the ability to rotate his back hip around the front hip while doing so, this indicates that he is able to completely finish the throw and can be allowed to continue throwing across his body. If he cannot show that he can do this, or if it is obvious that he could throw much harder or much more efficiently another way, I would then try to help him with his line to the plate.

High Glove Side

Another element of deception is the high glove side. Usually, a pitcher with an elevated glove side, as shown in figure 5.21, has the ability to hide the ball longer because the ball often appears to the hitter just after the glove side goes down, especially when the arm slot comes through the same pathway as the glove side. In a perfect world, setting the hip, which was described in detail in the previous chapter, is what elevates the front shoulder. If everything is on time and in rhythm, the elevated glove side creates leverage, angle, and deception for the pitcher.

Figure 5.20 This pitcher's delivery may hide the ball longer from the hitter because he is closed off to the plate, thus making it more difficult for the hitter to pick up the pitcher's release point.

Figure 5.21 The elevated glove side not only increases the pitcher's leverage for working against the slope of the mound, it may also make it more difficult for the hitter to pick up the release of the ball.

Throwing Arm Direction

A third deceptive quality is the manner, or direction, in which the throwing arm moves. Usually, the arm swing that is most deceptive to the hitter is one that is directly behind, is shorter, and does not pause or stop. The pitcher's body shields the ball from the hitter, and the ball often appears to come out of nowhere or off the top of the shoulder. The pitcher doesn't give the hitter anything to look at, and the ball has the ability to sneak up on the hitter. These guys are tough to hit!

Angle and Slot Change

The final deceptive quality is a change of the angle and slot from where a pitcher normally throws the ball—this is the sidewinder. Some people in baseball circles would say that sidearm pitchers are more difficult to hit because their ball moves so much, but I would disagree. I think they are tough to hit because they have a swooping spine change at the end, and the ball comes from a much different place than the hitter is accustomed to seeing it. The deception of the sidewinder is that he is upright and then makes a drastic posture change, delivering the ball from a very odd and low angle—something the hitter is definitely not used to seeing. This, coupled with the movement of the ball and the unusually sweeping movement of the breaking ball, makes the sidewinder extremely deceptive.

As with stepping across the body, these deceptive traits of the delivery make each pitcher unique, and the coach and the pitcher must determine at some point what stays in the delivery and what is adjusted and why. If there is a risk of injury, the pitcher should obviously make an adjustment. If the pitcher is on time and executes consistently, the coach must be careful not to make unnecessary changes.

The important thing for a pitcher to keep in mind when developing pitches is to master the basic pitches first and then let his pitches evolve naturally based on need, maturity, and skill level. Too often, a pitcher tries to do too much with his pitches instead of keeping his arsenal simple. Remember, hitting is difficult to do, and the pitcher has an advantage if he can hit a spot or throw a pitch consistently. In the end, the pitcher who has a simple arsenal of pitches or a simple pitch plan that he can execute consistently will outperform the pitcher who has a plan or a pitch that he cannot control.

The Role of the Catcher

No examination of pitching would be complete without a discussion of the role of the catcher. Fundamentally, the catcher is an extension of the pitcher and the pitching foundation, and the success of the pitcher is dependent on and directly related to the skills of the catcher. Many skills and attributes—for example, the way that he blocks, throws, and receives—are required to be a good catcher. But what separates the good ones from the great? This chapter covers the qualities that a great catcher possesses.

Qualities of an Excellent Catcher

A professional scout once told me that the very best catchers are the ones who go unnoticed throughout a contest. They catch every ball, lead positively, control the pace of the game, and work intelligently with the pitcher to produce desirable results. They are the gatekeepers of the pace and rhythm of the game, and good catchers have a knack of squeezing every ounce out of whatever skills a pitcher possesses. They are usually the unsung heroes of a winning team.

The catcher is two players in one—catcher first and hitter second. It's a bonus if a catcher is also an offensive threat, but the catcher must be able to separate the two roles. Show me a catcher who is unable to separate what just happened in his last at-bat from the task of skillfully guiding and interacting with his pitcher the very next inning, and I will show you a machine that is irreparably broken. The ability to *separate*—a term baseball folks use to describe the mental ability to compartmentalize the offensive side of the game from the defensive side—divides the average catcher from the good catcher, and the good from the great.

A catcher is not a dictator, even though some act that way. Although the catcher's job is to take charge, this should not include belittling or yelling at the pitcher, which would negatively affect what the pitcher is trying to do. This type of pitcher–catcher interaction will simply not work. The catcher must remember that pitching is very difficult to master and that many variables play on the effectiveness of a hurler's stuff and psyche during any given outing. This is also wise advice for the coach to remember as well.

PEN SESSION   Interacting With the Pitcher

Many young catchers make the mistake of believing that in order to take charge, they must show a tough exterior. Yelling the number of outs and constant communication are required, but the way the catcher handles individual pitchers will vary, and this is where a coach's help can greatly benefit the catcher. Each pitcher has a unique personality on the mound. For some pitchers, their game personality is completely different than their normal personality. For example, a kid who is extremely shy and quiet may suddenly come to life when he is on the mound. However, I have found that most pitchers' game personality and normal personality are very much aligned with one another, leaving coaches to constantly evaluate how they should approach their pitchers and how they can motivate them. A coach may find that one of his pitchers responds well to praise, while another responds well to constructive criticism. Some pitchers fare better when they are simply left alone. Whatever the case, the coach must share his findings with the catcher so that the catcher can be an extension of the coach during a game. I spend a great deal of time talking to our catchers about the personalities of our pitchers and how the catcher should talk with them during a game. The catchers will also share with me their ideas on each pitcher. Because the catchers are around the pitchers more—going to class with them, eating with them, training with them—they have a unique perspective that the coach does not.

Good catchers serve as an ambassador between the pitcher and umpire. This is another area where the catcher's communication skills come into play. A good catcher works the umpire by carrying on a casual dialogue throughout the game about the pitcher's stuff, his arsenal, and how the two will fit into the umpire's strike zone. The catcher may strategically alert the umpire about the shape of the pitcher's curveball or the movement on his fastball. In other words, the catcher "butters up" the umpire. Coaches and catchers need to remember that most umpires are simply human beings doing something they love. They will make mistakes, but they can also be influenced by the pitcher's ability to consistently hit spots and the catcher's ability to "steal strikes" with proper pitch framing and subtle, yet informative, conversation. Yes, the catcher is a salesman! With proper selling technique, the catcher can help expand the strike zone by a few inches, providing a distinct advantage for the pitcher.

Pitchers are, by trade, insecure creatures. They often need a good amount of reassurance, and the catcher is the point man for this during the game. The entire defensive front faces the catcher, so he must display positive body language and infuse positive energy toward the pitcher and the defense. Subtle hints, such as the catcher pulling his front shoulder in and pointing to it before throwing the ball back to the pitcher, can serve as a reminder that reinforces the idea of staying closed during the pitching delivery. A catcher pointing his glove in the pitcher's direction after a well-executed pitch can give the pitcher great confidence and reassurance that his stuff and pitches are working well. All of this body language, or gap movements, can be priceless for the psyche and soul of the pitcher.

Speaking of psyche, the catcher, through keen observation and hundreds of bullpen sessions, also becomes the resident team psychologist. A good catcher recognizes when the pitcher's mind or body is "sped up," and because he knows the pitcher both as an individual and as a baseball player, the catcher knows just what to do or say to get him back on track. He understands the rhythm of the pitcher, and he takes action when the pitcher's pitches are not doing what is intended. He knows when a mound visit is necessary or when he needs to slow the pitcher's processes down. When this happens, the catcher should ask the pitcher to breathe deep and should remind him of the game situation and the plan against the current hitter. Recognizing these warning signs in a pitcher takes practice, but it can be mastered through observation and coaching. Sometimes the best remedy is simply humor; easing the tension and helping the pitcher get out of his own way might be just what the doctor ordered!

Seven Intangible Attributes of a Good Catcher

Here are seven key attributes that are inherent in good catchers:

1. *Displays toughness*—He's a competitor in every sense of the word.
2. *Plays the role of servant leader*—He leads his team by serving his pitcher, coaches, and other players on the field.
3. *Communicates*—A good catcher isn't afraid to speak his mind; he is a general or leader on the field, in practice, and perhaps off the field.
4. *Separates*—As mentioned earlier, a good catcher has the ability to separate his offense from his defense.
5. *Displays good body language and presence*—A good catcher displays effective use of body language and establishes a presence. The catcher must remember that everyone on the field is watching him, so he must display control at all times.
6. *Demonstrates hustle*—The catcher must display the most hustle on the field. He must give the pitcher the confidence to throw the ball in the dirt, knowing he will block it, especially during crucial times in the game.
7. *Serves as psychologist*—A good catcher knows the personality of his pitchers and is able to reach them through words or actions.

Responsibilities of the Catcher

The catcher is a general or coach on the field. His responsibilities include catching the pitcher, moving players around the field for defensive positioning, and being the last line of defense to prevent the offense from scoring. It is sometimes said that the catcher wears the "tools of ignorance," referring to the padding that protects him from batted and thrown balls, but I would disagree with this description. The catcher is often coach, player, and resident psychologist all rolled into one; and a catcher who also has charisma, physical tools, and intelligence is definitely a winning player.

The catcher has many direct responsibilities to his pitchers that will greatly affect the amount of success they enjoy. Though I will not get into specifics on catching techniques or the physical abilities that a good catcher possesses, I will touch on them indirectly and how they pertain to the success of the pitcher. First, the catcher must have a solid understanding of the in-game goals that a pitcher is striving for. Basic in-game goals, such as throwing strike 1 and "winning" even counts (1-1, 2-2 counts—the goal will always be to throw a high-quality strike in these counts), can be used to serve the point. These goals are the basic framework for pitching success, and it must be established from the beginning that these goals are as much the responsibility of the catcher as they are of the pitcher.

The catcher's next responsibility is to give the pitcher a proper target. A pitcher's success starts with his ability to be precise with the pitches he throws. A great target— one that is early and big (glove up and open)—increases the chance for precision. As discussed in chapter 2, the pitcher needs to train his eyes in order to increase his ability to focus on a smaller point inside the catcher's mitt, but this skill is directly related to the type of target that the catcher provides. Many catchers get lazy with their target, show it late, or perhaps don't even show one at all. This is a detail of the game that cannot go unnoticed by coach or pitcher.

PEN SESSION Valuing the Target

At the beginning of each year, we have a meeting for our pitching staff and spend time talking about little things that make a big difference. The catchers are included in this meeting. Training the eyes is a major topic discussed at this meeting. The catchers are instructed on how to show a target and what the pitcher is trying to focus on. During our initial bullpens, we break down the way we would like the catcher to set up and how he should show his target. The pitchers will usually let me know if they don't think the catcher is setting up properly for them, or I will sometimes correct the catcher's setup and target in a bullpen session. We also film all of our games, and our coaches check the target and setup of the catchers. As discussed in chapter 5, the catcher needs to set up properly in the zone in order to give the pitcher the best chance to consistently hit the strike zone. If the pitcher is not a highly skilled strike thrower, the catcher will set up in the middle of the plate so that there is a big area to throw to. As the pitcher becomes more skilled, the catcher's setup can become more pointed to a specific location on the plate.

One of the necessary, yet tough, duties of the catcher is to catch the many bullpens that his pitchers throw. This often takes away from the amount of time a catcher spends on the offensive side compared to other positional players, but it is a vital piece to the success of his staff. Most important, catching bullpens gives the catcher an understanding of what type of pitcher he will be dealing with. The catcher becomes familiar with the movements and shape of each pitch, as well as the strengths and weaknesses of a pitcher's arsenal. In addition, by working together in the bullpen, the pitcher and catcher will answer questions such as how they will attack a left-handed hitter or what pitches they will throw in certain counts. Though the pitcher and coach will ultimately be responsible for the final game plan, the catcher's input is invaluable. His observation that a certain pitch isn't effective (particularly if it is one of the pitcher's primary pitches) could influence how the pitcher and coach approach the adjustments to the game or opponent.

Pitcher and Catcher: Working Together

A certain beautiful type of rhythm happens when a pitcher and catcher work in harmony together. I have found that this rhythm occurs more often when the pitcher and catcher are allowed to call the game—with limited interference from the coach. The battery of the pitcher and catcher see and feel things that the coach cannot, such as the movement and exact location of the pitch. With proper training, the pitcher and catcher will be able to make intelligent assessments and decide what pitch to throw next. Because we live in a "transfer of blame" society more than ever before, accountability and conviction are the main reasons that the pitcher and catcher should call the game. I want our batteries to be intelligent and responsible. Again, this is where bullpens and chalk talks between pitcher, coach, and catcher will pay off. As the pitcher and catcher become more competent in understanding what to throw and when, their effort takes on a natural rhythm. It is like a pendulum on a clock—consistent, smooth, and on time. The pace of the game increases, enhancing the alertness of the defense, as well as the trust that the pitcher puts behind each pitch. This is winning baseball.

Not only is a good catcher critical to the success of a pitcher, he also serves a vital role in communicating with the coaching staff. Among other things, the catcher has a distinct advantage over the coach in that he receives the ball thrown by the pitcher—so he sees it, feels it, and understands certain details that a coach cannot. Therefore, he becomes the eyes and ears of the coach, which makes him a very valuable tool.

If a team puts a high value on the catcher's role, input from the catcher becomes critical in decisions that the coach makes regarding pitching plans, mechanical or pitch adjustments, and tactical strategies. Another advantage that a catcher has over the coach is that he has most likely faced his pitchers as a hitter in batting practice or practice scrimmages, giving him yet another angle from which to help the coaches in making decisions. The coach can only speculate on what it's like for the hitters facing the pitcher; the catcher's information is based on actual experience.

During competition, the catcher is the closest person to the hitter—yet another advantage. As he is receiving pitches, the catcher is privy to certain changes in the batter's demeanor (e.g., confused or angry looks), or he may hear the hitter mumbling under his breath. Again, these subtleties are all things that the pitcher and coach might not be able to see and hear. This information can be quite useful in calling the next pitch, or it could even help expose a weakness that was not previously known.

To pick up this information, the only talent that the catcher needs is the ability to keenly observe the body language of the hitter. He should also learn to "think with" the hitter based on what he sees and hears.

The catcher should apply the same awareness when dealing with the pitcher. He faces the pitcher the entire game and has the opportunity to see certain things that a coach might not be able to see. Again, the only skill needed is for the catcher to stay alert and observe his pitcher's nuances. In many instances, my catcher has come in after an inning and told me that the pitcher is giving off bad body language after poorly executed pitches. This is something that I couldn't see from the dugout. For our machine to work properly, I must trust in what my catcher sees in order to educate the pitcher on how to cope with the game better. After all, if the catcher saw the negative body language, there is a good chance the hitter did too, and this might cause a pitcher to lose his edge against that particular hitter or in that particular inning. This problem must be resolved quickly if the pitcher is to return; if not, a pitching change may be in order.

You might wonder how a catcher can be trained to see and hear all of this action that is essentially going on at the same time. How can he see the reactions of the pitcher as well as the hitter? The coach must first educate the catcher about what to look and listen for. The catcher should then practice these skills in the bullpen and in practice scrimmages. The catcher practices the art of being alert. After receiving the ball, the catcher then throws it back while at the same time listening to the hitter and observing the pitcher. Next, he should quickly turn his attention to remembering the hitter's reaction to the pitch and scan for clues. If any are found, he then bases his next pitch call on what was previously thrown and the hitter's reaction to it. This is the "cat and mouse" game played by pitcher, catcher, and hitter. This is the game within the game!

As mentioned, one of the most useful tools for the catcher is to catch his pitchers in the bullpen. Besides the obvious advantage of getting to know his pitcher, the catcher is able to help the coach better understand if the adjustments that are being made are yielding results. During these moments, I find myself first asking the pitcher "How does that feel?" followed by asking the catcher "How does that look?" After all, if he truly knows his pitcher, the catcher will know that the throw looks, feels, or reacts either better or worse than previous throws. In the end, making adjustments becomes a three-pronged attack—the feel of the pitcher, the look of the pitch coming into the hitting area, and the coach's judgment of whether there is improvement or not. Two heads are better than one, as the old saying goes, so surely three heads are better than two.

After each outing, our pitchers are asked to evaluate their performance. Among other things, I want to know what they thought went well and what they think needs to improve in both the short term and the long term. True evaluation is a powerful tool for preparing for the pitcher's next outing—we will base his work week on what needs to be improved. Here, the catcher's perspective is vitally important and highly sought after. I want to know what he saw and what he thinks. For me, his thoughts serve as an outside perspective; he is not a pitcher or a coach, and his thoughts often come from a much different place than the thoughts of a pitcher. It's like when a lawn mower is broken and won't start. The coaches check the plugs and points, and they perhaps narrow it down to the crank shaft or the carburetor. The catcher walks up, checks the gas tank, and states that the mower is just out of gas. He keeps it simple. He "gets" it.

Lastly, because the catcher catches in the bullpen and during the game, he is a central component to the training versus trusting mode a pitcher finds himself in at any given time. You might remember that training versus trusting is one of the seven foundational elements to pitching that were discussed in chapter 1 and it serves the pitcher by separating the different thought processes he travels through between practices and games. In other words, it helps the pitcher "separate." The catcher sees and hears it all—from the training foundation that the pitcher has worked on in practice to what "shows up" during games. He is a constant, and because of this, he will likely have a good understanding of when the pitcher is crossing the line, either by thinking too much or thinking of the wrong thing.

The catcher is an extension of the pitcher and also serves as a coach on the field. He supports the pitcher with his physical skills (catching, blocking) and also helps keep the pitcher on target mentally. The actions and body language of the catcher can help give the pitcher confidence. In addition, the catcher, pitcher, and coach must work together—each bringing a different perspective—to plan and adjust the pitching strategy before and throughout the game. A good catcher can go a long way toward helping a pitcher achieve success.

SEVEN

Pitching With a Plan

Warren Spahn, hall of fame pitcher for the Milwaukee Braves, once said, "Hitting is timing; pitching is upsetting timing." Spahn was quite qualified to make that statement, winning a record 363 games by a left-handed pitcher in 21 years in the major leagues. Certainly, he was a man who knew what he was doing, and upsetting the hitter's timing was no doubt a large component of his success. But is pitching really that simple? Is upsetting a hitter's timing really all that is required of the pitcher to be ultrasuccessful and win as many games as the great Spahn did? Or are there other aspects of the hitter–pitcher confrontation that must be carefully considered?

A lot has been said and written about the mechanical, mental, and physical training of the pitcher; however, the most important element is often left out—how to retire the hitter. This chapter identifies what good pitchers often intuitively do to beat their opponent, and it helps create a template for the pitcher and coach to follow in developing a plan.

Before moving on to identifying and classifying hitters, it is important to note two foundational elements that are extremely important in retiring hitters consistently: balls and strikes and me versus me and me versus you. Balls and Strikes is a key concept when it comes to developing a plan. Strikes win in any league—the game cannot simply not be played without them. If the pitcher is fearless in the zone and possesses an aggressive mindset, chances are he gives himself and his teammates a very good opportunity to stay in the game with a chance for a win. Me versus me and me versus you is the root of baseball competition; it is a mentality that the pitcher must take seriously in order to have the best chance to be successful. The best plan and the best arsenal that is complemented with a weak constitution from the pitcher will likely result in mediocrity.

Traits of the Hitter

Many avenues could be taken in discussing the best ways to consistently get hitters out, but to help pitchers gain a better understanding of what they are up against, we'll start with an investigation of the hitters themselves. First and foremost, the pitcher must always remember that hitting consistently well is very difficult. Pitchers tend to give hitters too much credit before the battle has even begun. Too often, the pitcher nibbles at the strike zone or fears contact when he should realize that the percentages of the game almost always favor the pitcher and the defense. A pitcher should pursue an aggressive mind-set and should attack the strike zone—he must have the courage to fail!

Gaining an understanding of a typical batting order can be a solid first step in developing a plan. When making out a lineup, every coach tries to put his hitters into an order that suits the team best, both in the function of the position in the order and the individual style of the hitter. This being the case, the batting order can provide clues to the pitcher regarding what type of hitter each batter might be based on his position in the lineup. Table 7.1 lists the type of hitter that commonly hits in each spot of the lineup and identifies traits that each type of hitter often possesses. This information can provide clues to the pitcher and coach that may give the pitcher an advantage in the "me versus you" battle. As with all things in baseball, remember that abnormalities and individual differences are the rule rather than the exception.

The batting order may contain many combinations that fit the strengths and style of a particular team, but it can generally be split into three sections. The first three hitters are usually the best hitters in the lineup, and they most likely strike out the least. Hitters 4, 5, and 6 generally possess the most power on the team, and they are counted on to drive in the first three hitters with extra-base hits or deep fly balls for sacrifice flies. The last three hitters in the lineup are often good defensive players who can handle the bat (bunting or hit-and-run), and they may have the ability to run. Once the leadoff hitter gets on base, it is the number 2 hitter's job to somehow move him to second base so that hitters 3, 4, and 5 have a chance to drive in the leadoff man. For batters 7, 8, and 9, the primary role is to make the pitcher work harder by taking pitches; these hitters are also trying to find a way to get on base to start the cycle over again. Coaches have also been known to hide good hitters at the bottom of the order so that these hitters get to see more fastballs and surprise the opponent. The pitcher must be aware of these circumstances, as well as the fact that when he is pitching against a good team, the number 7 or 8 hitter may be well equipped to handle his best stuff.

Notice that in table 7.1, the hitters with the most power have more holes in their swing than those who are considered contact-type hitters. In the same way that power pitchers can dominate with overpowering stuff yet sometimes lack control, power hitters, feared for their ability to hit long drives and produce runs, swing and miss more often. A parallel comparison holds true for the finesse pitcher and the contact hitter: Just as the finesse pitcher's job is to fill up the strike zone with as many strikes as possible, the contact hitter's role is to simply put the ball in play. There is certainly a place in this game for both types of pitchers and hitters—which is one more thing that makes baseball so great!

Table 7.1   Hitter Types in the Batting Order

Batting order	Hitter type
1	• Good runner • Slap or contact hitter • Sees pitches and works the count • Handles the bat; bunts and hits behind runners
2	• Good runner • Handles the bat; bunts and hits behind runners • Sacrifices himself to get runners in scoring position • Understands game
3	• Team's best hitter • Flat-swing hitter; hits many pitches in many areas • Fewest holes in swing and approach • Potential power hitter
4	• Run producer • Potential power hitter • Holes; prone to strike out • Potentially the team's most dangerous hitter
5	• Run producer • Potential power hitter • More holes than hitters 3 and 4 • Prone to strike out
6	• Run producer • Potential power hitter • More holes than hitters 3, 4, and 5; similar to hitter 5
7	• Defensive player • Athletic • Sometimes a runner with holes in swing • Power potential is gap to gap
8	• Defensive player • Handles bat • Potential runner • Potential bunter
9	• Defensive player • Handles bat • Potential bunter • Potential runner • Similar to hitter 1

The Pitching Plan

Every pitcher should go into a game with a solid plan for how he will pitch based on the strengths of his arsenal coupled with information about the other team. Too often at the lower levels of the game, college included, the pitcher tries to beat the opponent by relying solely on exposing the hitter's weakness, even if that goes against the strength of his arsenal. This plan may have short-term value for the first time through the batting order or perhaps the second, but in the long term, this strategy does not usually yield consistent results. A pitcher who stays true to what makes him effective in the first place—whether it be throwing a fastball to a certain side of the plate or using off-speed pitches that he owns rather than rents—will have more success. A pitcher must also remember that at the beginning of the game, hitters are rarely truly ready to hit, so this is another good reason why a pitcher should use his strengths the first time through the batting order.

QUICK PITCH

Pitchers should use a three-pronged approach in understanding how to attack a hitter:

1. *Pitcher's strengths*—Matching the pitcher's strengths against the hitter's strengths.
2. *Game situation*—Paying attention to the score of the game, the inning, who is up, who is on deck, the history of how the hitter has fared against the pitcher in the past, and so on.
3. *Hitter's weaknesses*—Attacking the hitter's weakness (if it fits into the pitching scheme) based on the situation and with the intent to win the game. This should be done after first targeting pitching to a hitter's strengths. The pitcher needs to realize that in almost every situation he has an advantage over the hitter.

As the game progresses and more information is obtained by both parties (hitter and pitcher), the pitcher may realize that he needs to use alternatives and switch gears in order to be successful the second time through the batting order. A good general rule is to pitch "backward," or pitch differently than what the hitter saw his first time at bat, *unless* an obvious hole was exposed. The hitter who primarily saw fastballs in his first at-bat may see more breaking balls or changeups the second time around, or he may see pitches on a different side of the plate than before. The pitcher must be careful not to overthink the situation and attack the hitter if there is an obvious hole. For example, if the pitcher primarily throws fastballs to a hitter in his first at-bat, and the hitter struggles to catch up with the pitch, it would be foolish to show him anything different that is hittable until he proves that he can hit the fastball. If the pitcher wants to throw him something different—whether for the purpose of changing the pace or simply giving the hitter a different look—the pitch should be thrown outside of the strike zone and into the pressure zones (see the sidebar Pressure Zones for more information). By throwing softer pitches (changeup or breaking ball) into the pressure zones rather than through the strike zone, the pitcher can disrupt the hitter's timing yet still maintain adherence to the original plan of beating the hitter with the fastball.

Pressure Zones

Pressure zones refer to the areas just outside the strike zone, as shown in figure 7.1. The pressure zones are areas that the pitcher wants to visit often, but not live in. By throwing the ball to these zones, especially when the pitcher is ahead in the count (e.g., 0-1, 1-2, 0-2), the pitcher forces the hitter to make a decision on whether to swing or not. Approached correctly, pressure zones give the pitcher a huge advantage because hitters rarely make consistent, hard contact in these areas; swings and misses and weak contact are much more prevalent. An incorrect way to deal with pressure zones would be to throw to them too frequently or too early in the count. When a good hitter sees these pitches being thrown early in the count or too often, he will find a way to discipline himself to stop swinging at them, thus forcing the hand of the pitcher to throw a strike more to the hitter's liking. In this case, a coach will often tell the pitcher, "You are picking at the zone" or "You are being too fine." Both statements are correct, and the pitcher must strive to first challenge the hitter with strikes located inside the strike zone. Once he can do this, the pitcher earns the right to throw his pitches into the pressure zones.

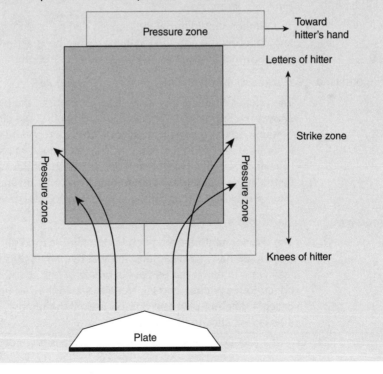

Figure 7.1
Pressure zones.

The third time through the batting order can prove to be tricky for various reasons. By this time, the pitcher has most likely lost a bit of velocity or "stuff," and the hitters have had ample time to observe the pitcher's repertoire and idiosyncrasies. How a pitcher operates in this stage of a game is what separates the craftsman pitcher from the common or ordinary pitcher. Adding a third pitch into the mix here gives the pitcher an added edge, provided he used this pitch conservatively or did not need to throw it earlier in the game. Obviously, the pitcher should only throw the third pitch if conviction and trust are involved; throwing a third pitch that is rented by the pitcher is fruitless. Another possibility for the pitcher would be to show a completely different pattern of pitches or revert back to an earlier pattern that the hitter may have forgotten. Both could be promising alternatives to use the third or fourth time through the lineup, and these strategies can still be executed within the framework of pitches in a pitcher's comfort zone. See table 7.2 for a basic pitching plan based on batting order.

This plan can be quite useful if the pitcher makes sound decisions based on his strengths and weaknesses. The pitcher must also have the ability to switch gears, because every game will present different circumstances and challenges. As an old coach of mine used to say, "If baseball were easy, everyone would play it." In other words, the pitcher's livelihood depends on his ability to adapt and overcome.

Table 7.2 Basic Pitching Plan for Batting Order

Time through batting order	Pitcher's focus*
First time	*Pitcher's strengths*
	The pitcher should throw the pitches that he is skilled at throwing and should throw them to the locations where he is skilled at throwing them—even if these pitches and areas are strengths for the hitter.
Second time	*Backward from first time, unless obvious hole*
	The pitcher should show something different to the hitter than was shown the first time up unless it is obvious that the hitter can't hit a certain pitch or a certain location. Information should be taken from the first at-bat and used accordingly. The pitcher might attack the hitter with breaking balls the second time up because he attacked the hitter with fastballs the first time. A different plan can only be implemented if the pitcher is skilled enough. If he is not, stick to the basics.
Third time	*Backward from backward*
	The pitcher might save a pitch for the hitter's third at-bat. If the pitcher used a fastball and changeup the first two times through the order, he may want to mix in the use of his breaking ball as the hitters start to adjust to his pitches and his locations. Like the second time through the order, a different plan can only be used if the pitcher is skilled enough—if he is not, stick to the basics.

*Relief pitchers should always pitch to their strengths each time through the batting order.

PEN SESSION Game Planning for the Reliever

Relievers need to use a different approach than starting pitchers. When relievers enter the game, the final outcome is usually still in question, and they must have the ability to establish their pitches very quickly. Relievers need to come out of the gates with "guns blazing," so to speak, and they must pitch to their strengths. At this point in the game, the hitter will have to make adjustments from the last pitcher to the new one, and the reliever's job will be to get comfortable as quickly as possible. Because of this, it makes sense for relievers to throw the pitches they are most adept at throwing. Remember that percentages in the game of baseball favor the pitcher, so throwing good strikes with the highest level of conviction and trust will help keep these percentages on the reliever's side. When in doubt, the pitcher should always throw his best pitch in his best location, even if that means throwing "into the teeth" of the hitter.

Hitter Awareness

Once the pitcher's basic plan has been established, the pitcher can move on to more specific in-game adjustments and techniques used to keep hitters off balance, out of rhythm, and out of time. Making those adjustments requires an ability to read the clues that a hitter supplies based on his position in the batter's box and by the way he swings the bat.

There are five words that pitchers don't want to hear: "The hitter is on you." This is baseball terminology referring to the hitter being on time with his bat to a pitch or a series of pitches. It means that the hitter has coordinated the delivery of his swing in time and in rhythm with the pitch being thrown, creating a good opportunity for solid contact—he is "seeing the ball well" against the pitcher. Hard contact can result in outs (remember, the percentages favor the pitcher), but hard contact can just as easily result in hits, extra-base hits, and balls being mishandled for errors—a recipe for scoring runs! Telltale signs of the hitter being "on" the pitcher, other than an obviously hard-hit ball, would be a ball that was fouled straight back to the screen or a ball that was hit very deep but foul. Less obvious signs of the hitter being in rhythm with the pitcher can be found in his reaction, whether it's his body language after taking a pitch or something verbal that he utters between pitches. And sometimes, it is simply a feeling or hunch that the pitcher has after throwing a pitch. Having a gut feeling can sometimes be just as important as something that's visible. I advise our pitchers to not dismiss hunches, because intuition will serve the pitcher very well in most situations.

So, the hitter is on the pitcher, and now the pitcher must decide what to do. The pitcher has four options to choose from. The first—and the most widely used—is to simply change the type of pitch he throws next. For example, if a batter hits a long foul to his pull side on a fastball, this should prompt the pitcher to throw an off-speed pitch next. Another option would be to throw the same pitch, but to a different side of the plate. Using the previous example, let's assume the pitcher threw an inside fastball that the hitter pulled foul. Locating a fastball on the outside part of the plate on the next pitch may change the hitter's swing and the timing of that swing. This can result in weak contact, perhaps a fly ball in play or a ground ball to the pull side.

The third option is probably the least used because it may be the most difficult to execute. Using the same example of a loud foul to the pull side on an inside fastball, the third option calls for the pitcher to throw the same pitch in the same spot but to change speeds on the pitch. In chapter 5, two types of fastballs besides the normal fastball were described: the BP fastball and the extra fastball. If the pitcher was to throw the extra fastball after the inside fastball that was pulled foul, the one- or two-mile-per-hour jump in velocity may be all that is needed to jam the hitter. The BP fastball may not work quite as well in this situation unless the pitcher wanted yet another foul ball, because this pitch would make the hitter's swing even earlier. However, the BP fastball could work in tandem with a fastball away because the hitter would likely mis-hit the ball but put it into play weakly in fair territory.

The final choice that a savvy pitcher will employ is to throw the very same pitch as his last, except he throws the ball farther in or farther away than the previous pitch. This tactic is designed for the pitcher with exceptional skill, so it may not be appropriate for the beginner or intermediate pitcher. In this instance, the hitter pulls a fastball on the inside part of the plate into foul territory. On the next pitch, the pitcher throws farther inside, perhaps in the gap area between the hitter and the plate. Because the hitter just saw and swung at this pitch, he will often swing at it again. The location of this ball makes it very difficult for the hitter to keep the ball fair and can result in another foul ball or a weak ground ball to the infield.

Sometimes subtle differences create large dividends, as would be the case with choice number 2, 3, or 4 if properly executed. These four choices—different pitch, same pitch different side of the plate, same pitch different speed, and same pitch farther in or away—are all designed to keep the hitter from being "on" the pitch and to give the pitcher wiggle room to be creative and stay within the strengths of his arsenal.

QUICK PITCH

The catcher can also help in gathering information during the first pass through the batting order. Because of his proximity to the hitter, the catcher should be mentally noting where each hitter stands in the batter's box as well as the foot positions that each hitter uses in his batting stance. Both things can provide clues about what the hitter is looking for and what he can or cannot hit.

Another baseball axiom, "Pitch a hitter with long arms in, and pitch a hitter with short arms away," also makes perfect sense. I'm not sure whom to give credit for this quote, but I first heard it from Tom House at a clinic several years back. Hitters who like to extend on their swings (long arms) should be attacked on the inside part of the plate, while hitters who stay inside the ball—or have a short, quick swing (short arms)—should be pitched away. Of course, these are generalities, because both types of hitters can often be pitched to on both sides of the plate, but pitchers should still pay attention to not only the hitters' physical appearance but also where hitters stand in the batter's box. Much can be gained by watching the opposition take batting practice and paying close attention during their first at-bats of the game. Not every high school and summer league team takes batting practice on the field, but if the opposing team does, pitchers should observe this activity so that they can come up with a plan based on stance, stride, and swing. As a side note, this is also a good way to find out the other team's bunters and runners. Good bunters become good bunters by practicing bunting. Poor bunters spend very little time on the craft, so they don't work on it during batting practice.

Just like the delivery of the pitcher, the hitter's stance and nuances can help him attack the pitcher or can cause him to show weakness on certain pitches or in certain locations. These weaknesses are also known as holes. If observed and understood correctly, these stances and nuances can be used against the hitter, provided the pitcher can execute certain pitches that will attack the holes.

QUICK PITCH

An important thing to understand and implement into the pitcher's plan is the fact that most hitters have trouble hitting the pitch away from them. Most hitters exhibit their strongest and fastest swing when trying to pull the ball that is close to them. The ball away presents challenges to the hitters because they often hit the ball on the far end of the bat or they are too early and hit a pull-side ground ball that has a good chance to be defended. For this reason, pitchers must be able to throw the ball inside to the hitter to make him think and react to the ball close to him; when this happens, the ball away from him becomes even more difficult to hit.

Stance, Stride, Swing

Here is a typical baseball scenario: The hitter saunters up to the plate, receives whatever sign the coach might give him, and begins the preamble for the "me versus you" battle that is ready to occur. He adjusts his batting gloves, then his helmet, and he taps the bat lightly on the opposite side of home plate. As he goes into his initial stance, war is declared between pitcher and hitter, and the confrontation begins. As the pitcher hurls the ball toward home, art and science mesh into a single unit; the pitcher is doing his thing, and the hitter is doing his. For the pitcher, this confrontation all boils down to whether or not a high-quality pitch is executed. If he executes the pitch, the pitcher has done his job and must now rely on his catcher and fielders to finish the play and record an out. Of course, the hitter's job is the opposite—hit the pitch that best suits him or wait for the pitcher to execute incorrectly and then hit the resulting mistake.

The hitter's swing, much like the pitcher's delivery, is dependent on synergy of movement and timing. Luckily, the pitcher dictates the timing of the hitter's swing (nothing can happen until the pitcher throws a pitch) and also has the ability to occasionally alter his swing, further complicating the hitter's main objective. This is done by throwing pitches on different sides of the plate, throwing different pitches, and throwing pitches at different speeds. Though it almost sounds unfair (to the hitter, that is), good hitters have a knack for putting the barrel of the bat on the ball, so the pitcher needs to collect as much information as possible so that he may attack properly. This section covers some of the clues that a pitcher can get from a hitter.

Position on the Plate

Although the location where a hitter stands in the box may only give a slight indication of how to approach the hitter, it is nonetheless the first thing that a pitcher can notice during the game. Most hitters do not arbitrarily stand in the batter's box without a reason for their position. They usually stand at a certain place to hide or minimize a weakness. For instance, the hitter who stands close to the plate is usually not afraid of the pitcher pitching him inside, but he *might* be afraid of not being able to cover the outer part of the plate. This type of hitter is often a pull hitter with a quick bat. When confronted with this scenario, the pitcher can do two things: get the hitter off the plate by throwing pitches in and in off the plate (see figure 7.2*a*), and then follow up by expanding the outside part of the plate (see figure 7.2*b*). The pitcher's job in this case is to make the hitter uncomfortable by throwing pitches that are close enough to him to force him to move, followed by pitches that may start in the strike zone but move into the pressure zone areas referred to earlier. Against this type of hitter, the pitcher will spend the majority of his time pitching the ball to the outside part of the plate, keeping the hitter uncomfortable. Remember, the hitter stands there for a reason, yet this is why it is vital for the pitcher to show the ability to pitch inside. The pitcher pitches inside in order to get the hitter out with pitches away.

If a hitter stands off the plate, this indicates that he is a hitter who likes to get extension. This type of hitter likes the ball out over the plate, either in the middle or just slightly on the outside part of the plate. The first cue that the pitcher should look for with this sort of hitter is whether or not he can cover the outer third of the plate with his swing. If he cannot, the pitcher can attack this spot consistently. However, if the hitter shows that he is capable of outer third coverage, the pitcher should then attack the inside part of the plate. This will inhibit the hitter's chance to extend his arms and will likely keep his swing "locked up." Tall, rangy hitters with long arms are often hitters who stand off the plate.

The hitter who stands in the back of the box is generally afraid of getting beat with velocity, so he puts himself in a position to see the ball as long as possible. Conversely, the hitter who stands at the front of the box generally concerns himself with hitting off-speed pitches. The pitcher can attack these two types of hitters in the same manner but with a slightly different thought process. The pitcher will attack the hitter by first throwing what the hitter wants to see and then throwing what he does not want to see. The pitcher should first show velocity to the hitter who is standing in the back of the box and observe how prepared he is to hit velocity. The hitter who stands in the front of the box should receive off-speed pitches for the same reason.

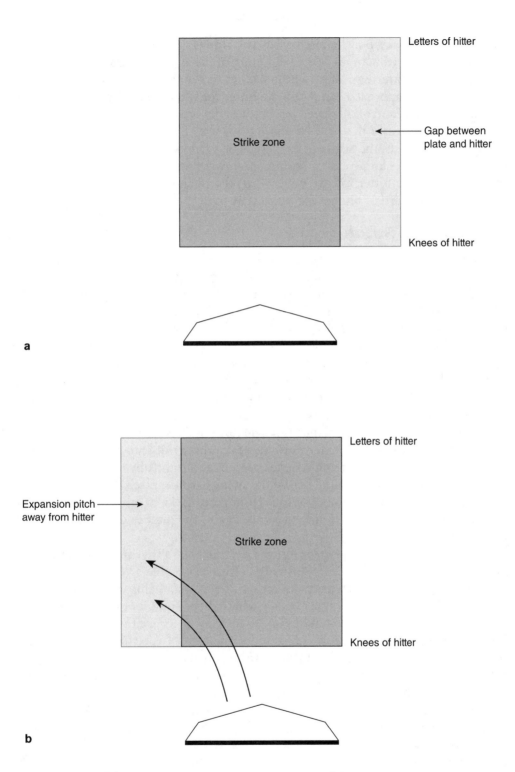

Figure 7.2 *(a)* Pitcher throwing in and off the plate; *(b)* pitcher expanding the outside part of the plate.

This may sound risky, but the pitcher has two things working in his favor. One, the hitter may not be ready to hit at the beginning of the at-bat. He may take or foul off the pitcher's first offerings, allowing the pitcher to get ahead and also gain information. Second, this approach can set up the hitter for what the pitcher will do next. If the hitter who is afraid of off-speed pitches sees the breaking ball first, he will surely be late on the velocity that will be coming his way. Similarly, if the hitter who is afraid of velocity sees the fastball first, he will be surprised by the breaking ball later in the count. This is known as "speeding up, slowing down" the hitter. This method can also set up the hitter for the next at-bat; the pitcher can confuse the hitter by switching the pattern of pitches for his next at-bat.

Stance and Stride

Another observable characteristic of the hitter is how he stands and strides before initiating the swing. Generally, hitters use three basic kinds of stances, each of which can reveal different information to the pitcher. Other clues throughout the swing will lend insight on how to use off-speed pitches. The first and most basic stance is the straight-on stance (see figure 7.3*a*). The hitter's feet are in line with one another, and the width of the stance will vary according to the comfort of the hitter. Very little information can be learned from the basic stance, unless the stance is unusually wide. In this case, the pitcher must question how much rhythm and timing a hitter will have in what looks to be a nonathletic position. Wide-stance hitters often have trouble starting the swing; therefore, they are often late on velocity or pitches that are inside. If the stance is normal by baseball standards (approximately shoulder width), then the pitcher must also take the stride into account. An early, short stride is what most hitting coaches preach, and rightfully so. The heel of the front foot must be on the ground before the swing can take place. An unusually long stride or a stride that prohibits the foot from getting down on time is a sign that the hitter will not be ready to hit, and once again, the pitcher should use velocity to beat the hitter.

A hitter with an open stance (see figure 7.3*b*) is usually a rhythm hitter with many moving parts before launching the swing. This has become a very popular stance because people believe that the positioning of the head helps the hitter see with both eyes. Again, the pitcher must decide whether the front foot gets down in time to launch the swing, but he should also be looking at where the front foot lands. Because the stance is open, it is common for the hitter to stay open when getting the front foot into the ground. This used to be called "stepping in the bucket," and if the hitter is out of alignment when he strides (stays open), the pitcher should attack the outer half of the plate. Some open hitters can get to this pitch, but many cannot, so it is well worth the pitcher's time to attack away and make the hitter prove he can get there.

The last type of stance is the closed stance (see figure 7.3*c*). The closed stance has become less popular for the opposite reason that the open stance is in vogue; theoretically, a closed stance makes it more difficult for the hitter to see, and it could impede the front hip from fully opening on the swing by virtue of the body's positioning. The closed stance is a nonfactor as far as revealing any information, unless the stride is misdirected. Often, the closed-stance hitter will also stride closed, opening up the inside part of the plate for the pitcher to attack. Throwing pitches to the inside of the plate will keep the hitter's front hip locked into place and prevent him from opening up to swing the bat. This produces jam shots and mis-hit balls, which are both be welcomed by the pitcher. Hitters can also have crossovers in their stance and stride. The open-stance or even-stance hitter can overstride and dive into the plate, allowing the pitcher to attack the inside part of the plate. The closed-stance or even-stance hitter can step into the bucket, which opens up the outside part of the plate.

Bat Speed

Besides their stance and stride, hitters can reveal many clues to pitchers and coaches with the way they swing the bat. Bat speed of the hitter is a good place for the pitcher to begin planning his attack. A hitter with poor bat speed can generally be attacked with velocity and well-executed off-speed pitches; however, off-speed pitches that are lazy or soft in the zone can accidentally "run into" the hitter's bat, basically doing the hitter a huge favor. We call these pitches "cripples," and the pitcher will need to stay away from these as much as possible when facing slow bats. Well-executed off-speed pitches (located breaking balls and changeups) as well as off-speed pitches that travel into pressure zones should work fine, unless the hitter proves he can hit those. The pitcher also shouldn't be afraid to throw in on the hitter with poor bat speed. A good old-fashioned challenge pitch is always applicable to this type of hitter.

The hitter with above average bat speed is a hitter who must be "pitched" to. This hitter will be able to get the barrel of his bat on most of the pitches within the strike zone, so the pitcher must change lanes (inside or outside to the hitter), levels (up or down to the hitter), and speeds (faster or slower) of the various pitches in his arsenal. As a general rule, the pitcher should attempt to attack this kind of hitter with a backward approach. This hitter is likely to see off-speed pitches in fastball counts and see fastballs in off-speed counts. For example, if the pitcher goes to a two-ball, no-strike count on this type of hitter, the hitter will be sitting "dead red" and expecting a fastball. In this case, the pitcher might throw a breaking ball or changeup instead.

When throwing the fastball, though, the pitcher must do a good job of locating the pitch as well as disrupting the hitter's timing by making the fastball appear slower and faster. This is done by changing lanes, levels, and speeds (BP, regular, and extra fastballs). The pitcher may need to be a bit more careful on the inside part of the plate to this type of hitter, unless his pitches possess late movement, because hitters with quick bats will be more apt to hit velocity. However, the pitcher can throw the fastball in off the plate into a pressure zone. The ball close to the hitter or toward the hitter's eyes will make the ball appear faster and will force the hitter's reaction to be faster, allowing the pitcher to set the hitter up for the next pitch. The next pitch may then be an off-speed pitch away from the hitter or a well-located fastball on the outside part of the plate, both of which will destroy the hitter's timing.

QUICK PITCH

The ability to change speeds and execute pitches to different areas of the strike zone—lanes and levels—is what makes a pitcher a pitcher instead of a thrower. A skilled pitcher makes the hitter responsible for various locations, heights, pitches, and speeds. If a pitcher can throw a fastball to both sides of the plate and both high and low, the fastball essentially becomes four different pitches in the hitter's eyes. These differences are what pitching is all about! If a pitcher's current skill level is not adequate enough to throw to certain locations in the strike zone, a good old-fashioned low strike in the middle of the plate is a great place to start. The pitcher has the advantage more often than not if he can simply throw strikes with aggressive conviction.

Swing Plane

The swing plane of the hitter may also help the pitcher decide how to attack. A slap-type hitter often uses a downward swing without loading his hands. This hitter is trying to hit the ball on the ground. In this case, the pitcher should say, "Have at it; hit as many ground balls as you possibly can!" With this kind of hitter, the pitcher should simply let his defense work behind him and should try not to do too much. On the other hand, the hitter who drops his back shoulder and swings the bat in an uphill manner will usually have trouble with off-speed pitches down and away from him, as well as pitches that are up or underneath his hands. The hitter who has a flat swing is generally the hitter who can best manipulate the barrel of the bat and keep the bat head in the strike zone longer than the other swing types. Much like the hitter with above average bat speed, this type of hitter must be "pitched to," either through side of plate, height of pitch (up or down), speed changes or by pitching backward. Note that when a pitcher sees a hitter who doesn't start his hands (no-load approach), the pitcher will often be able to beat him with velocity away in tandem with breaking pitches away from him. The hitter with the no-load approach will often have to cheat to start his swing, thereby causing flaws in his swing.

Other Considerations

After taking in all these nuances and idiosyncrasies of hitters and hatching a plan, what next? What other considerations must the pitcher take into account when determining how to best retire the hitter? First, the score of the game is a good starting point. A pitcher may have to pitch a hitter differently than he originally planned simply because of the score of the game. Pitching with a big lead may change the approach of the pitcher, making him take fewer risks and allowing him to use his defense more without making it too easy for the hitters to hit.

PEN SESSION **Pitching With a Lead**

Pitching with a big lead may be one of the most difficult things for a pitcher to do. Many coaches make it out to be easy, but it is not. This scenario involves a mental hurdle that many pitchers cannot overcome. They let down, let up, or try to cruise, and the next thing you know, the opposition climbs back into the game. I instruct our pitchers to always pitch as if it is a 0-0 game. The pitcher's job, regardless of the score, is to simply execute his pitches. Toward the end of the game, pitchers may be required to throw more balls to the outside of the plate to limit mistakes that might be hit for extra bases. There will also be many crucial spots in the game where the pitcher cannot afford to let the momentum swing from his team to the opponent. Sometimes pitching to the opposition's best hitter late in the game may not be the best tactic that the pitcher could employ (e.g., with a runner in scoring position, first base open, and a one-run lead). At other times, it might be the right thing to do (e.g., late in the game, score tied, and the pitcher doesn't want to put the winning run on base with a walk). The point is, the variables in the game are almost endless, and an educated guess or a gut feeling is often all the information that a pitcher has to rely on before making the next pitch.

Count

Making pitches based solely on the count—as opposed to the situation and how the hitter reacts—is a very bad idea. But using the count to apply pressure to the hitter and to give the pitcher an idea of what type of pitch he needs to execute is indeed beneficial. The count can be viewed as a template or framework that helps identify what kind of pitches the pitcher can throw in order to put himself in the best position to be consistently successful. However, remember that the hitter will be using the count against the pitcher as well, so many of the strategies presented here are designed to counter what the hitter is trying to accomplish.

Even Counts (0-0, 1-1, 2-1, 2-2, 3-2)

The even counts present the opportunity for the pitcher to get ahead or dispose of the hitter. Strike 1 in baseball is very important because it sets the tone for the at-bat and gives the pitcher more options deeper into the pitch sequence. Most baseball experts will tell you that the 1-1 count is the most important count in an at-bat; if the pitcher throws a strike, he is way ahead of the hitter, but a ball will swing the count to the hitter's advantage. The 2-2 count is a tricky count. The hitter has seen a few pitches, which aids him in timing the pitcher, and the pitcher would like to stay away from full-count (3-2) situations as much as possible. The pitcher's job in even counts is quite simple. Execute good pitches! If the pitcher can command the fastball low in the zone and on both sides of the plate, the pitcher can potentially force the hitter to swing at pitches that he cannot hit hard consistently. If the pitcher can command his off-speed pitches in these counts, he again puts the hitter on the defensive. Staying solid in even counts by throwing high-quality strikes will help the pitcher set up the next pitch.

Advantaged Counts (0-1, 0-2, 1-2)

Advantaged counts are the counts that pitchers strive to be in. Being ahead in the count means the pitcher has more options and possibly more weapons at his disposal. These counts give the pitcher the chance to expand the strike zone by throwing pitches in the pressure zones just outside of the strike zone. Batting averages are very low against pitches in these areas and in these counts, so it is safe to assume that most hitters become very defensive and will expand their zone to try to put the ball into the field of play. I tell our pitchers that the pitches thrown in this count should start off looking like a strike to the hitter but then become a ball because of late movement or spin. Some good pitches to throw in these counts include expanded fastballs on either side of the plate, elevated fastballs, extra fastballs, and "chase" breaking balls and changeups.

Disadvantaged Counts (1-0, 2-0, 3-0, 3-1)

Before we discuss disadvantaged counts, notice that I left the 2-1 count out of this category and included it in the even-count section. This is not a mistake. The 2-1 count does not put the pitcher at a disadvantage; he still has two balls to walk the hitter or two strikes to strike him out. This makes it even. Some may think this is a ploy to trick the mind, and perhaps it is, but by throwing a strike in this count, the pitcher puts the hitter in a two-strike situation, and most hitters are less effective with two strikes.

In disadvantaged counts, pitchers must become ultracompetitive. They must not give in to the hitter and throw pitches that are easy to hit. In these counts, the pitcher must take a down-zone approach and use speed, location, and movement to his advantage. This is where pitching backward comes into play. The hitter will be looking for a fastball, and he very well may get one, but at a different speed or with a different movement than the normal fastball. The changeup is a good pitch in these counts, and the breaking ball is fine as long as the pitcher has the confidence and command to throw it. Whatever pitch is decided on, the pitcher must truly believe in what he is throwing, command the pitch downstairs, and *never give in to the hitter* (unless the game situation dictates it). Some pitches that may be good options in a disadvantaged count include the BP fastball, the located fastball at the bottom of the strike zone, the sinker, the cutter, the changeup, or the breaking ball.

It is easy to see that a lot of factors are in play when a pitcher is developing a pitching plan and gaining a better understanding of how to attack certain types of hitters. This information can only be useful, however, if the pitcher has a complete understanding of what makes him a good pitcher in the first place (his strengths) as well as an aggressive approach in throwing strikes. It goes back to the game being about "balls and strikes" and the "me versus you" mentality that successful pitchers employ.

Spahn's wisdom about the essence of pitching is truly on the mark. If the pitcher can disrupt the timing of the hitter, chances for solid contact lessen, and the hitter is retired. For the pitcher and coach, it's a matter of collecting the proper information about the hitter and then applying it in a game situation. Applying it in the game is the not-so-simple chore of executing pitches. The foundational principles of joy, balls and strikes, intent, and me versus me and me versus you all being implemented into one pitch—simple and complex, elegant and chaotic, all at the same time.

EIGHT

Fielding the Position

Deland, Florida, a sleepy little town, is home to Stetson University, a school where I coached for four very rewarding years and whose fans are crazy about their baseball. On one particular spring day, we were clinging to a one-run lead in the top of the ninth inning. Our closer was in the game, and after recording the first out of the inning, he got himself in a bit of a jam by giving up a base hit and a double. He was now facing the other club's four-hole hitter with men on second and third. Coach Dunn, Stetson's head coach and one of the very best I have had the pleasure to serve under, asked me to signal to the catcher for an intentional walk so that we could set up the double play. As I made the call, it suddenly dawned on me that we hadn't bothered to spend time practicing intentional walks in our preseason work. It was an area that I had overlooked. After a shaky ball 1 and ball 2 were thrown by our closer, his third attempt came too close to the plate and was hit for a lead-changing, two-run double. Yep, you guessed it, we lost the game . . . and it was absolutely, positively my fault!

This incident led me to strongly believe in the concept of the complete pitcher, an approach that leaves no stone unturned in the enhancement of a pitcher's development or the evolution of his game. Becoming a successful pitcher is much like following a cooking recipe; in the kitchen, too much of one ingredient or not enough of another makes a dish taste not quite right. Too much emphasis placed on one area of pitching and not enough on another will lead to a pitcher having chinks in the armor, and these become areas that an opponent can attack. Unfortunately, pickoffs, pitchouts, and fielding plays are usually the ingredients that coaches omit from the pitching recipe—as evidenced by my lack of attention to details leading to that ninth inning at Stetson. Reasons for this may include time constraints in practice or the belief that working on other parts of the game (e.g., doing bullpen work, developing arm strength, enhancing a pitch, or performing weight training) is more important. The pitcher and coach simply run out of time, or they place a higher priority on other aspects of the craft. This is definitely not a winning recipe! This also speaks to one of the foundational elements—balance. A complete pitcher possesses the skills and abilities that will put him in the best position to win. Often pitchers ignore the skill that it requires to field his position well, and in the end when the game is often on the line, they fail to execute a bunt play, pickoff, or even something as simple as an intentional walk. These inadequacies will get pitchers beat all the time!

A good place to start a discussion of the other responsibilities of pitchers is by talking about some of the skills they will need to use most often: attacking the running game and making pickoff moves to first and second base. Next in level of importance are the plays that the pitcher will likely need to execute during the course of an ordinary game, such as starting a double play or fielding a bunt. In baseball circles, this is referred to as PFP, or pitcher's fielding practice. Trick plays or those used in special circumstances are addressed at the end of this section.

Attacking the Running Game

I've heard many people speak on aspects of the running game, and the general consensus seems to be that the pitcher's main function in this area is to *control* the running game—that is, the pitcher's primary job is to keep the runner close, somewhat pay attention to him, but spend the majority of time concentrating on the hitter. On a fundamental level, I agree wholeheartedly. The pitcher should indeed focus his attention on the hitter first and the runner second. After all, the pitcher's main function is to throw a good pitch and retire the hitter. But on many levels, this approach makes the pitcher aggressive in one area and passive in another. The opponent smells a weakness and exploits it by turning the basepaths into a running track. The pitcher, helpless in his efforts to control the running game, becomes defenseless on all fronts, including his ability to execute pitches.

Pitchers can be more successful in this aspect of the game by thinking of it as "attacking the running game" (rather than controlling the running game). This places the pitcher into an aggressive mode, and it helps emphasize the importance of the running game and the magnitude of its effect on the outcome of the game. In the attack mode, the pitcher will follow three simple steps: understand the situation, vary the cadence, and pick or pitch. If the pitcher can follow these three steps, which are really mind-sets, he will be able to cope with any attacks brought on by the opponent.

Understand the Situation

Stealing bases is generally predicated on the type of runner and the score of the game. A good base runner usually possesses speed or instinct, and the pitcher should be aware of stealing threats either through statistics or scouting. More often than not, teams will not use the running game as a weapon when they are losing the game or when their best hitters are at the plate. Occasionally though, with a top hitter at the plate, a coach will give the green light to the runner within the first two pitches so that the runner will be in scoring position for the hitter to drive him in. Because coaches fear and want to avoid running into outs with run producers at the plate, this scenario generally happens with zero outs. Thus, understanding the score of the game, the number of outs, and the current situation will greatly improve the pitcher's decision-making skills regarding how aggressive he should be with the running game and what tactics he should use in undermining the opponent's efforts.

Understanding when the runner might try to steal is also beneficial. Assuming that the score, the number of outs, and the situation are all favorable for the opponent to attack, the "plus" base runner—one who possesses speed and instinct—may run any time during the at-bat, while the average runner might choose to run in a count where the pitcher is apt to throw a breaking ball or changeup. The off-speed pitch arrives slower at the plate, thus increasing the base runner's chances to arrive at the next base safely.

Vary the Cadence

A major topic of chapter 2 was rhythm. The pitcher wants to connect the upper half of the body with the lower half in order to be on time to make the pitch. It is the synergy of his movements that makes the pitches he throws more efficient and increases the chances for the pitch to be thrown harder and with greater accuracy. Obviously then, rhythm is very important, but in the running game, it can ultimately be the pitcher's undoing. As the pitcher searches for the correct rhythm and tempo of his delivery in his quest to throw strikes, he can fall into a predictable cadence that the runner can prey on. The pitcher will come to the set position, wait for a certain amount of time or look at the base runner a certain number of times, and then make his pitch. The pitcher's predictability in delivering the pitch gives the runner the advantage in getting a great jump to steal the base, leaving the pitcher and catcher virtually helpless.

If the pitcher wants to prevent the base runner from taking advantage of this scenario, he must practice controlling his looks at the runner and varying the time between coming set and making the pitch. The easiest way for a pitcher to practice this is to simply make it a part of the protocol for bullpen sessions and scrimmage games. The pitcher should become comfortable being *out* of rhythm before starting the delivery (varying counts and looks), yet fall *into* a rhythm once he begins to make the pitch. Again, with proper practice, the pitcher should have no trouble properly executing cadence as well as executing pitches—the best of both worlds.

Pick or Pitch

For the pitcher to be highly successful, he must pitch with a clear mind and razor-sharp focus—that is, he must pitch with intent. The same mind-set should be used in determining whether to attempt a pickoff move or deliver a pitch to the plate. The pitcher should have already decided to "pick or pitch" by the time he arrives in the set position out of the stretch. This is a solid practice because it keeps the pitcher's focus from being split between the runner and the hitter. I have yet to find a pitcher who could split his concentration between the two and still execute properly, so making this decision early gives the pitcher the best chance to successfully attack the runner or the hitter.

The pitcher can assess the situation before stepping on the rubber (runner, count, and situation) and decide to pick or pitch; however, the pitcher may also gather information about the runner when arriving at the set position and may change his decision at the last second. This is important because many things might happen in between these two points. The runner may shorten or lengthen his lead, causing a change in plan by the pitcher. The left-handed pitcher has the best advantage in this situation because he is facing the runner, but the right-handed pitcher can also assess the runner's intention by using his peripheral vision. Any time the pitcher is unsure or cannot commit to the pick or pitch rule, he should step off, clear his mind, and start over.

QUICK PITCH

A pitcher's mind cannot be split into two processes at one time. If he completely ignores runners who reach base, the opponent can expose this weakness and put more people in scoring position. If the pitcher is too consumed with the runner, he will likely not execute good pitches consistently. This is quite a quandary. For this reason, the pitcher must make his decision and then act with aggression and conviction—he cannot put himself in the middle.

Also note that the pitcher can use other tactics in order to aggressively address the running game, such as delivering the ball quicker to the plate (through the use of a flex step or slide step), holding the ball, or executing a pitchout. Quickness to the plate is not easy to address because it is a physical act carried out by the pitcher, but by being quicker in a running situation, the pitcher gives his catcher the best chance to throw a runner out at the next base. In quickening his rhythm, the pitcher must shorten his normal delivery into a more compact one; he can do this using the slide step or flex step, which were discussed earlier. As pointed out in chapter 2, the faster a pitcher can be to the plate without jeopardizing stuff or accuracy, the better chance he has of controlling the running game.

Holding the ball is another very effective way to keep the runner in check. As the pitcher comes into the set position, the runner is anticipating when he can break for the next base. As mentioned, the pitcher's main objective here is to disrupt the anticipatory skills of the runner by varying the time he spends in the set position (cadence). Holding the ball for an extended time (three or more seconds) may disrupt the runner's timing to the point that a steal becomes impossible, or at the very least, improbable.

The pitchout is probably the least used weapon for tempering the running game because most coaches do not want to waste a pitch if they guess wrong; however, if the coach guesses right and the opponent runs into an out because of the pitchout, very few teams will try to steal many bases for the rest of that particular game. There is just something about the idea of "getting caught at your own game" that steers most coaches away from gambling again.

Making Pickoffs

Picking a runner off at first or second base is a very exciting defensive play in baseball. It lessens the chance of the opposition scoring because it negates a base runner, but it also provides a psychological edge. A baseball game has many momentum changes during the course of the contest, and a pickoff may be the most effective play for deflating the momentum that an offense is trying to mount. Probably more important, baseball is a game of inches, and pickoff moves between the pitcher and runner are the battle for those inches. Even if a pickoff move is unsuccessful and the runner is safe, it may still help the pitcher win the battle of inches by making the runner shorten his lead or become less aggressive in his quest to get to the next base. This gives the defense a chance to further win inches because if the runner shortens his lead or becomes timid, the catcher has a better chance to throw the runner out if he does steal, or it gives the infielder a little more time to get to second base on a force play for the out. In either case, the defense has won the battle for those precious inches.

Pickoffs at First Base

Once the pitcher has decided to attempt a pickoff throw to first base, he needs to do it well. Baseball is a game of angles, distances, and times, so the pitcher's main goal is to deliver the ball to the first baseman as quickly and as accurately as possible. Taking too much time or making inaccurate throws often means the difference between the runner being safe or out. In that regard, pitchers should work on specific areas in order to improve their pickoff skills. The details for these areas will differ depending on whether a pitcher is right-handed or left-handed, so separate information is provided here for each type of pitcher.

First-Base Pickoffs for Right-Handed Pitchers

As the pitcher comes to the set position, the pitcher's head should remain locked on the plate area. The pitcher can use his peripheral vision to check the runner, but the head should remain virtually still. The reason for this is that a pitcher's head movements often tip off the runner regarding whether the pitcher is going to the plate or attempting a pick. Eliminating head movement decreases the chances of the runner gaining an advantage.

The footwork must be short and quick; more specifically, the feet must stay under the pitcher so that a quick move can be executed. The feet should move the body closer to first base, not away from it, which is a mistake that many pitchers make (see figure 8.1). In addition, if the pitcher executes the footwork properly, he will be in a direct line to throw to first base.

The arm action of the pickoff move must be quicker and shorter than that of the regular pitching motion.

Figure 8.1 The pitcher's feet should move closer to first base rather than away from it during a first-base pickoff.

This shorter action can be achieved by keeping the hands together longer while the feet move toward first base. Another way for the pitcher to execute a shorter arm action is to take the ball to the ear before throwing, much like a catcher or a shortstop (see figure 8.2). This will ensure that the arm action is shorter than the normal delivery.

In close plays where the runner and the ball arrive at first base at approximately the same time, the difference between safe and out will largely depend on the accuracy of the throw. In this case, the best throw is one that arrives on the fair-territory side of first base in an area between the first baseman's knee and chest, which is called the box (see figure 8.3). A throw that is higher than the box area will cause the first baseman to take longer to apply the tag; a throw that is below the knee risks hitting the runner or being misplayed by the first baseman.

Figure 8.2   Right-handed pitcher bringing the ball to his ear before throwing a first-base pickoff, thus allowing him to execute a shorter arm action.

Right-handed pitchers can use various specific pickoff moves when executing a pickoff to first base. Here are some of the common pickoffs used in this situation.

Figure 8.3   Pitcher making a throw to the fair-territory side of first base and to the box area on the first baseman.

Out of Hand   This pickoff is for the pitcher who starts with the ball behind his back and in his throwing hand. The pitcher gets the sign from the catcher and then abruptly turns and throws to the first baseman *before* moving into the set position (see figure 8.4). The element of surprise makes this pickoff effective because most moves happen after the pitcher comes to the set (resting) position.

Figure 8.4   Out-of-hand pickoff to first base.

Top of the Set   This pickoff begins as soon as the ball touches the glove as the pitcher starts into the set position (see figure 8.5). Like the out-of-hand pickoff, this pick can surprise the runner because of its timing.

Figure 8.5   Top-of-the-set pickoff to first base.

Bottom of the Set This pickoff is easily the pick that is used most by right-handed pitchers (see figure 8.6). Pitchers who use this move exclusively or without variation are usually the easiest to steal off of because, as mentioned earlier, pitchers become slaves to their own rhythm and cadence. If this is the main pickoff employed by the right-hander, he should take steps to vary the cadence between coming set and attempting the pickoff or pitch.

Figure 8.6 Bottom-of-the-set pickoff to first base.

Best or Balk Move We use the term *best move* to describe the pickoff move that the pitcher uses when he needs to be as quick and accurate as possible with his feet and arm. The best move will most likely be a variation of one of the moves that have already been discussed, but the pitcher performs it with an understanding that he must make the move as fast as possible. The pitcher may also employ a "balk move" toward first base, which is intended to further deceive the runner. The balk move can be implemented by executing a subtle flinch or bend of the front knee or front shoulder followed immediately with a quick pickoff move.

Runners are taught to focus on the pitcher's front knee or front shoulder as a way to determine when the pitcher is throwing the pitch, because both of these body parts turn inward and toward the plate if the pitcher is delivering the pitch to the plate. Therefore, the pitcher can deceive the runner by flinching the front knee or shoulder and then turning to attempt the pick. This is a difficult pickoff to master but very effective if executed well. Technically, this move is considered a balk and may be called accordingly, but the good pitcher will always work to the edges of the "gray area" to gain an advantage. This is not cheating; this is competing. If a balk is called, the pitcher will shrug it off and focus on executing the next pitch.

Set and Hold   This is the most useful pickoff move against an aggressive runner. The pitcher goes to the set position, holds the baseball for 3 to 5 seconds, and then attempts a pickoff. Any move can be used after holding the ball, but the most effective seems to be the best or balk pickoff move. Again, the pitcher holds the ball to disrupt the runner's rhythm. In trying to anticipate when the pitcher will start his delivery to the plate, an aggressive runner may lean or, better yet, make a break toward second base, giving the pitcher a window of opportunity to pick the runner off.

Right-Handed Pickoff Exercises

Pitchers can practice their pickoffs in daily sessions by starting with the arm only, then the feet only, and finally, bringing the whole body together:

1. *Arm only*—The pitcher works on shortening the length of his arm action to first base. During this pickoff drill, the pitcher focuses solely on the arm and the arm action.

2. *Feet only*—The pitcher works on quickening his feet on the move to first base by keeping a solid base underneath him as he turns to throw. He also works on gaining ground to first base, thereby shortening the actual distance of the throw he is making. During this pickoff drill, the pitcher focuses solely on the quickness and path of the feet, with no concern for arm action.

3. *Arm and feet together*—The pitcher works on combining the shorter arm path that he worked on in drill 1 with the foot quickness and proper path of the feet that he practiced in drill 2.

First-Base Pickoffs for Left-Handed Pitchers

The easiest way for a runner to know that a left-handed pitcher is attempting a pickoff is a change in the pitcher's tempo. The pitcher's pickoff move is usually slower and will include a lean toward the first-base bag. Changes in the height of the leg lift may also expose the pick attempt and should be avoided.

The NCAA Baseball Rule Book states that the pitcher must step directly and gain ground toward a 45-degree angle measuring from the pivot foot toward the base the pitcher is throwing to or feinting a throw (NCAA Baseball Rule Book, 2010). Whether a pitcher steps on or within the 45-degree line is a judgment call by the umpire, so there is a good deal of gray area for the pitcher to work with. In most cases, the home plate umpire will make the balk call on the left-handed pitcher when there is no space between the feet (see figure 8.7); therefore, the lefty must be sure to lengthen the stride so that the umpire sees space. The first-base umpire usually makes the balk call when the pitcher steps over the 45-degree angle toward home plate. To cover this angle, the pitcher will step on the 45-degree line, as shown in figure 8.8, or slightly in front of it. The pitcher then steps back over the imaginary line after throwing the ball. Some people may think this is simply cheating, but until this rule becomes less ambiguous and a 45-degree chalk line or other objective measure is taken, it is no different than a catcher framing a borderline pitch or a shortstop decoying a runner at second base. It's all part of the game!

Changes in head movement and head direction at leg lift and during the course of delivery can help the pitcher develop a good pickoff move. The general rule for the left-handed pitcher is that the head must go to the plate *with* the glove for maximum deception (see figure 8.9). One way that the lefty pitcher gives his pickoff move away to the runner is for his head to immediately go to the plate, creating a choppy, unnatural look to his delivery.

For the lefty, the glove side, the position of the chest, and the tempo are the three greatest factors in developing a good pickoff move. If the glove side can mimic what it normally does during the delivery, and if the chest can stay open to the runner, the chances for a good pickoff move are very high. A bad pickoff move will feature the glove side not doing what it normally does in the delivery (usually shortening up), or the front arm will turn more toward the first-base bag, thus closing off the chest. One easy way for the pitcher to make his glove side and chest maintain their delivery position is to hold his hands together longer. Because tempo and arms are so important, holding the ball longer will make tempo speed up and make the arms move in a similar manner to the delivery.

Because runners usually run on first movement, the better the move and the earlier the read on the runner, the better the chance for a pickoff. I want our pitchers to predetermine whether they will pick, read the runner for any signs of running, and be able to adjust if the runner does run. We may sometimes be called for a balk

Figure 8.7 No space between a left-handed pitcher's feet when attempting a first-base pickoff. This will result in a balk.

Figure 8.8 To ensure that space is seen between the feet, the left-handed pitcher steps on (or over) an imaginary 45-degree line.

Figure 8.9 Left-handed pitcher's correct head position when executing a first-base pickoff.

after adjusting, but our theory is that, in this situation, the runner would have easily stolen the bag anyway. The pitcher just needs to make sure there is no one else on base when using the read and adjust technique!

Left-Handed Pickoff Exercises

Several exercises can be used by left-handed pitchers to improve their pickoff ability. Here are a few effective exercises:

1. *Stride to the 45-Degree Line*—This is strictly an upper-body exercise. Working with a partner, the pitcher strides to the 45-degree line and then uses upper-body technique to execute the pickoff (shorter, flip type of throw to the partner; glove side going to the plate; chest open to the runner).

2. *Suspended 45-Degree Line*—The pitcher keeps his hands together and suspends his foot about 12 inches (30.5 cm) off the ground at a 45-degree angle (see figure 8.10). As he goes forward and lands, he attempts to move his arms in a delivery fashion, keeping his chest open to the runner.

3. *Hanging Knee to the 45-Degree Line*—The pitcher hangs his knee and strides to the 45-degree line (see figure 8.11), keeping his chest open and his hands together as long as possible, before moving the arms in a delivery fashion.

Figure 8.10 Suspended 45-Degree Line: Left-handed pitcher suspends his foot 12 inches off the ground.

Figure 8.11 Hanging Knee to the 45-Degree Line: Left-handed pitcher hangs his knee and strides to the 45-degree line.

(continued)

Left-Handed Pickoff Exercises (continued)

4. *Full-Motion Pickoff*—Starting in the stretch, the pitcher combines parts of the body for a pickoff attempt. Points of emphasis here include timing the head and glove arm to reach for home plate simultaneously, using the proper length of stride, and walking over the 45-degree line to receive the throw from the first baseman.

5. *Step-Off Pickoff*—Instead of a normal pickoff where the pitcher lifts the leg and attempts to deceive the runner by making it look like a pitch to the plate, the step-off pick is used to surprise the runner and make him retreat back to the base quicker. This pickoff is essentially a short step off the rubber with the left foot followed by a snap throw (see figure 8.12). The step-off pick can be used at any time during the set portion of the delivery and can complement the other pickoff moves quite nicely.

6. *Mixed Moves*—In this exercise, the lefty pitcher mixes in the various pickoff moves in his arsenal. Most of the lefties who have good pickoff moves are able to set the runner up by showing him a bad move or two, thereby making the runner confident that he can steal a base. Then, just as the runner is feeling comfortable, the lefty uses his best move and catches the runner leaning or leaving the base prematurely.

Figure 8.12 Step-Off Pickoff: Left-handed pitcher steps off the rubber with the left foot.

Pickoffs at Second Base

There is something very special about picking a runner off at second base. It is a sure-fire way to kill a rally for the opponent and can spark your team to grind out a few more outs or muster a few more hits to achieve victory at the end of the ball game. It is indeed a momentum shifter.

Most aggressive and savvy base runners would agree that stealing third base is actually easier than stealing second base. Stealing third is often easier for two reasons, one of which is the fault of the pitcher, while the other falls on the shoulders of the middle infielders. Both parties must work in tandem to effectively hold the runner.

In this situation, the pitcher's main task in holding the runner revolves around the cadence or rhythm of his delivery. If the pitcher simply comes set, looks back at the runner, and then pitches, the runner will have an easy time stealing the bag because it will be simple for him to time his jump. The middle infielders, for their part, must apply pressure to the runner at second by holding him close to the bag and then retreat back to their position once the pitch is delivered. If one or both of these functions are neglected or unsynchronized, the advantage goes to the runner.

For the middle infielders and the pitcher to work as a unit, a system must be put into place. The shortstop should communicate with the pitcher and second baseman via hand or verbal signals about how many looks back the pitcher will give or how long the pitcher will hold the ball. This will give the middle infielders a solid idea about when and for how long to hold the runner at second base and when to retreat back to their position. It will also provide the pitcher with a plan for varying his looks and counts between each pitch.

After gaining an understanding of how to work as a unit, the pitcher and middle infielders can begin to work on executing specific pickoffs. Many types of pickoffs can be used at second base, but the two most common are the daylight pickoff and the inside move.

Daylight Pickoff

The daylight play has proven over time to be the most valuable pickoff for controlling the running game at second base. This is most likely because of the spontaneous nature of the play and how it is designed. The play starts with communication (hand signals or verbal signals) between the pitcher and middle infielder. As the pitcher comes set and looks back at the runner for his predetermined number of looks, the infielder holds the runner by casually staying directly behind his right hip. When the infielder is ready *and* the pitcher is looking (an important distinction because it will affect the timing and effectiveness of the play), the shortstop will flash his glove, signaling the pitcher to turn and throw to the base (see figure 8.13).

a   b

Figure 8.13   When the shortstop flashes his glove, the pitcher knows to throw to that base.

If the play is run efficiently, the ball and runner should arrive to the bag at about the same time, resulting in a bang-bang play.

The daylight play can be run by either the shortstop or second baseman. The shortstop is usually responsible for holding the runner at second, so getting the second baseman involved can be extremely effective. Variations of this pickoff are virtually endless; the pick can be worked off of timing or a specific number of looks, so it is a pickoff that can create endless deception if approached creatively. For the pitcher, the mechanics of the throw to second base are much like the mechanics of the right-handed pitcher's pickoff throw to first base in that the feet and arm must be short and quick and the throw must be accurate. The pitcher will spin to the glove side, keep his feet underneath his body, and make the snap throw to the third-base side of the bag in the imaginary box between the shoulders and knees of the receiver (see figure 8.14).

Figure 8.14 A well-executed pickoff at second base is very much like the right-handed pitcher's pickoff at first base: The pitcher must use short, quick feet and a quick arm. He must get rid of the ball! Baseball is a game of inches!

Inside Move

The inside move provides a different type of deception than the daylight pick because the pitcher camouflages the move by lifting the leg as if delivering a pitch, only to spin farther inside and throw to second (see figure 8.15). This move usually works off of timing and is best disguised when the pitcher's head is facing toward home plate (as if he were to pitch). This move is also a good way to expose the opponent's short game by causing the hitter to tip off whether or not he is bunting.

Figure 8.15 The inside pickoff move is a good move when the pitcher can disguise the first part of his delivery to make the runner at second base think he is pitching the ball to the plate. If the pitcher can replicate the first part of the delivery, this may be just enough to fool the runner.

A pitcher will often perform an inside move to second base late in the ball game with a potential bunter at the plate. The defense is trying to determine if the batter will attempt to bunt, so the pitcher makes an inside move, trying to prompt the batter to square around and thus expose the offensive plan. When this occurs, the defense may then realign itself to defend the bunt.

As a pickoff play, the inside move is most useful against an ultra-aggressive base runner. If the middle infielder observes the runner getting a big secondary lead toward third base as the pitch is being delivered, the inside move can be a handy weapon to employ. The pitcher's primary objective is to sell the beginning part of the move to make it appear that he is delivering a pitch. He does this by keeping the leg lift, leg height, and speed of the delivery the same as if he were truly pitching. This will make the runner more apt to continue to take large secondary leads. Once this happens, the shortstop or second baseman can slide behind the runner in the direction of the base; and the pitcher will spin, set his feet, and make the throw to second. At first, this throw can be a bit awkward, but in time and with practice, the pitcher can make this an effective tool for attacking the running game.

Pitcher's Fielding Practice (PFP)

Once the pitcher delivers the ball to the plate, he then becomes an infielder, and as such, he must cover various areas of the field and possess certain skills to help defend the opponent's short game. Because so many games are won or lost by the pitcher's ability to react to the bunt, suicide bunt, or ball hit right back to him, his value as a fielder cannot be overstated. The reality is that the pitcher stands closer to the hitter than any other infielder, so he must react and make decisions quicker than anyone on the field.

The following are "quick hits" covering the plays that a pitcher will regularly encounter as well as photos of the correct techniques used to execute each play. A pitcher must understand that proper and consistent execution of these skills requires purposeful practice and application. There are no shortcuts here—just plain, old-fashioned hard work.

3-1s

The 3-1 play is named for the score book symbols representing the defenders involved in the play (3 is the first baseman, and 1 is the pitcher). On this play, the ball is hit to the first baseman and then flipped to the pitcher covering first base. The 3-1 is probably the most common play in the PFP directory. Any time a ball is hit to the right side of the diamond, the pitcher should run a direct route to the first-base bag until he's certain he won't have to cover the base (see figure 8.16). As he reaches the area in front of the bag, he should then create a "fishhook" to square himself off to receive the throw. The pitcher should raise both hands to give the first baseman a target to throw to, and after receiving the ball, he should touch the inside of the base with his right foot (see figure 8.17). If there are multiple runners on base when this

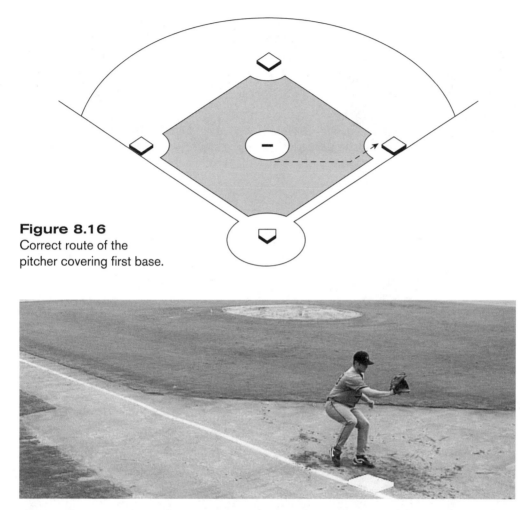

Figure 8.16
Correct route of the
pitcher covering first base.

Figure 8.17   The pitcher providing a target for the first baseman.

play occurs, the pitcher should quickly transform from fielding to throwing mode and turn back to the infield in case he needs to make a throw to another base (see figure 8.18).

Comebackers to First and Second Base

When the ball is hit back to the pitcher, the pitcher is often forced to make a reactionary play where he uses his reflexes to protect himself, much like a hockey goalie saving a puck from the net. Occasionally, the ball is mis-hit and is chopped directly back to the pitcher. In either case, the most important thing is for the pitcher to get an out. With no one on base, the pitcher has two options when the ball is hit back at him. If the ball is hit and it carries the pitcher toward first base, the pitcher can run the ball over and flip to the first baseman (see figure 8.19). If the force of the

Figure 8.18 The pitcher must be ready to throw to another base if there are multiple base runners.

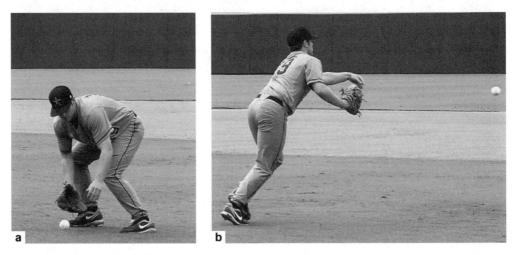

Figure 8.19 The intermediate throw is tough for a pitcher because he is used to throwing at full speed. With this in mind, it may be easier to flip the ball underhand.

ball keeps the pitcher on the mound or makes him move toward third base, he will simply field the ball, perform a shuffle step, throw the ball using an infielder's arm action, and then follow his throw (see figure 8.20). The pitcher's throw to second base is identical to the throw to first with one exception. Obviously, the pitcher's back is turned to second when he fields the ball, so he must turn to make the throw, and his eyes must find the target that he will throw to. The mechanics of the throw (the shuffle step, infielder's arm action, and finishing the throw) are exactly the same.

Figure 8.20   If the pitcher is going to make an overhead throw, he should throw the ball like an infielder–short and quick.

Bunts

On a bunt, the pitcher's main objective—just as on a comebacker—is to get an out . . . anywhere, somewhere, but get an out! Late in the ball game or when the game is on the line, the defense is usually set to throw out the lead runner; however, the pitcher must remember to simply get an out, because outs are precious at that point in the game. Once the bunt defense has been set (a team may use many possible variations) and the ball is bunted in a specific area, the pitcher needs to field the ball and throw to a base. Figure 8.21 shows the zones where bunts generally end up. In each zone, there are specific things that the pitcher needs to do. In zone 1,

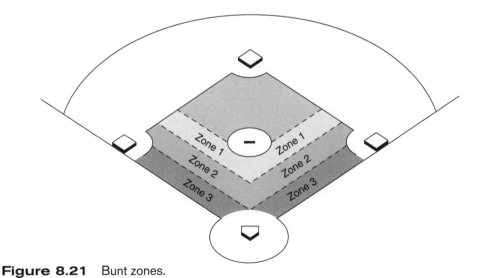

Figure 8.21   Bunt zones.

Figure 8.22   Pitchforking a ball that has stopped moving ensures that the pitcher can get a grip.

the pitcher has plenty of time to field the ball, take a crow hop or shuffle step, make the throw, and keep the feet moving in the direction of the throw, which is called finishing the throw. In zone 2, the pitcher has less time, so he will field the ball, secure the ball to his belly while staying low to the ground, take a shuffle step, and then deliver the ball with an infielder's arm action. Zone 3 is obviously the toughest area to field a bunt; a bunt in this zone is a good or great bunt, and the pitcher has a long way to go in order to field the ball and make the play. In zone 3, the pitcher will field the ball, secure it to his belly button while rocking onto his back foot, and make the throw. If the ball has stopped moving when the pitcher gets to it, he will "pitchfork" the ball into the ground, ensuring a good grip, and then make the throw (see figure 8.22). If the ball is bunted into zone 3, the pitcher basically must sell out in a do-or-die fashion—field the ball, find the target with his eyes, and make an athletic throw.

Suicide

On a suicide squeeze bunt, the pitcher has two options. He can use the glove and flip the ball to the catcher on the third-base side of home plate (see figure 8.23), or he can use the bare hand to shovel pass the throw to the catcher (see figure 8.24). The key here is for the pitcher to make sure he doesn't hang the flip to the catcher—the

a   b

Figure 8.23   The pitcher uses his glove to scoop the ball to the plate.

Figure 8.24   The pitcher barehands the ball and flips it to the plate.

arm should never go above the shoulder when making the flip. After flipping to the catcher, the pitcher will peel toward the first-base side of the plate. This is another do-or-die play, so the pitcher must sell out and get to the ball as quickly and as athletically as possible.

Cutoffs and Relays

When runners are on base and a ball is hit to the outfield, the pitcher should read the ball and listen for the call made by the catcher before deciding where to line up to back up a throw to third or home. When in doubt, the pitcher should split the middle by going in between home and third base; he should then move to the appropriate base once he is sure where the throw is going. He should take up a position on line with the throw and deep. A general rule is that if the ball is hit directly to the outfielder or in close proximity, the pitcher will back up two bases ahead. So, if a ball is hit directly to the center fielder with a runner on first base, there will likely be a play at third base, prompting the pitcher to back up third. If the ball breaks the perimeter of the outfield, the pitcher will go to the middle between third and home; he will then read the ball and listen for the call.

Pitchout

In the pitchout, a pitcher should use a normal delivery and throw waist to chest high to the catcher in the opposite batter's box (see figure 8.25). The catcher will give the sign and then set up on the outside part of the plate, ready to receive the throw. At approximately the point when the pitcher squares around to throw, the catcher will move out and up simultaneously at a 45-degree angle. The pitcher should deliver the ball as a normal fastball thrown with a four-seam grip so that the catcher can catch, transfer, and throw to second all in one motion.

Figure 8.25 The ball should be delivered to an area that allows the catcher to catch, step, and throw all in one motion. The best place to throw the ball is right at the catcher's chest as he is coming out of his crouch position.

Intentional Walk

Ah, we return to the scene of the crime and the play that my team was beat on several years ago! To properly execute this important play, the pitcher should use a normal leg lift (or whatever leg lift he is comfortable throwing with) and throw a 75 percent fastball to the catcher in the batter's box opposite the hitter (see figure 8.26). The pitcher should throw the ball on a line (no lobs). In addition, the catcher cannot move out until the pitcher turns his shoulders to throw the ball to the plate. Any movement made by the catcher before this time can be considered a "catcher's balk," the only balk not induced by the pitcher that is covered within the rules of the game.

5-3 Move

This is a technique used with runners on first and third base. The right-handed pitcher will start a normal delivery and get to his matched position. This will help sell the move. His lead leg will go down the 45-degree angle line, and his chest will stay square to the third-base runner. As the pitcher touches the lead leg down, he will use the ground to pivot back toward first base, keeping his arm up in a throwing position, and look to see if he has a play on the runner at first. This play is useful when the pitcher thinks that the runner at first base is being too aggressive in getting a secondary lead. It may also be used if the pitcher thinks the offense is considering an early-break steal, trying to score the runner at third by using the runner at first

Figure 8.26   The intentional walk looks easy, but it is an intermediate throw that many pitchers have trouble executing.

as a decoy (drawing a throw on the runner trying to take second so the runner at third can score).

QUICK PITCH

Over time, the pitcher should develop a high level of intuition, or savvy, in regard to attacking the running game and defending the short game. Experience and repetition will be the pitcher's greatest allies in this case, just as ignoring these skills or practicing them without a purpose will be his Achilles' heel. In most cases, a pitcher will get out of this proposition exactly what he puts into it. The pitcher can draw from the foundational principles of skill and ability as well as the principle of balance in that a lot of different ingredients are required to be a complete pitcher. Weaknesses will be exposed as the pitcher transitions to higher levels of the game. It is up to the pitcher to become complete.

A final consideration for this chapter is that the pitcher and team are only as good as their weakest link. A staff of pitchers who cannot hold runners or field their position put themselves at risk of faltering at crucial times of the game. Bunting and running often occur when the game is on the line, and if weaknesses are exposed, these tactics can result in runs for the opponent. When runs are scored late in the game, momentum switches occur, and that can be the end for many teams or pitchers. This is a poor way to lose and can easily be remedied with time and practice. Being unprepared or deficient in these areas is inexcusable as the pitcher moves up in levels of the game.

NINE

The Mental Game

Baseball players are very superstitious people. From Wade Boggs eating chicken before every game (because he thought it made him hit better) to Nomar Garciaparra making multiple helmet and batting glove adjustments before settling into the batter's box, ballplayers adopt unique methods when preparing for battle. I once played on a team that won 11 games in a row and did so primarily because everyone refused to wash their uniform—at least that's what we thought. We believed that the laundry detergent or a clean uniform would somehow wash away the luck and thus end the streak. I've even seen players who boasted about not being at all superstitious yet seemed out of sorts if their routine was somehow broken. I suppose they were superstitious about not being superstitious.

Baseball is clearly a thinking man's game, full of important moves and decisions made continually throughout the course of the contest. Yet in its most natural state, the game seems to be best played when a player has a sense of clarity, thoughtlessness, and flow—just like in backyard baseball when you were a kid. Being able to manage this tug-of-war between the analytical, sensible, thoughtful mind and the instinctive, creative, free thinking mind is most likely what separates the supreme ballplayer from the average one. This notion may be difficult for most to believe, but it is supported routinely in baseball at all levels. How can two pitchers with equal size, stuff, and ability throw the same pitches to the same hitters but get drastically different results? Better yet, how can a pitcher with much less size, stuff, and ability seem to be able to get everyone he faces out, while a pitcher with superior tools fails repeatedly? This is a million-dollar question filled with variables, but the answer most likely lies in the difference in mental capacity of the two pitchers.

Understanding the Mental Aspect of the Game

Today, players and coaches at every level understand the importance of the mental game. What might have been considered to be hocus-pocus 20 years ago is now often the rule rather than the exception in the way players approach, practice, and implement the mental game. Anyone who observes or is involved in the game will see many manifestations and variations of mental practices taking place. Major-league organizations often use the services of sport psychologists throughout their minor-league system as well as with their main club. These sport psychologists help players by giving them coping strategies and exposing them to methods for improving consistency. Many college coaches have also started employing outside services that come in for a weekend or two and work with their players on the mental aspects of the game. In these sessions, the players learn ways to "slow the game down" or develop effective mental routines in an attempt to upgrade their level of play. Even at the high school and summer league levels, players often use techniques such as diaphragmatic breathing and visualization to help them with the mental side of the game.

QUICK PITCH

The balance of understanding oneself and the battle between the pitcher and hitter is where the "me versus me and me versus you" principle was spawned. The pitcher must first attempt to get himself right, free of the mental chains that may bind him, and then he can move toward the ensuing battle between himself and the hitter. If these two things occur, optimal performance is possible.

So, in a perfect baseball world, the triumvirate of body, mind, and spirit would all morph into a single, well-oiled machine called the complete baseball pitcher. This pitcher would be a coach's dream. Able to analyze without paralyzing, adjust easily and swiftly, and execute precisely, this pitcher would surely never lose. But for those of us who play or coach this game, we know that the perfect baseball world does not exist, so instead we continually search for ways to incorporate the mental game more manageably and usefully. That is what this chapter deals with.

Implementing mental practice can be both a good thing and a bad thing. On one hand, it makes no sense to consistently practice the physical skills of baseball yet leave the mental skills to chance, hoping that somehow the pitcher can become equipped to handle the adversities that crop up during the game. Some people believe that "the game is the best teacher" and that players will automatically learn the mental skills by playing. However, if the goal of the pitcher is to pitch with an easy demeanor—free of analytical thought and full of creativity—the pitcher must learn to strike a proper balance between when he should be thinking and when he should not be thinking during the game. Because many of the current methods for mental training do not address this balance, they often seem gimmicky and can sometimes get in the way of the competitor instead of helping him. Like in most other areas of baseball, a pitcher's individual style and personality must be taken into account when implementing the mental techniques. Keeping the mental approach simple can help pitchers use this part of the game to their advantage.

PEN SESSION Defining Mental Toughness

Before getting into the tools used to manage the mental side of the game, let's define what "mental toughness" means and how it relates to the pitcher. The term *mentally tough* is often misused. If a pitcher has physical prowess or a certain "look" about him, people will often anoint him as mentally tough. The pitcher looks tough, he acts tough, and he even talks tough—therefore, he must be tough, right? But the real question is, does he think tough? Mentally tough pitchers can come in various shapes and sizes, and it is the bite of the dog that makes him tough, not the bark. The mentally tough pitcher must have the heart and soul of a wild warrior, but also the tact and knowledge of the expert assassin. Can the pitcher train his mind to stay quiet in the face of adversity? Can he take a proverbial punch and get right back to his feet? Can he choose to target certain thoughts rather than succumb to sporadic or errant ones? If the answer to these questions is yes, then indeed the pitcher is tough minded. His exterior shell, regardless of how impressive and tough talking it may be, is of minimal consequence.

The Three Ps

A couple of years ago, I was looking for a way to simplify some of the mental processes that our pitchers were trying to apply. The pitchers were not having a great deal of success implementing these processes. It had become apparent to me that even though our pitchers were working diligently to stay within their routines and "keep the game small," many of them seemed uncomfortable. Instead of letting these techniques sink in and become useable, the pitchers were trying to think their way through them. As a result, instead of freeing up the pitchers' minds, the techniques were actually having the reverse effect.

One thing that I noticed about our pitchers during this time was that it seemed to take them a very long time to make the next pitch. Dictating the pace of the game has always been one of our goals. The faster the pitcher and catcher work, the more times a hitter will become impatient or uncomfortable, which can result in weak swings or swings and misses. But after the pitchers worked on these mental exercises, this wasn't happening as often. During this time, I also observed that many of the pitchers were starting to second guess themselves. This was "paralysis by analysis" at its finest, so I decided to take action; I introduced the three Ps—pace, presence, and pitchability.

The first two of these have a strong bond with the mental side of the game, even though each requires some physical action from the pitcher. Pitchability, though important to the grand scheme of pitching, fits with the mechanical aspects of how to pitch, what pitch to throw, and so on. As mentioned previously, *pace* refers to how the pitcher and catcher can dictate the speed of the game. But pace is not just about working fast to make the hitter susceptible to taking bad swings; it is also a way for the pitcher to avoid overthinking or using improper thinking about the task at hand.

Pace means being clear in purpose and pitch selection, trusting preparation and intuition, and letting it rip!

Initially, we used the term *presence* to describe a pitcher's demeanor on the mound, and this had been a staple in our mental vocabulary for quite some time. Our pitchers worked on trying not to show emotion on the mound, or if they did have an outburst, to dispose of it quickly. Both teams, the opponent and the pitcher's defensive teammates, are always watching the pitcher closely. If a pitcher has poor presence, this could swing momentum from one side to the other, giving an edge to the opposition without them earning it. But the word *presence* has a much greater meaning than just body language, and if thought of and implemented properly, the idea of presence can help the pitcher pitch "in the now" as well as keep his emotions in check. The word *presence* suggests "presently," which suggests "now," so it is a constant reminder for the pitcher to be in the present moment in order to make the next pitch. This isn't simply a play on words. Ask any pitcher what he was thinking during his finest games, and most likely he will tell you the following: "Nothing. I was simply throwing the ball. It was easy." Therefore, if the pitcher's goal is to be completely immersed in the present moment, to completely trust the pitch he is about to make, and to think purely and simply, then staying focused on the present moment is of the highest importance. Present thinking can free the pitcher's mind from clutter, so he should practice bringing his thoughts to a close just before making the pitch. Used in tandem and practiced deliberately, pace and presence can free the pitcher from unwanted and irrational thought.

PEN SESSION **Implementing Gap Movements**

We refer to the time in between pitches as the gap. During the gaps, a pitcher's actions often make it easy to recognize that the game has "sped up" on him. His movements become fast, often in the form of constant adjusting and readjusting of his uniform or cap. It may also be seen in the way he proceeds back to the mound. Usually, this is very apparent to those watching, but it may not be apparent to the pitcher. Because of this, we practice what is known as gap movements. During the gaps, a pitcher who is in control of himself is generally slow moving, free flowing, and breathing at a normal rate. So that is exactly what the pitchers should practice. Gap movements can be practiced during catch play, on a bullpen mound with or without a ball, or when the pitcher is standing in his room right before bedtime. The pitcher should be instructed to breathe deep and move slower in hopes that the physiological response will trigger the proper mental response. During a contest, if the pitcher hears the word *GAPS* coming out of our dugout, that is his cue to slow the gap movements down considerably.

Me Versus Me and Me Versus You

Many tools can be used to formulate a mental foundation. An entire book could be devoted to this theme, but a solid place to start is with the principle of "me versus me and me versus you" that was discussed in chapter 1. As mentioned, the "me versus me and me versus you" mentality is the root of competitiveness at the heart of the pitcher–hitter confrontation. This concept is so important that when the pitcher is truly armed with it—when he truly believes and trusts in his stuff and himself—there isn't much that will stand in the pitcher's way, including the hitter.

For a pitcher to develop this mentality, it must be repeatedly ingrained into the pitcher through deliberate practice. And, deliberate practice is directly related to intent, which is another one of the foundational principles discussed in chapter 1.

Intent gives the pitcher a clear purpose and a deep sense of caring about what and how he is practicing. The intent in the work that a pitcher carries out will enable him to take a very abstract premise (the thought of "me versus you") and create a tangible and useable mental strategy. One player who provides a good example of this is David Price, the number 1 draft choice of the Tampa Bay Rays in 2007. During his rookie season, David called me on the phone after a poor outing against the Rangers. I could hear the despondent tone in his voice, and it was apparent that he was really searching for answers. After listening to him, I asked him if he still thought of the hitter as someone who was trying to take something away from him. Had he taken the battle with each hitter personally as he had done so many times in college? Was he still thinking *me versus you*? After a bit more discussion, David decided that in his next few outings he would try going back to the mental strategy that he used in college. As a result, he won his next five games in a row. A while later, I asked him what some of the differences were. He said that he focused on taking the confrontation between himself and the hitter personally—and that this made him more aggressive, helped him clear his mind of all the so-called important things he thought he needed to be thinking about, and allowed him to simply make pitches. This situation demonstrates that "me versus you" needs to be a habit and a lifestyle; it must be something that the pitcher uses all the time as opposed to once in a while. It is not a quick fix or a gimmick to trick the mind; rather, it is a root foundation that enables the pitcher to establish a mind-set for the game.

So how does a pitcher inject this type of thinking into his weaponry to use against the enemy? As every Chicago Cub fan says, "You gotta believe!" The pitcher must believe in this concept so strongly and use it so often that it simply becomes a part of him. It is a concept that can be continually revisited, as in David Price's case, to get back on the proper course and boil the game down to its simplest, yet most important, ingredient—competing against the hitter. So often the pitcher is drowning in thoughts. *What do I throw? How do I feel? Why is my breaking ball not breaking? If I don't throw well this time, Coach might not pitch me again.* The thoughts go on and on until the pitcher forgets the most important thing—taking the confrontation against the hitter personally and showing him that the pitcher is better than him! The pitcher should stay focused on these three little words: *me versus you*. He should forge ahead with courage and trust, implement the three Ps deliberately, and then watch his game rise to a new level!

Routines

For the most part, people are creatures of habit. They generally rise at the same time each day, eat the same types of food, and participate in the same activities on a regular and very predictable basis. When one or more of these activities are altered, either by time or circumstance, a person can become out of sorts and distracted, and he will usually not function up to his normal capabilities. The same is true for a pitcher. Pitchers need to become comfortable in perceived uncomfortable situations. Notice that I used the word *perceived*. The pitcher who is clear thinking chooses how he perceives threatening situations; he is proactive in his approach rather than reactive. This allows him to compete against the hitter by limiting the effect of external circumstances or internal thoughts that would otherwise distort or disorient his thinking. How does the pitcher stay comfortable in uncomfortable situations? How does he limit distractions? He does this by implementing routines.

QUICK PITCH

Pitchers need to have a flexible mind-set, as opposed to a mind-set that is reactive. The reactive pitcher acts out of fear, though fearing something suggests that it has not happened yet. The flexible pitcher chooses to delay his reaction, waiting for more information so that he may make a better choice. Remember, we have a choice in everything that we think, say, or do. Champion pitchers are champion thinkers. They are flexible.

Wade Boggs' practice of eating chicken before every game was a routine, as was Nomar's ritual before stepping into the batter's box. Routines are like "home." They make the pitcher feel safe and help keep his game simple by preventing external and unnecessary circumstances from arising before and during a competition. They put him in the right frame of mind. Routines promote consistent performance because they cause the pitcher to regularly place himself in situations that will arise during the game. Nothing will surprise him.

Practice Routines

Practice should be well planned based on need, adjustments from the previous game, or the current training cycle of the player. This applies to practices directed by the coach or when the player is working on his own. A good practice contains segments that are staples for the pitcher; these daily staples may be physical exercises or mental techniques such as visualization practice, breathing exercises, or simply getting the mind right through deliberate thinking. A staple for our pitchers is the way that we warm up and stretch, perform tubing and pitcher-specific stretches, and perform catch play. These exercise routines will be explained at length in the chapters that follow. The pitchers perform these routines at the beginning of our practices and during pregame warm-ups at the same time and in the same manner with no exceptions. The routines are meant to set the stage for ensuing activities, put the pitcher in a specific mind-set, and send the message, "It's time to go to work."

Pregame Routines

As mentioned, prepractice routines are also implemented on game days, so activities such as warm-up, stretching, tubing, and throwing are done the same way each game. Because pitchers have different roles and pitch at different times in the game, a different set of routines must be put into place for the starting pitchers and the relievers. In these cases, the best method may be to let the individual pitcher formulate a specific plan based on personal preferences and needs (as long as the plan fits the parameters of the coach's principles). Bullpen routines, as well as the running and throwing before the bullpen starts, can certainly be tailored to fit the needs of the starting pitcher. Relief pitchers must have the ability to get ready very quickly, so a routine must be designed to give them the best chance to be successful. Small details such as having spikes on and knowing where his glove and jacket are located will help ensure that the relief pitcher can get ready as fast as possible. Again, the pitcher must understand himself in order to create routines that help make him ready to compete.

Prepitch Routines

Once the game starts, the pitcher's primary goal is to stay in the present, clear the mind of as many distractions as possible, recognize when he is uncomfortable, and have the wherewithal to combat those uncomfortable feelings. Most important, he must execute the next pitch free from the chains of the last one. Then, after that pitch, he must be able to do this for the next pitch, and then the next, until the game is over. The objective is to keep the game as small and as manageable as possible, and the pitcher must try his very best to be "all in" for the next pitch. At the beginning of each season, I use a hypothetical situation to help the pitchers put this task in the proper perspective. I first ask the pitchers how long it takes to deliver a pitch from start to finish (starting the delivery, executing the pitch, and then finding out if it was a ball or strike.). They usually respond by guessing 2 or 3 seconds per pitch, depending on the outcome. Next, I ask them how many pitches a starter would normally throw in a game, to which they usually reply, "Approximately 100." I then stress that if each pitch and outcome takes approximately 2 or 3 seconds and the pitcher throws 100 pitches, then the pitcher must be ready to focus intently and stay present for approximately 200 to 300 seconds, or 3.3 to 5 minutes, per game. I point out that this is very obtainable! I finish by explaining that the pitcher can spend the rest of the time using positive self-talk, practicing white noise (nothingness), or planning for the next inning while sitting in the dugout.

How does the pitcher channel his thoughts during the long time in between pitches? How can he quiet his mind to stay present and then calm his mind into a "nothingness" just before starting the delivery? Again, this can be done by deliberately practicing a set routine that breeds familiarity and comfort. Like all of the other routines, this routine should be unique to the individual and designed to fulfill his specific needs. However, I have also found that a template can be useful as a starting point. An approach that my pitchers have had success with involves three basic actions: assess the situation; agree with the catcher on the pitch and trust it; and then take a deep breath, quiet the mind into nothingness, and execute the pitch.

This simple routine helps a pitcher use the time between pitches wisely. For a pitcher, assessing the situation is nothing more than identifying what just happened, recognizing if something is physically or mentally wrong, and then thinking about what might happen next. Let's look at an example. The hitter just hit a double, putting the tying run on second base. The pitcher hung a slider and is upset with himself, and the hitter coming to the plate has been hitting the pitcher all day long. In this situation, the pitcher is rattled and should stay off the mound until he puts things back into perspective. How should he be thinking so that he can get back on the right track? His thoughts should go something like this: *I can't do anything about what just happened. Yes, I hung that pitch, but I am still in a position to get this hitter out if I make good pitches. I also know that if I get behind in the count, I could always pitch around him (with a base open) and pitch to the next guy. I am one pitch away from getting out of this.* Putting things in perspective is often the most difficult thing to do because emotions rise during the heat of battle and often take on a personality of their own; these emotions detract from the pitcher's ability to recognize what is happening and to coach himself in a constructive manner. That is a good reason why a practice routine must be set in place and then worked on repeatedly.

Once the pitcher has put the game in perspective and is ready to step back on the rubber, he stops self-coaching, agrees on the pitch, and places trust in it. Placing trust in the pitch (focusing his intent) puts the responsibility directly on him and his intuition. This is one reason why pitchers should call their own games. Throwing the wrong pitch with conviction is much better than throwing the "right" pitch without trust. For the pitcher to develop trust, he must be placed into a practice environment where he learns to use his intuition and take responsibility for the pitch. A pitcher becomes much more aggressive under these circumstances, and the quality of his pitches improves. Letting the pitcher call the pitches is a frightening thought for most coaches because it takes them out of control of the situation. However, allowing pitchers and catchers to make the decisions on pitches shows them that the coach trusts them, and this can pay huge dividends! The final piece of the prepitch routine is the pitcher calming his thoughts to nothingness, thereby signaling that it is time to start the delivery and that he is all in. The pitcher has his thoughts in perspective, he agrees on and trusts in a pitch, he takes a deep breath and calms his mind, and he executes the pitch. In this stage, like any other aspect of baseball, the pitcher must be able to apply intent to the skill.

Postgame Routines

Regardless of the outcome or how good or bad the performance, a pitcher can learn a lesson from each game. It is the pitcher's duty to put the game in perspective by trying to understand what went right, what went wrong, and what adjustments he must make before his next outing. Pitchers often make blanket statements such as "I am terrible. I haven't pitched well for two weeks. My curveball stinks." The casual fan or even the coach can make those same statements, but they provide no valuable information to the pitcher on ways to improve. Just as it is easy to criticize when things go wrong, it is equally simple to become complacent when things are going well. "Man, I pitched a great game today. I'm cruising. I can't be beaten"—these are all famous last words! Generally, a pitcher is never as bad as he thinks he is, nor is he as good as he thinks. There are always ways to improve performance and ways to improve the process.

Research into the psychology of sport is being conducted daily, and a chapter in a book can hardly scratch the surface of this discipline. More is being learned about the mind every day, and the new advances are exciting. But these findings can also be confusing and make the pitcher and coach feel overwhelmed or underprepared to take on new challenges. Much of the information, though, is common sense and can be applied to everyday life circumstances. If a person gets cut off by another driver on the interstate, he can learn to deal with it, or he can go "bananas" and find himself in a threatening situation. It is his choice; he can control it, or it can control him. A person can become upset that he has to pay more taxes this year than last, or he can accept it as being out of his control, pay the money, and then set a strategy for next year.

Each person has the freedom to choose what he thinks, how he responds, and what he will do next time. A person is free to be however he wants to be; therefore, he is free to be whomever he wants to be. It then becomes a matter of deciding, planning, and acting.

Too often, people and ballplayers, especially pitchers, play the victim, when in actuality it is their thoughts that victimize them, not the situation. These same people often try to control things that are simply beyond their control. This is a recipe for chasing your own tail. Look at this chapter as an outline; it is a simple overview of the many things that a pitcher must prepare for in a game setting. Breathe life into it and make it your own. A pitcher must keep things small and manageable and must stay in the "now." He must create his own recipe for consistency. He must be "all in."

Lastly, we should go back to one of the foundational principles in chapter 1—training versus trusting. The game is a time when the pitcher must trust the work he has put in beforehand on the various skills and abilities it takes to play the game. These skills and abilities are not limited to the physical side of the game; practicing the mental side is as important, perhaps even more so. But as the game starts, the pitcher must go out and let it rip; he must trust his training. After all, if he is truly prepared, then how can he fail?

PART III

Conditioning for Pitching

Arm Strength and Injury Prevention

Dana Cavalea

If you've been around the game in the last 8 to 10 years, then you are aware of the priority that has been placed on preventing pitching injuries. Solid advancements have been made in reducing arm injuries, and some of the brightest minds in sports medicine are working to implement new strategies at the youth level to educate parents, coaches, and players on ways to prepare and preserve the pitching arm. Also during this period, significant improvements have been made on the methods for developing arm strength. Younger players are throwing harder than ever before, and it seems that we are only scratching the surface of the potential that is there for greater gains in the future. Yet the reality is that pitching a baseball is very much a risk–reward endeavor. Variables that can't possibly be accounted for during training and preparation can rear their ugly head at a moment's notice and cause injury. This is simply the chance that a young person takes when he decides to take up a sport: a risk of being injured in pursuit of fun, glory, and greatness on the battlefield or in the arena. If an athlete wants a guarantee of not being injured, then he should choose an activity that requires absolutely no physical exertion, one in which all variables can be consistently accounted for and controlled. May I suggest chess or checkers!

This chapter deals specifically with some of the methods that are currently used to strengthen the arm and reduce the risk of injury. As mentioned earlier, many variables play into injury; this chapter identifies some of the more common ones and then prescribes drills and exercises that can help prevent them.

Prevalence of Arm Injury in Pitchers

Chronic overuse and repetitive motion trauma have increased by as much as 50 percent since the 1990s (Peterson 2009), supporting the notion that younger players are simply playing too much baseball. Research studies provide further evidence of this: "Last spring, (Dr.) Andrews and his colleagues conducted a study comparing 95 high school pitchers who required surgical repair of either their elbow or shoulder with 45 pitchers that did not suffer injury. They found that those who pitched for more than eight months per year were 500 percent more likely to be injured, while those who pitched more than 80 pitches per game increased their injury risk by 400 percent. Pitchers who continued pitching despite having arm fatigue were an incredible 3,600 percent more likely to do serious damage to their arm" (Peterson 2009).

Even though little data exist regarding pitching injuries at the amateur level in the 1980s and early 1990s, I can give a personal account of what it was like then, which can provide a frame of reference for how far baseball has changed in just a short amount of time. During my high school and college years (late '80s and early '90s), the standard modality for curing a sore arm was rest and ice therapy. If a pitcher's arm still hurt after the prescribed rest period, he would extend the rest time and apply more ice. If this therapy didn't work, the pitcher would have a choice between early retirement or trying to bear through the pain in the hope that somehow the arm would fix itself. Jobe exercises (shoulder exercises using small dumbbells that were invented by Dr. Frank Jobe, the famous physician who performed the first Tommy John elbow surgery) were also used as a strengthening tool for the rotator cuff. Many pitchers came out of this situation okay and were able to continue pitching; others were not as fortunate.

Today, we have entered the age of pitch counts and mandatory rest time in between starts or appearances on the mound. And enforcing these new restrictions is definitely a good idea. But these restrictions are simply not enough. If they were enough, we wouldn't be seeing the astronomical number of injuries that are still occurring.

Perhaps baseball people need to look at the results of the studies from a different perspective and approach this situation from a different angle. What if throwing too much for too long a period of time wasn't the only culprit in pitching injuries? What if pitchers were trained to handle the stress that was placed on their arms by all of the pitches they threw and during all of the innings they logged? What if a reasonable pitch count and recovery time were coupled with a solid throwing regimen that was established before the start of the season, followed by a training routine that functionally "prehabbed" the arm through the course of the season? Would this training implementation completely eliminate all the throwing injuries reported in the studies? Probably not, but the reported numbers would certainly not be nearly as bad. This sort of regimen has worked for many pitchers, and it is the basis for what follows in this chapter.

A good way to approach this new plan is by starting with the principle of "throwing precedes pitching" (skill versus ability) as the foundation of a pitcher's training. As mentioned earlier, in order to become a proficient pitcher, a player must first become a proficient thrower. He becomes proficient at throwing through throwing. By focusing on progressive and daily throwing with intent, the pitcher will establish a solid throwing base, enabling his arm to become more durable and capable of handling the stress of throwing and pitching a baseball.

A bonus to this approach is that the pitcher can simultaneously increase velocity. After the player establishes a foundation and a throwing base, he will then begin to apply his skills on the pitching mound. Currently, many players seem to be doing the opposite: playing an extreme number of games over an extremely long period of time with little or no practice or preparation time devoted to developing the foundation.

Eight or nine months of playing with little or no practice and preparation time is a recipe for disaster—and the injury numbers prove it.

Assessment and Correction

Another ingredient in helping a pitcher train the arm to handle the rigors of competitively throwing a baseball is assessment and correction. The process of assessment and correction has the potential to reduce injuries, or at the very least, decrease the odds of getting hurt. Though a complete discussion of assessment and correction is well beyond the scope of this book, a few words on this topic are necessary.

Baseball is a very one-sided sport. Hitters and pitchers repeatedly swing and throw in the same direction, causing one side of the body to become stronger than the opposite (nondominant) side. This causes imbalances, and these inefficiencies lurk and prey on various areas of the body. The kinetic chain relies on stabilizing and mobilizing joints to work in tandem to move the body, providing a series of checks and balances of sorts. The ankle is a mobility joint, supported by a stabilizing knee joint, which in turn stabilizes a mobile hip joint. The lower lumbar region and scapula (especially in overhead throwers) serve as the stabilizers in the upper body while the thoracic spine and shoulder joints serve as mobilizers. In the lower arm, the elbow is the stabilizer, and the wrist joint is the mobilizer. Looked at this way, it is easy to see that one joint can affect the next in line and the corresponding muscles if it is not functioning properly. The pitcher strives for symmetry and harmony of muscles and joints in order to efficiently throw the ball. A poorly functioning ankle can lead to muscles and ligaments being forced to compensate, thus placing greater strain on the pitcher when throwing. Assessment and correction involve finding those flaws and implementing strategies for increased strength, flexibility, mobility, and stability.

As pitchers begin to understand the kinetic chain and understand the basic functions of the joints working up the chain, they will also understand the importance of "connection" in the pitching delivery. If one area of the chain is weak or not used properly, it directly affects the next part of the chain, which in turn affects the next, and so on. It is amazing to think of the dynamic intricacies that all of the body parts must coordinate together to produce movement—and produce extraordinary connection.

Arm Strengthening Exercises and Routines

Through the years, countless exercises, programs, and workouts have been developed for pitchers. Most of these training tools are designed to strengthen the pitching arm, improve durability, and decrease injury. The exercises and routines included here are the ones that I have found to be most effective. This is by no means an exhaustive list; however, for pitchers who are looking for a new arm strength routine, the exercises and stretches that follow will be invaluable. Even pitchers who already have an effective conditioning program will find valuable exercises that can be incorporated into the routine.

Resistance Tubing and Pitcher Stretch Exercises

Various stretching protocols can be used to properly warm up the body before beginning a throwing activity, some of which will be covered in chapter 11. The important thing is that stretching and a total-body warm-up *must* be done before throwing the baseball, not the other way around. For the pitcher's arm to respond properly and have the ability to handle the stress of any type of throwing activity, the pitcher must first get the arm ready. Resistance tubing exercises, pitcher stretch exercises, and perhaps even general agility training are all suitable activities to engage in before throwing; these activities "grease the grooves," prepare the neural pathways, open up and heat the body, and generally prepare the body to handle the demands that throwing a baseball places on it. Too often, players simply go out and warm up by throwing instead of warming up to throw. This is the equivalent of lifting a heavy weight without preliminary warm-up sets or running a sprint without prior running.

Resistance Tubing Exercises

After a proper general stretch that raises the core temperature of the body, the pitcher should engage in resistance tubing exercises. Resistance tubing is available in various tensions, so a pitcher or coach should identify the desired level of resistance before purchasing. I usually buy Thera-Band brand tubing, but there are many kinds out there that are comparable in both price and quality.

The band needs to be placed at the proper height before starting the tubing program. This will ensure that tension is not misplaced or altered, thereby ensuring that the greatest amount of tension is given across the range of motion. The band will be tied or clipped (carabiners work very well) at either hip or knee height depending on the exercise, and it can be tied to almost any fence or hook. Much of the tubing that is sold today comes in various resistance levels and often comes prepackaged with clips to hook onto the fence. Exercises should be completed using strict form and in a slow and controlled manner. The pitcher should strive for a large range of motion throughout the exercise. Tubing exercises must be completed before throwing every day, and 12 to 15 repetitions should be performed for each exercise. Note that some exercises require the use of two pieces of tubing. Handles and wrist cuffs are optional. Many of the tubing exercises you will find here are designed for the throwing side of the body, however, it should be noted that they can be done on both sides of the body for optimal strength gains.

Straight-Arm Horizontal Adduction

Secure the resistance band at knee height. Hold the band in the pitching hand, keeping the elbow and wrist straight (see figure 10.1a). Pull across the body, stopping at the hip on the opposite side (see figure 10.1b). Slowly return to the starting position. Repeat.

Figure 10.1   Straight-arm horizontal adduction.

Straight-Arm Horizontal Abduction

Secure the resistance band at knee height and on the opposite side of the pitching arm. Hold the band in the pitching hand with the thumb facing the ground. Keep the elbow and wrist straight (see figure 10.2a), and pull across the body, pulling the thumb to the sky slightly above shoulder height (see figure 10.2b). Slowly return to the starting position. Repeat.

Figure 10.2 Straight-arm horizontal abduction.

Bent-Arm External and Internal Rotation

For external rotation, hold the band in the pitching hand with the elbow bent at a 90-degree angle and about even with the ribs (see figure 10.3a). Keeping the pitching arm at your side, pull the resistance band away from the body (see figure 10.3b). Slowly return to the starting position. Repeat.

For internal rotation, hold the band in the pitching hand with the elbow bent at a 90-degree angle and about even with the ribs. Keeping the pitching arm at your side, pull the resistance band across the belly. Slowly return to the starting position. Repeat.

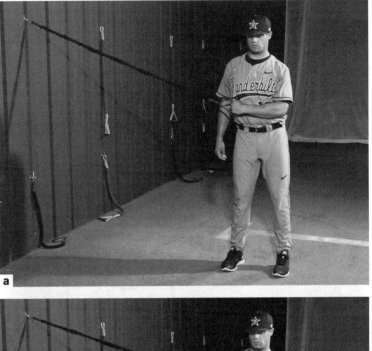

Figure 10.3   Bent-arm external rotation.

Backward Straight-Arm Hyperextension

Secure the resistance band in front of you. While leaning forward, stand with feet shoulder-width apart and with the arm in front of you (see figure 10.4a). Pull the band behind you (see figure 10.4b) and then return to the starting position. Repeat.

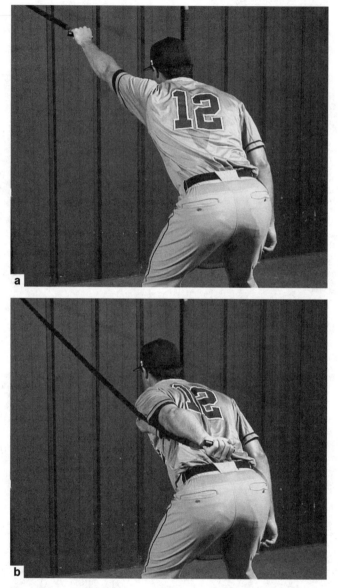

Figure 10.4 Backward straight-arm hyperextension.

Overhead Triceps Extension

With the resistance band underfoot, or secured to a wall at knee level, grab the band over the pitching shoulder; the elbow should be pointing forward, bent at 90 degrees (see figure 10.5a). Keeping the elbow still, straighten the arm toward the ceiling (see figure 10.5b). When fully extended, slowly return to the starting position. Repeat.

Figure 10.5 Overhead triceps extension.

Forward Side-to-Side

With the resistance band securely attached behind you, spread the legs apart with one foot forward and the other behind. Raise both arms above the head and lean the body from one side to the other (see figure 10.6). Keep the back arched and do not rotate the body. Repeat. This stretches the oblique and hip flexor.

Figure 10.6 Forward side-to-side.

Backward Side-to-Side

With the resistance band securely attached directly in front of you, spread the legs apart with one foot forward and the other behind. Raise both arms above the head and lean the body from one side to the other (see figure 10.7). Keep the back arched and do not rotate the body. Repeat. This stretches the oblique and hip flexor.

Figure 10.7   Backward side-to-side.

Forward Pitcher

With the resistance band securely attached behind you, simulate the throwing motion to pull the band back and over the front pitching shoulder (see figure 10.8). Keep the back slightly arched and the feet apart. Return to the starting position. Repeat.

Figure 10.8 Forward pitcher.

Backward Pitcher

With the resistance band securely attached directly in front of you, begin in the finish position of the delivery (see figure 10.9a). Reverse the throwing motion, leading with the elbow and pulling the band back and over the pitching shoulder (see figure 10.9b). Keep the back slightly arched. Return to the starting position. Repeat.

Figure 10.9 Backward pitcher.

Pitcher Stretches

Once the pitcher finishes with the resistance tubing exercises, he will further prepare his arm to throw by performing a series of stretches designed to target some of the smaller muscles in the shoulder, elbow, forearm, and wrist. These are muscles that might otherwise be neglected in a normal stretching routine. The following stretches are fairly simple and easy to remember, and the pitchers seem to enjoy doing them.

Arm Circles

The pitcher moves his shoulders and arms in small, medium, large, and extra large forward circles. Once the pitcher completes these forward circles, he then reverses the procedure and moves through extra large, large, medium, and small forward circles. The pitcher then follows the same progression using backward circles (see figure 10.10).

Figure 10.10   Arm circles.

Pot Stirs

This stretch is done by spreading the legs wide, bending over, and depressing the shoulder capsule down into the socket. The arms are held straight, with the fingers spread and the hand hyperextended (see figure 10.11a). The pitcher then makes a stirring motion with the hand in both a clockwise and counterclockwise manner (see figure 10.11, b and c). This stretch obviously stretches the shoulder, but it also provides a stretch for the fingers, wrists, and forearms if done properly.

Figure 10.11   Pot stirs.

Teacups

This is a pitcher favorite. It mimics a movement used in the martial arts and does a fantastic job of stretching the entire arm as well as the lower back and upper thoracic region. The pitcher holds an imaginary cup of tea in his hand, and through a series of twists and contortions, he moves the cup around his body and delivers it to the front, all the while trying not to spill a drop of the tea (see figure 10.12). The movement will be done both forward and backward.

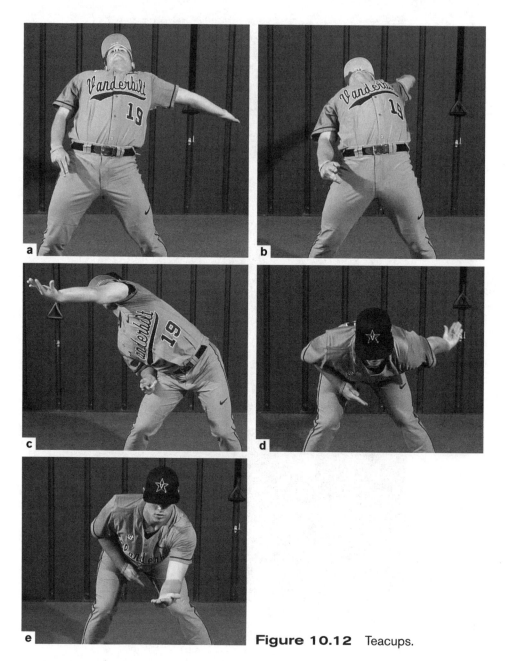

Figure 10.12 Teacups.

Sleeper Stretch

This stretch is easily the most technical and probably the most important. The sleeper stretch is a self-administered internal rotation stretch. Poor internal rotation can be a precursor for glenohumeral internal rotation deficit (GIRD), which is as debilitating as it sounds. GIRD is when the shoulder loses some of its capacity to internally rotate, leading to a loss of the total arc of the throwing motion. This condition usually comes with a loss of velocity and control, and it increases the chance for shoulder and elbow problems. The stretch is done lying on the throwing side as if sleeping with the head in line with the spine. The pitcher uses the opposite arm to gently stretch the throwing arm into internal rotation (see figure 10.13). The pitcher will generally hold this stretch for 10 to 15 seconds and perform 3 to 5 repetitions on the throwing side only.

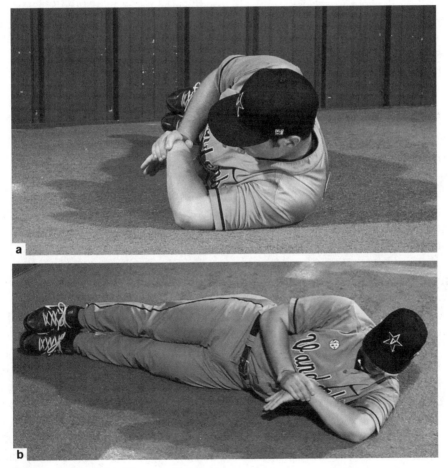

Figure 10.13   Sleeper stretch.

Throwing Routines

By this time, the pitcher's body and arm are prepared to throw, and that's what he will do. While throwing, too many pitchers get caught up in conversations about a variety of subjects, ranging from what they did last night, to homework, to what movie they will see tonight. This makes throwing a shallow activity at best, and because intent is vital (and throwing precedes pitching), this type of throwing does not help the pitcher develop. Of course, the pitcher should have fun, and a small degree of chatter is acceptable, but when the pitcher begins to throw the ball, all focus MUST be on the present moment—on the act of throwing itself! This is practicing deliberately.

Our throwing routines are broken into two categories: catch play and long toss. Catch play is the daily routine that our pitchers use for throwing at the beginning of practice and is designed to be performed for a limited amount of time. The long toss, which can also be performed during practice, is a way for the pitchers to practice throwing without the time limitation. Both routines work well for helping a pitcher develop a base level of throwing, and the pitcher can use one or the other during different times of his training or throwing cycle. The routines should be used in conjunction with one another to provide a total training solution.

Understanding Levels of Discomfort or Pain

After an initial general warm-up, resistance tubing exercises, full-body stretches, and pitcher stretches, the pitchers should be able to throw from 45 feet (13.7 m) apart with good intent and good velocity. However, sometimes pitchers experience discomfort that can interfere with this plan. At the start of each season, I try to educate the group on the differences between being stiff, sore, and hurt and how those degrees of pain can be managed when throwing. The pitchers need to develop a mentality that enables them to throw "to tolerance." Stiffness is just that—the body or arm is stiff, similar to when a person wakes up and his joints and muscles creak and don't move as well until he is up and has moved around a bit. Stiffness can and should be worked through, and stiffness is usually a sign that the pitcher hasn't warmed up and prepared properly. The pitcher should still be able to throw even when stiff.

Soreness can be related to how the athlete's body feels the day after a lift; the soreness comes from the "belly" of the muscle and, again, usually dissipates in time. The last degree of pain is hurt. Hurt, by our definition, doesn't go away. It is an acute, perhaps persistent, shooting pain through the arm or a dull pain that seems to linger throughout. When a pitcher's pain falls in the category of hurt, the pitcher must shut down throwing for the day or possibly a few days and then try again. If the pain persists, the pitcher should then seek medical attention. When pitchers understand this and how it relates to their own arms, they will be able to identify their individual tolerance levels.

Catch Play Routine

Figure 10.14 provides the details of our daily catch routine. This routine is used by our pitchers for their throwing at the beginning of practice. We call it catch play because it is essentially "playing catch." Ideally, time limits would not be placed on how long a pitcher will throw, but time constraints of practice and NCAA limitations prevent most college coaches from taking this approach. The catch play routine is a good way for the pitcher to get the benefits of throwing without taking up too much valuable practice time.

Catch play will typically last approximately 17 to 22 minutes. On the day after throwing in a game, a pitcher may throw to tolerance; otherwise, normal throwing protocol is expected. The foundational element, intent, is a very important aspect of catch play, especially if time is limited. For best results, each ball should be thrown with good intent. Remember if the pitcher wants to throw harder, better, faster, he must train his arm.

Figure 10.14 Catch Play Routine

Throws at 45 feet (2 min.)	Focus on spotting.
Throws at 60 feet (2 min.)	Focus on lift, rhythm, and tempo.
Throws at 75 feet (1-2 min.)	Focus on stepping into the throw, momentum, and backside drive.
Throws at 90 feet (2 min.)	Focus on stepping behind on the throw and the finish.
Throws at 120 feet (2 min.)	Focus on stepping behind on the throw and the finish.
Throws at 150 feet (2 min.)	Focus on stepping behind on the throw, lower-half crow hop, and the finish.
Throws at maximum distance (1 min.)	Focus on executing proper form on throws at maximum distance.
Compression throws (2 min.)	Focus on compression throws where pitchers move closer to their partner in 10-foot increments, starting at maximum distance and moving in until 90 or 75 feet.
Pitches at 90 or 75 feet (1-2 min.)	Focus on development of the changeup.
Pitches at 45 feet (1-2 min.)	Focus on spin on the breaking ball.

Long-Toss Routine

Figure 10.15 provides the details of our long-toss routine, which differs from the catch play routine in that there are no restrictions of time or distance on the throw and these elements will vary from pitcher to pitcher. The general rule is to throw the ball as far as possible, as hard as possible, for as long as possible, always maintaining body control. This routine was adopted from Alan Jaeger's program with a few minor modifications to fit our needs. The routine can best be summarized through two of its characteristics: As the pitchers move out and gradually increase the distance between themselves and their partners (stretching and distance phases), arm endurance is the main focus, but during the compression phase (moving closer together), the pitchers are focusing on arm strength and arm speed. Essentially, compression throwing means that the pitcher will take his longest throw during the distance phase and "compress" it into a shorter throw. For example, if the pitcher reached a maximum distance of 300 feet for his longest throw, he would retain the intensity of the 300-foot throw at whatever distance he is throwing from (120 feet, 110 feet, 100 feet, and so on) during the compression phase until he reaches his final destination. Throughout the compression phase, he would be decreasing the arc at which he throws the ball—throwing the ball on a line. Note that the final destination should be around 75 feet (22.8 m). Command of the ball should be a strong consideration for this exercise, but it should not be the primary focus, especially during the distance phase of the routine. The pitcher should try not to make his partner move more than 3 feet (91 cm) in any direction to catch the throw. When a pitcher's command is so poor that the partner must move farther than 3 feet, the pitcher is likely trying to throw too far, and inefficiencies are occurring during the throw. In that case, the partners should move closer together to a point where they can meet the 3-foot rule.

The long-toss routine is a great tool for the serious pitcher. However, if the routine is not done properly, long toss can become counterproductive. Though it would be nice if every pitcher could throw the ball 300 feet and then compress that throw into one that is 60 feet 6 inches, the reality is that not every pitcher will be capable of doing so. Because of a lack of strength or a lack of coordinated and connected movement patterns, the pitcher's throwing mechanism will often break down, and poor movement patterns (i.e., the stuff the pitcher is trying to fix or eliminate) will appear. As a result, in trying to gain arm strength, he is fortifying faulty movements and jeopardizing proper mechanics.

The pitcher and coach must ensure that the long-toss routine is executed in a way that increases arm strength while also enforcing proper mechanics. To do this, the pitcher should perform the long toss in a range that will allow his arm to breathe and extend without jeopardizing efficient movement patterns. Glove-side action is a great example of this. If the pitcher goes beyond the distance where his glove side can stay connected with the rest of his body—that is, if the pitcher begins to spin or pull his lower half and glove to recruit more strength in order to make the longer throw—then this throw is counterproductive. The pitcher should move in closer and throw more efficiently. Once the shorter distance is mastered (perhaps it is 250 feet instead of 300 feet), the pitcher can then progress back to a longer distance. A good rule of thumb to ensure quality throws would be to make sure the pitcher can land solidly and get out over his front side. See the enclosed DVD for video of this routine.

Figure 10.15   Long-Toss Routine

Arm circles (1 min.)	See page 182 for full description of this exercise.
Resistance tubing exercises (10-15 reps)	See page 172 for full description of these exercises.
Stretch phase	The pitcher throws at a comfortable distance (for distances past 120 feet, he should use a step behind) to let the arm stretch itself out. By learning to throw through a stretch, the pitcher will let the arm "open up," and arm speed will increase. During this phase, the pitcher keeps these things in mind: Let the arm stretch itself out; no misplaced effort. Allow the arm to throw as far as it wants to provided that it "feels" good. Arc or ball height is not an issue, but a general rule is to throw the ball with a 30- to 45-degree arc. Be aware of mechanics, especially the finish portion of the throw.
Distance phase	As the arm builds endurance, the pitcher will not only need to throw more often, but also with more distance. For example, in the stretching phase, a pitcher's throws may have been at 150 feet, whereas in this distance phase, the throws may be 250 feet. The pitcher must give himself time to develop.
Compression phase	This phase helps generate arm speed, arm strength, and a lower release point. The pitcher moves in 10 feet closer after each throw. In this phase, the pitcher should focus on trying to generate as much arm speed as possible with the right type of effort and intent. He works on the last 10% of wrist snap and limits the arc of the throw. In other words, he starts throwing the ball more on a line. Also note that if the pitcher wanted to stretch his arm out on the second day after pitching, he could simply follow the long-toss routine (after his day 2 ACE routine [see page 194]) and eliminate this compression phase; we call this the easy long-toss routine. It's great for the pitcher who is recovering from his last start and training for his next.

Velocity Training

Velocity training, or weighted-ball training, has gained a good deal of momentum since the late 1990s and early 2000s. The vehicle behind the momentum has likely been Ron Wolforth's Athletic Pitcher program that has become a staple in many high school and college programs. The Athletic Pitcher program employs a vast array of medicine ball, agility, and explosive exercises that are designed to enhance the overall athleticism of the pitcher. Ron's program is responsible for many young men making considerable velocity gains and athletic improvements.

One part of the Athletic Pitcher arsenal deals with overload-underload training. Though it has become popular with Wolforth's program, this type of training has been researched and developed over time by men such as Dr. Coop DeRenne, Tom House, and Dr. Mike Marshall, to name a few. In one study, DeRenne et al. found conclusive evidence that using weighted implements, both heavier and lighter than the traditional five-ounce ball, increased velocity over a 10-week period for 225 high school and college aged pitchers (DeRenne et al., 1994). This is only one study, but it does typify the results of many of the other studies that have been conducted. Coaches and pitchers who are considering an overload-underload (weighted-ball) regimen should read the current research and determine if this type of training is appropriate for their situation.

Weighted-ball training started to make sense to me when I heard Paul Nyman, whom I mentioned earlier, speak at a clinic. When talking about weighted-ball training, Paul explained quite logically that players throw a "weighted ball" every time they throw a baseball—and that five ounces, the weight of a baseball, is an arbitrary weight. Science never concluded that five ounces was the exact weight that a baseball should be. Paul spoke of how a javelin and a football weigh considerably more and are both thrown overhead. This helped me understand how using heavier and lighter weighted balls to train could make pitchers more efficient and explosive when they were throwing a five-ounce baseball.

So why and how does overload-underload training work? When throwing the heavy ball, the arm must recruit more muscle fibers to work so that the ball can be thrown. So over time and practice, the overload training acts much like weight training; the more one lifts, the stronger one becomes. In underload training, because the ball is lighter, this enables the arm to move faster than it does when throwing a regulation weighted ball. The two types of throwing training—underload and overload—then combine for the best of both worlds: the recruitment of more muscle activation throughout the arm and body, along with the arm traveling faster than normal. This is a nice recipe for strength and velocity.

The velocity training routine shown in figure 10.16 follows what is called the ROUR principle: regular, overload, underload, regular. The pitcher will perform each exercise by throwing the different balls in a specific order: regular baseball, overload (heavy) baseball, underload (light) baseball, and finish with regular baseball.

Figure 10.16 Velocity Training Routine

On knees with "go" call	Facing a net, the pitcher is positioned on his knees. On the coach's "go" command, the pitcher throws into the net using weighted balls. This segment focuses on the pitcher's anticipatory skills in throwing the baseball. By waiting for the "go" command, the pitcher's arm is on "high alert" to throw the ball; the pitcher is recruiting muscle fiber to throw the ball and training his arm to move faster. Because the pitcher starts on the knees, this drill emphasizes and isolates the arm action. ROUR: 5 oz, 21 oz, 14 oz, 7 oz, 3.5 oz, 5 oz.
Standing with "go" call	Facing a net, the pitcher stands with feet side by side. On the coach's "go" command, the pitcher throws into the net using weighted balls. This exercise also focuses primarily on arm action, but because the pitcher is in a standing position, a small portion of lower-body support and power will be used. ROUR: 5 oz, 14 oz, 7 oz, 3.5 oz, 5 oz.
Final arc	Facing a net, the pitcher stands with one foot in front of the other. He throws into the net using weighted balls. This segment isolates a very important position for the pitcher. It goes from release point back to external layback (pitcher's arm is cocked and ready to catapult forward) and then through release of the pitch. This is a vital area where hand and arm speed are at their highest. ROUR: 5 oz, 21 oz, 14 oz, 7 oz, 3.5 oz, 5 oz.
Turn-arounds	Facing a net, the pitcher stands in a release point position. He throws into the net using weighted balls. From the release point position, the pitcher uses a full turn and elbow action with no pauses or stops. Essentially, he is making a full turn to his throwing side to make the throw. ROUR: 5 oz, 14 oz, 7 oz, 3.5 oz, 5 oz.
Hands out	The pitcher starts with his glove side facing the net. His hands are directly out in front of him, and he makes a throw by pulling his arms back into his body. This action initiates the scapular movements that must fire to execute the throw. ROUR: 5 oz, 14 oz, 7 oz, 3.5 oz, 5 oz.
Hands up	The pitcher starts with his glove side facing the net. His hands are up by his face. He makes the throw by letting his hands drop, initiating the scapular movements that must fire to execute the throw. ROUR: 5 oz, 14 oz, 7 oz, 3.5 oz, 5 oz.
Step behind with crossover	The pitcher starts with his glove side facing the net. A step with the front foot initiates the movement. After the initial step, the back foot steps behind and both arms cross in front of the pitcher simultaneously as the throw is made. This movement focuses on coordination, rhythm, and power of the throw. ROUR: 5 oz, 14 oz, 7 oz, 3.5 oz, 5 oz.
Hot feet	The pitcher starts in an athletic position with his glove side facing the net. The pitcher initiates the movement by rapidly moving his feet up and down, then he takes a step toward the net and makes a throw. This movement focuses on lower-half power and connection into the throw. ROUR: 5 oz, 14 oz, 7 oz, 3.5 oz, 5 oz.
Turn and burn	The pitcher starts by facing away from the net. He then takes 3 or 4 steps backward (almost a run), turns, and makes the throw. This movement focuses on coordination, timing, and rotational power to make the throw. ROUR: 5 oz, 14 oz, 7 oz, 3.5 oz, 5 oz.

Arm Care Exercises (ACE)

As mentioned, for pitchers at the amateur level 15 to 20 years ago, arm care was a gamble at best. Jobe exercises were the predominant preventative exercises used to keep the pitcher healthy, and weight training for baseball was in its formative years. Some people believed in weight training, while others did not, so the athlete was basically left to his own accord, fumbling his way through what to do or what not to do. As a first-year coach who just finished my playing days, this did not satisfy me one bit. I knew there had to be better measures that could be used to make the arm more durable and keep the pitcher healthy. The routines in this section contain a collection of exercises that have been defined, refined, and redefined over the course of 15 years. I have borrowed ideas from just about everybody—including Ron Wolforth (Athletic Pitcher and Combat Pitcher programs), Tom House, Mark Verstegen, and Vern Gambetta—as well as added a few that were possibly edited versions of other exercises that I saw along the way.

One of the best features of the ACE program is its versatility. Exercises can be mixed and matched, and relief pitchers' routines can be designed based on the volume of throwing or upcoming throwing events. Exercises can also be pulled from the routine to address any issues related to strength, mobility, or stability that the pitcher might have, either by adding more sets or reps of one exercise or by deleting others. Intensity is at a premium during these exercises, and, as with all things, the pitcher will get out of this program exactly what he puts into it!

Day 1 ACE Routine

The day after he pitches, a pitcher should complete the day 1 ACE routine (see figure 10.17). During the season, this will be the only day that the pitcher participates in long-distance running; subsequent days will include sprint or interval training. Day 1 is more of a full-body routine and includes a good number of two-hand exercises along with exercises that target the small muscles in and around the elbow and forearm.

Figure 10.17 Day 1 ACE Routine

Run (30 min.)	The pitcher embarks on a 30-minute run. The run is designed to be a low- to moderate-intensity run, flushing the body and mind.
Foam roller (8-12 sec. each body area)	The pitcher lies on the foam roller, slowly moving his body over select muscle areas to increase recovery.
Tissue regeneration (as long as needed)	The pitcher places a baseball between specific body areas and a wall. The pitcher leans into the ball to keep it from dropping and slowly moves his body so the ball rolls over muscle areas to stimulate tissue regeneration.
Resistance band exercises	See page 172 for full descriptions of these exercises.

Overhead medicine ball on two feet (2 × 25)	The pitcher faces a wall and stands on two feet. He bounces a medicine ball overhead against the wall. This exercise promotes full range of motion and is an excellent shoulder exercise that benefits the elbow as well.
Overhead medicine ball on one foot (2 × 25)	The pitcher faces a wall and stands on one foot. He bounces a medicine ball overhead against the wall. This exercise promotes full range of motion and is an excellent shoulder exercise that benefits the elbow as well.
Chest medicine ball on two feet (2 × 25)	The pitcher faces a wall and stands on two feet. He bounces a medicine ball from the chest against the wall. This exercise is an excellent shoulder and core exercise that benefits the elbow as well.
Chest medicine ball on one foot (2 × 25)	The pitcher faces a wall and stands on one foot. He bounces a medicine ball from the chest against the wall. This exercise is an excellent shoulder and core exercise that benefits the elbow as well.
Side-to-side (2 × 20 sec.)	The pitcher stands with his back to a wall and bounces a medicine ball from side to side against the wall.
Diagonals (2 × 20 sec.)	The pitcher stands with his back to a wall and bounces a medicine ball from high to low and low to high against the wall.
Woodchopper (2 × 20 sec.)	The pitcher stands with his back to a wall and bounces a medicine ball above his head and between his legs against the wall.
Pitcher torques (1 × 10)	The pitcher stands with one foot in front of the other while holding a medicine ball. The pitcher "torques" the ball to his nonthrowing side, then torques the ball to his throwing side, followed by an explosive throw against the wall.
Overhead soccer throws (1 × 10)	The pitcher makes a throw with the medicine ball much like the way a soccer goalie throws the ball into the field of play.
Medicine ball sit-ups (2 × 35)	The pitcher lies on the ground in a sit-up position, and a partner stands at his feet facing him. As the pitcher performs sit-ups, he and his partner pass the medicine ball back and forth between them.
Side-to-side sit-ups (2 × 35)	While lying in a sit-up position, the pitcher moves the medicine ball from one side of his body to the next with his feet, keeping his feet off the ground. This is a great rotational and abdominal exercise.
Feet-off sit-ups (2 × 35)	The pitcher starts in a seated prone position with a partner. With his feet off the ground, the pitcher tosses the medicine ball back and forth with his partner. The standing partner should pass the ball to each side and over the head of his partner, forcing him to tighten his core.
Rice routine	Using various grips and hand positions, the pitcher moves his throwing hand in a bucket of rice to help strengthen his wrist and hand. The pitcher should do each grip and position as long as he can; typically this is 30 seconds or longer.
Wrist rollers	Using a broomstick with a weight tied to it with a rope, the pitcher holds the broomstick and rolls the weight up to it as many times as he can.
Light toss	With a partner, the pitcher makes a series of light throws. The distance will vary based on how far the individuals can throw; for example, some pitchers may throw 90 feet while others throw just 45 feet.

Day 2 ACE Routine

The pitcher performs the day 2 ACE routine on the second day after he throws (see figure 10.18). This routine is designed to place stress on the arm with one-arm medicine ball throwing and trampoline throwing. The two-hand exercises are designed to facilitate explosion, and the pitcher finishes the routine by targeting the small rotator cuff muscles with dumbbell and Bodyblade exercises. Pitchers who do not have access to a Bodyblade can simply skip this segment of the routine.

Figure 10.18   Day 2 ACE Routine

Foam roller (8-12 sec. each body area)	The pitcher lies on the foam roller, slowly moving his body over select muscle areas to increase recovery.
Tissue regeneration (as long as needed)	The pitcher places a baseball between specific body areas and a wall. He leans into the ball to keep it from dropping and slowly moves his body so the ball rolls over muscle areas to stimulate tissue regeneration.
Resistance band exercises	See page 172 for full descriptions of these exercises.
One-arm pitches (1 × 5-8)	The pitcher stands in front of the wall with one foot in front of the other in the release point position. He lays back his throwing arm without turning his hips, and then forcefully throws a one-pound medicine ball (or heavier) into the wall.
One-arm pitches (1 × 5-8 at 90 degrees)	The pitcher stands in front of the wall at 90 degrees away from being completely squared off to the target. He lays back his throwing arm, turns his hips toward the wall, and then forcefully throws a one-pound medicine ball (or heavier) into the wall.
Backward granny	In the outfield or another open area, the pitcher throws a medicine ball up in the air as high as he can but slightly behind him. Then he immediately turns to retrieve the ball.
One-arm pitches (1 × 5-8 at 135 degrees)	The pitcher stands in front of the wall at 135 degrees away from being completely squared off to the target. He lays back his throwing arm, turns his hips toward the wall, and then forcefully throws a one-pound medicine ball (or heavier) into the wall.
Forward granny (1 × 10)	In the outfield or another open area, the pitcher throws a medicine ball up in the air as high as he can but slightly in front of him. Then he immediately goes to retrieve the ball.
One-arm negatives (1 × 5-8)	With his back facing the wall, the pitcher stands with one foot in front of the other. He again lays his arm back, but he forcefully lets go of a one-pound medicine ball (or heavier) into the wall behind him.
Two-arm medicine ball slams	The pitcher stands in an athletic position with an 8- to 10-pound medicine ball in his hands. The pitcher forcefully throws the ball with both hands to the ground as if he is swinging a sledgehammer. He then repeats this on the other side of his body.

Tramp throws (3 × 25)	A partner holds a minitrampoline against a wall. The pitcher throws a medicine ball into the trampoline, catches it as it returns, and immediately bounces it again.
Ground tramp (2 × 10)	The pitcher bounces a medicine ball on a minitrampoline that's on the ground. He catches the ball as it returns and immediately bounces it again.
Bodyblade exercises	See page 195 for full descriptions of these exercises (note that if the pitcher doesn't have access to a Bodyblade, this part of the routine can be skipped).
Dumbbell exercises	See page 200 for full descriptions of these exercises.
Easy long-toss routine	See page 188 for a full description of the long-toss routine and eliminate the compression phase.

Some of the day 2 ACE exercises include the use of light dumbbells and a piece of equipment called the Bodyblade. These exercises specifically target the smaller muscles in the shoulder and arm (such as the rotator cuff) that help stabilize and propel the arm to throw the ball. These smaller muscles must be strengthened on a consistent basis so that the pitcher can remain injury free. The Bodyblade forces the muscles in the shoulder and arm to contract rapidly, and Bodyblade exercises also have strengthening benefits. Our pitchers really like the way this type of exercise makes their arms feel. Bodyblade work flushes and massages the arm, and the pitchers report a sense of looseness after completing these exercises. The following sections describe some Bodyblade and dumbbell exercises that are effective for pitchers.

Bodyblade Exercises

A rather new device, the Bodyblade, has become a very useful tool in the pitcher's training program. Bodyblade exercises help defend against injury, and they also strengthen and tone the arm. The Bodyblade is a very simple device to use. Pitchers seem to love using it, and it is portable, which is a must for the training of pitchers. Our pitchers say that they feel as if they are shaking the muscles in the shoulder, arm, and forearm until they loosen. The pitchers also say that they experience a massagelike feel when they have completed the exercises.

Essentially, using this piece of equipment helps to fire muscles of the arm while forcing other areas of the body to stabilize and coordinate, which leads to greater efficiency over time. This applies to the following Bodyblade exercises for pitchers. When performing exercises using the Bodyblade, pitchers should keep these points in mind:

- Each exercise should be performed to burnout. Some positions may lead to burnout in 10 to 15 seconds, and some may take 60 seconds or more.
- When doing full-range exercises, such as those that simulate the pitching motion, the pitcher should strive to make it through the range of motion three to five times while remaining balanced and in control without taking a break.

- Correct positioning ensures correct form and causes the muscles to be used more efficiently and in similar positions to throwing.
- The pitcher should keep his shoulders depressed and keep his head and chest up. He must not slouch!
- Practice makes perfect.

Shoulder Flexion Series

The shoulder flexion series includes the horizontal shoulder flexion, vertical shoulder flexion, and changeup shoulder flexion exercises.

Horizontal Shoulder Flexion

Hold the Bodyblade at chin level and shake the blade vigorously until burnout (see figure 10.19). If this becomes easy, move through an entire range of motion from hip to overhead level. This is done with the throwing arm only.

Figure 10.19
Horizontal shoulder flexion.

Vertical Shoulder Flexion

Hold the Bodyblade at chin level and with the thumb up and shake the blade vigorously until burnout (see figure 10.20). If this exercise becomes easy, perform each set for a longer duration. This is done with the throwing arm only.

Figure 10.20
Vertical shoulder flexion.

Changeup Shoulder Flexion

Hold the Bodyblade at chin level and with the thumb down and shake the blade vigorously until burnout (see figure 10.21). If this exercise becomes easy, perform each set for a longer duration. This is done with the throwing arm only.

Figure 10.21
Changeup shoulder flexion.

Shoulder Abduction Series

The shoulder abduction series includes the horizontal shoulder abduction, vertical shoulder abduction, and behind-the-back horizontal shoulder abduction exercises.

Horizontal Shoulder Abduction

Hold the Bodyblade at chin level and shake the blade vigorously until burnout (see figure 10.22). If this becomes easy, move through an entire range of motion from hip to overhead level. If this second version of the exercise becomes easy, perform each set for a longer duration. This is done with the throwing arm only.

Figure 10.22
Horizontal shoulder abduction.

Vertical Shoulder Abduction

Hold the Bodyblade at chin level and with the thumb up and shake the blade vigorously until burnout (see figure 10.23). If this exercise becomes easy, perform each set for a longer duration. This is done with the throwing arm only.

Figure 10.23
Vertical shoulder abduction.

Behind-the-Back Horizontal Shoulder Abduction

Hold the Bodyblade about 4 inches (10 cm) from your rear end (see figure 10.24). With the elbow locked, shake the blade front to back vigorously until burnout. Remember to keep the shoulders depressed and not shrugged up as you fatigue. If this exercise becomes easy, perform each set for a longer duration. This is done with the throwing arm only.

Figure 10.24
Behind-the-back horizontal shoulder abduction.

Diagonal Movement Series

In the diagonal movement series, the pitcher will pass the Bodyblade through multiple planes and zones, mimicking his pitching delivery. Once he passes through his forward pitching motion (diagonal pitching motion), he will then retrace his movement backward, all the while keeping the Bodyblade moving (reverse diagonal motion).

Diagonal Pitching Motion

Hold the Bodyblade in a reverse C position with the arm all the way back and fully extended in to the cocked position. You can begin this on one foot (as shown) or on both feet in a pitching position. Begin shaking the Bodyblade and moving through the pitching motion, finishing on the landing leg and continuing through to a half squat (see figure 10.25). Then return all the way to the beginning position without stopping. Do 3 to 5 repetitions, start to finish.

Figure 10.25
Diagonal pitching motion.

Reverse Diagonal Motion

Hold the Bodyblade in front of the body with the elbow in front of the face. Move the Bodyblade diagonally until the arm is extended with the palm facing away from the body at approximately waist level (see figure 10.26). If this exercise becomes easy, perform each set for a longer duration. This is done with the throwing arm only.

Figure 10.26 Reverse diagonal motion.

Dumbbell Exercises

Dumbbell exercises should be a staple in every pitcher's prehab or rehab routine. These exercises target and isolate the small muscles that make up the rotator cuff—muscles that cannot be targeted with traditional lifting. The only equipment needed is small, low-weight dumbbells, which can generally be purchased cheaply at almost any discount store. For people who might be on an even tighter budget, empty tennis ball cans filled with sand (and then taped) also work nicely.

Pitchers must use correct form when performing these exercises and must lift and lower the weight in a slow, controlled fashion. Going faster or not using strict form will decrease the amount that the pitcher can isolate the rotator cuff muscles, thereby lessening the effect of the exercises. These exercises can be performed after throwing and can be repeated frequently. Throughout the course of the season, our pitchers generally perform these exercises as part of the day 2 ACE routine and then one other time during the week. Here are some general guidelines for the progression of sets, reps, and weight:

1. The pitcher should begin with 1 to 3 pounds, progressing up to a 5-pound maximum (in most cases), and should start with 2 sets of 15 reps for *each* exercise.
2. If the pitcher can finish 2 sets of 15 reps—with correct form and posture—then he should move up to 3 sets, and so on, up to a maximum of 5 sets.
3. When the pitcher can finish (with correct form and posture) 5 sets of 15 reps with a certain weight, he should move up 1 pound only and go back down to 3 sets of 15 reps with that weight, again following these procedures to advance.

Standing Dumbbell Exercises

In the standing dumbbell exercises, the primary focus is to target the small muscles that make up the rotator cuff. The rotator cuff muscles must be isolated in this fashion because larger muscles—primary movers—often do the bulk of the work when a person is lifting weights or moving. These exercises take the primary movers out of the equation and target the rotator cuff muscles.

Straight-Arm Flexion

Hold the dumbbells in an overhand grip, and stand with good shoulder posture (see figure 10.27*a*). Keeping the arms straight, flex the shoulders to raise the arms up to about chin level (see figure 10.27*b*) and then lower them under control.

Figure 10.27   Straight-arm flexion.

Straight-Arm Abduction

Hold the dumbbells in an overhand grip, and stand with good shoulder posture (see figure 10.28a). Keeping the arms straight, abduct the shoulders to raise the arms (like flapping wings) until they are parallel with the ground (see figure 10.28b) and then lower them under control.

Figure 10.28   Straight-arm abduction.

Straight-Arm Scaption

Hold the dumbbells in an overhand grip, and stand with the arms extended near the hip (see figure 10.29a). With the thumbs pointing up, raise the arms in the plane of the scapula to about chin level (see figure 10.29b) and then lower them under control.

Figure 10.29   Straight-arm scaption.

Carryover Biceps Curl

Holding the dumbbells with an underhand grip near your sides, begin a biceps curl up and then return to the starting position. When you return to the starting position, turn the wrist over and perform a biceps curl with the hands in an overhand grip (see figure 10.30). Repeat the exercise in this manner for a specified number of reps.

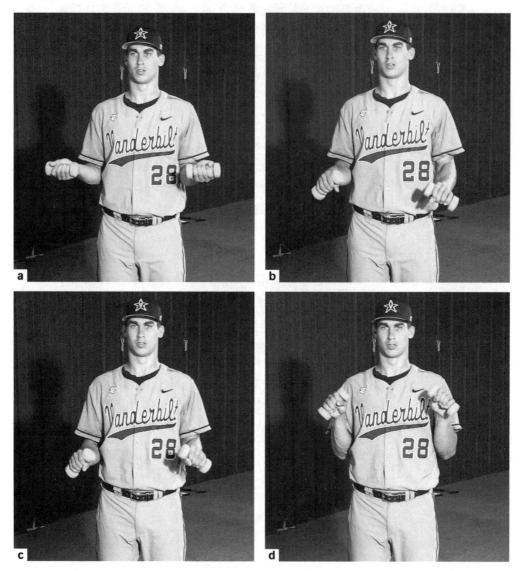

Figure 10.30 Carryover biceps curl.

Elbows-In Triceps Extension

Hold the dumbbells in a hammer grip behind the head (see figure 10.31*a*). Flex the shoulders to straighten the arms and raise the dumbbells all the way up, trying to keep the elbows close together (see figure 10.31*b*), then lower them back down.

Figure 10.31   Elbows-in triceps extension.

Lying Dumbbell Exercises

Several dumbbell exercises can be done from a lying position. The focus for the lying dumbbell exercises is the same as for the exercises done in the standing position—to isolate the rotator cuff muscles. Note that this section also includes an exercise called push-up plus, which does not involve dumbbells, along with some wrist exercises that are done using a baseball bat.

Prone Shoulder Flexion

Lie on your belly on a table or bench and hold the dumbbell in a hammer grip (see figure 10.32a). Keeping the arm straight, flex the shoulder to raise the arm to tabletop level (see figure 10.32b). Concentrate on pinching the shoulder blades together and doing the exercise slowly and under control. You can use both arms at the same time if the table is narrow enough. If not, switch arms.

Figure 10.32   Prone shoulder extension.

Prone Horizontal Abduction

Lie on your belly on a table or bench and hold the dumbbell in a hammer grip (see figure 10.33*a*). Keeping the arm straight, horizontally abduct the shoulder to raise the arm to tabletop level (like flapping wings; see figure 10.33*b*). Concentrate on pinching the shoulder blades and doing the exercise slowly and under control. You can use both arms at the same time if the table is narrow enough. If not, switch arms.

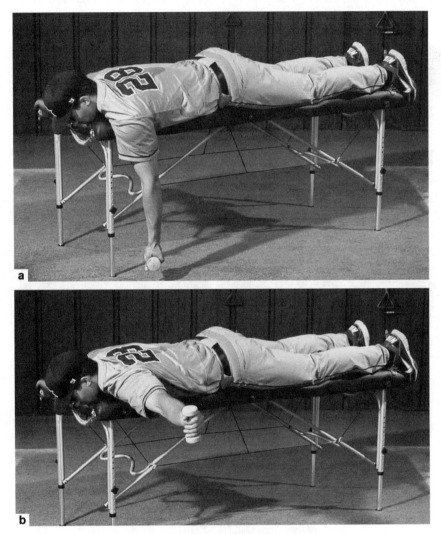

Figure 10.33   Prone horizontal abduction.

Prone Four-Step Extension

Lie on your belly on a table or bench and hold the dumbbell in a hammer grip (see figure 10.34*a*). Keeping the arm straight, extend the shoulder to raise the arm to the hip (see figure 10.34*b*). Next, in a plane parallel to the ground, abduct the shoulder so the hand moves about 12 to 24 inches (31 to 61 cm) from the hip (see figure 10.34*c*). Then, adduct the arm in the same plane (see figure 10.34*d*) and lower the weight slowly and under control (see figure 10.34*e*). You can use both arms at the same time if the table is narrow enough. If not, switch arms.

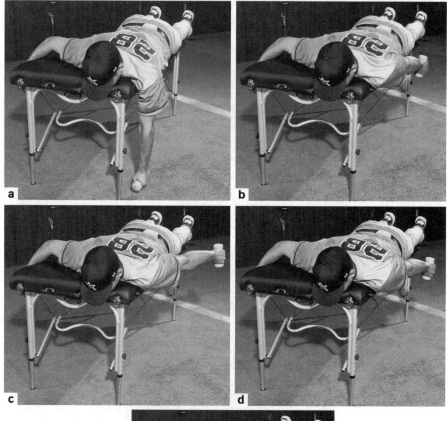

Figure 10.34
Prone four-step extension.

Prone External Rotation

Lie on your belly on a table or bench and hold the dumbbell in an overhand grip (see figure 10.35a). Perform a row movement (horizontally extend the shoulder and bend the elbow to 90 degrees; see figure 10.35b), externally rotate the shoulder (see figure 10.35c), and finally, reverse the steps. Lower the weight slowly and under control (see figure 10.35d). You can use both arms at the same time if the table is narrow enough. If not, switch arms.

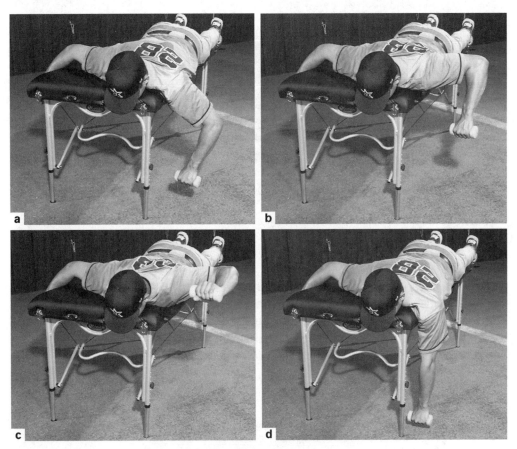

Figure 10.35 Prone external rotation.

Side-Lying External Rotation

Lie on your side, with one arm resting on a folded towel; hold the dumbbell in an overhand grip and flex the elbow to 90 degrees (see figure 10.36a). Externally rotate the shoulder to raise the dumbbell (see figure 10.36b). Do the exercise slowly and under control.

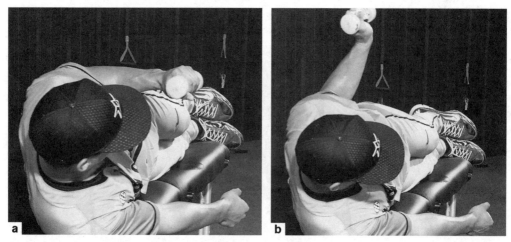

Figure 10.36   Side-lying external rotation.

Push-Up Plus

Assume a push-up position (see figure 10.37a), and using proper push-up form, perform a push-up (see figure 10.37b). At the top of the push-up, protract the shoulder fully and extend all the way up (see figure 10.37c).

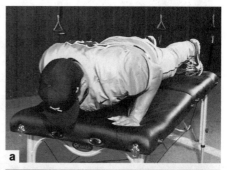

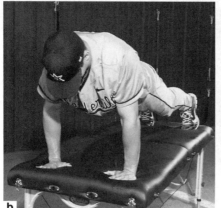

Figure 10.37
Push-up plus.

Wrist Exercises

Another area that the pitcher should attempt to strengthen is the wrist and forearm. A main goal of the ACE exercises is to strengthen and stabilize the areas of the body that are used by the pitcher. Obviously, the wrist and forearm are heavy traffic areas for a pitcher. Strengthening these areas can help protect the elbow—and ultimately the shoulder—because the weak area usually leads to compensation and can place undue stress on vital areas of the shoulder and elbow.

Wrist Deviations

With the arm resting on the table, hold a bat as near to the bottom as possible (see figure 10.38a); if the bat is too heavy to hold from the bottom, choke up accordingly. Lower the bat from vertical as far as possible (see figure 10.38b) and then bring it back to the starting position (see figure 10.38c). Next, from a standing position, hold the bat behind your body (see figure 10.38d), lower the bat as far as possible (see figure 10.38e), and bring it back up to the starting position. Switch arms and repeat.

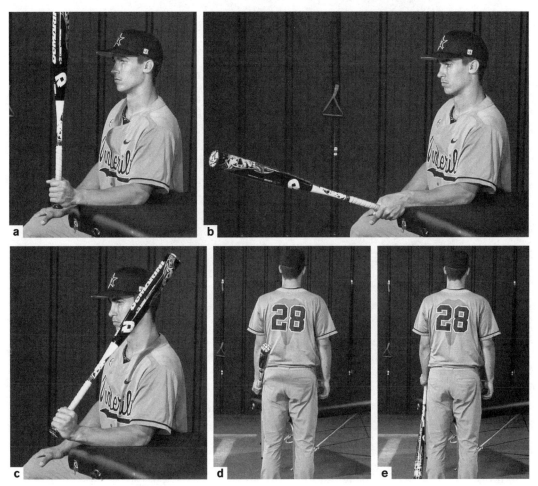

Figure 10.38 Wrist deviations.

Wrist Pronation and Supination

With the arm resting on the table, hold a bat as near to the bottom as possible; if the bat is too heavy to hold from the bottom, choke up accordingly. Rotate the bat out as far as possible (see figure 10.39*a*), then rotate it back in as far as possible (see figure 10.39*b*). Switch arms and repeat.

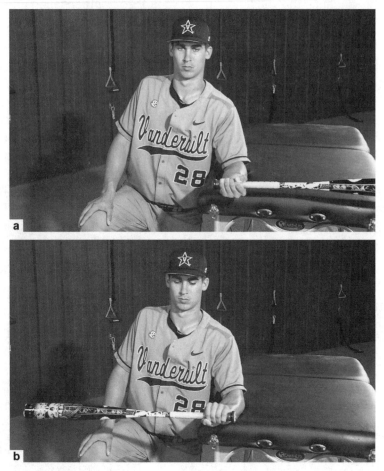

Figure 10.39   Wrist pronation and supination.

It should be fairly obvious after reading this chapter that arm strength and injury prevention are full-time jobs for the pitcher, and the training involved spans the various seasonal cycles that a pitcher will go through. Accountability from the pitcher is imperative for this type of training because it often requires time outside of the practice scope. I often tell pitchers that I refuse to hover over them and make sure they do every rep of every set of this kind of training because ultimately it is *their* arm and *their* career that they are trying to protect so it falls upon their shoulders to complete the training in perfect form and function. With this type of training, there is no magic formula for success—It simply goes back to purposeful and focused repetition, what we call *intent*.

Total-Body Conditioning for Pitchers

Weight training has been around for ages, but it was largely taboo for baseball players and especially for pitchers up until the late 1980s. People thought that weight training would make ballplayers too bulky, and that for pitchers, weight training would stiffen joints, decrease fluid motion, and increase the chance of injury. In many cases, these theories were based on factual accounts—the way that players were training did indeed make them stiff and vulnerable to injury.

The key word here is the *way* that players, specifically pitchers, train. With advances in technology and increased knowledge about weight training, pitchers are now able to use strength and conditioning protocols to increase their levels of strength, stamina, and flexibility to unparalleled heights. Essentially, baseball people got smarter in their approach to strength and conditioning, and pitchers are more athletic than ever before.

Emphasizing Athleticism Before Skill

Behind every great athlete's skill lies the engine that drives the skill. The performance characteristics that drive the athlete are based on several key variables. These variables include the following:

1. *Work capacity*—The ability to sustain work over an extended period of time.
2. *Strength*—The ability to recruit a large amount of muscle fibers to do the work requested.
3. *Power*—The ability to recruit a large amount of muscle in the shortest time possible to do work.
4. *Speed*—The ability to move in a linear fashion without wasted movement that would alter force angles.

5. *Stability*—The ability to use stabilizing musculature to support and assist larger muscles, allowing the athlete to reduce excess movement and to be more grounded and stable.

6. *Coordination*—The ability to produce dynamic symmetrical movement.

7. *Balance*—The ability to sustain postures in a variety of positions with and without movement.

8. *Prevention*—The ability to ensure that the right side of the body is equal to the left in regard to posture, movement, range of motion, and muscle function.

These eight variables are what lead to great performance of skills. Without each of these variables functioning synergistically, efficiently, and effectively, athleticism and skill will be compromised. As sport science and athletic movement are studied more, we are learning where glitches in performance originate. This provides coaches and pitchers with a new angle from which to approach training. However, this angle often gets lost in the shuffle of the parts of training that are considered more fun.

As contract figures for professional players continue to soar higher, many young athletes have chosen to focus on playing a single sport, no longer participating in multiple sports. This specificity has become more common, and it has led to a decrease in overall athleticism and finesse. Players have become much more one-dimensional. Coaches will sometimes say, "All that guy can do is pitch." In addition, some players want to focus continuously on the skill part of the game (i.e., throwing bullpens, flat grounds, dry sides, and so on) and not spend much time on the training (ability) side of the equation. As the great Alex Rodriguez once said, "Focusing on the skill side of the game prior to placing extreme focus on your training is like eating your dessert before eating your vegetables. It is the easy way out."

Today, many of the pitchers who are making their way to "The Show" lack the ability to move off the mound, play defense, and cover the bag without causing the athletic training staff to cross their fingers. Many pitchers go down with injuries on simple plays. This is a result of high forces colliding with a body that lacks stability, coordination, and balance.

QUICK PITCH

Balance—the ability to be a complete pitcher—is one of the seven foundational principles for a reason. Games are often won and lost on the pitcher's ability to execute fundamental plays in crucial spots of the game.

In theory, sport specificity seems to make sense for athletes because the more they practice something, the better they get. The problem with overplaying or only playing baseball as a young athlete is that it is somewhat detrimental to the body and athletic development because baseball is a one-sided game. This one-sidedness creates an adaptation (imbalance of strength) on one side of the body and not on the other. As a result, one side of the body is shortened while the other is lengthened, leading to altered posture, movement, and strength. This scenario is a recipe for injury. Coaches (and strength and conditioning professionals) should look for this imbalance when assessing a pitcher so that they can create an exercise prescription that will reduce the risk of injury.

The focus on athleticism does not begin with doing more agility drills, more strength training, or more medicine ball throws. It does not begin with simulating pitching in the gym. It begins with establishing a baseline and creating a program from this true beginning. Before a pitcher can begin a training program designed to increase athleticism, an assessment must be completed to identify the components of athleticism that the pitcher is missing and those that need to be enhanced.

Establishing a Baseline

As mentioned, every great training program begins with the establishment of a baseline. Establishing a baseline will allow for the development of a plan that is clear and focused on enhancement. There is no reason to focus on a pitcher's strengths when his weaknesses are the things holding him back. For a player who has tight hip flexors but loose hamstrings, the focus should be on releasing the hip flexors rather than continually stretching the hamstrings. For a player who has a strong rotator cuff but a poorly functioning scapula, the focus should not be on more isolated rotator cuff work; rather, the focus should be on assessing the movement and function of the scapula and the musculature that may be weak or tight that is inhibiting its function.

A global assessment should not be focused just on speed, strength, and power—or performance variables—but should also include a scouting report. To create a specific program focused on the athlete's needs, the coach should consult the player's pitching coach regarding the player's needs in the area of skill. Our pitching coaches often provide me with details on a pitcher's east-west delivery or a pitcher's habit of "falling" toward the plate. These are indications of an unstable landing or drive leg; at a deeper level, they may indicate a dysfunctional hip that could potentially lead to an episode of back pain.

QUICK PITCH

East-west delivery refers to a pitcher who spins and works around the plate instead of to the plate. Falling refers to a lack of lower-half usage—this pitcher basically throws with all arm. See part I of this book for tips on how to prevent these faulty movement patterns.

When completing an assessment on our pitchers, we include the following components:

- Scouting report of skill needs (developed by pitching coach)
- Postural assessment (head position, shoulder position, hip position, foot position)

- Single-leg balance assessment
- Single-leg power assessment
- Internal and external hip rotation assessment

Including all of these components makes the assessment extremely comprehensive and provides greater insight into the pitcher's current strengths and weaknesses. For tests such as the internal and external hip rotation and posture assessments, a certified athletic trainer or physical therapist can be very helpful in interpreting the results. These days, most coaches have access to trainers through their school or athletic leagues. Many coaches may also know a physical therapist through social or coaching connections. These practitioners are usually happy to engage in this type of assessment because it allows them to create relationships with players who may become future clients.

Scouting Report

The term *scouting report* is very common in baseball. Coaches often complete scouting reports on players either formally or informally. These reports include strengths, weaknesses, tendencies, comments, and concerns. They reflect the coach's viewpoint of a player. When the pitching coach is completing the scouting report on a pitcher as part of the assessment process, the coach should assess the following areas:

- Balance
- Stride
- Load
- East-west or north-south delivery
- Arm position at front-foot landing
- Position at landing
- Overall strengths and weaknesses

By dissecting and analyzing these skill variables, the coach gains greater insight that will help in the design of a training program that focuses on the pitcher's needs. Programming will begin with the areas where weakness is seen.

Postural Assessment

The key areas for the postural assessment are the head, shoulder, hip, and feet (see figure 11.1). If the head is forward, this affects the pitcher's perception and center of mass. Forward rounded shoulders affect the pitcher's ability to transfer force through the core and create efficient rotation. When the hips are tilted anteriorly or posteriorly, this affects the pitcher's ability to transfer power from the base to and through the core. When the feet are turned out, this gives the pitcher less surface area to push off of in order to create and generate force. Posture is a very important part of program design, but it is often overlooked. Many programs designed for athletes feed right into these negative postural adaptations rather than correct them.

This type of postural testing can also be done by an athletic trainer, physical therapist, or strength and conditioning professional.

Figure 11.1
Four key assessment points on the pitcher's body: head, shoulders, hips, and feet.

Single-Leg Balance Assessment

Maintaining single-leg balance plays a big role in a pitcher's ability to control the body and ultimately the ball. When the knee shifts inward or outward, this affects how the pitcher's weight is distributed through the foot and hip. When the knee shifts inward, weight shifts to the inside of the foot, which can cause the pitcher to fall or lose balance (see figure 11.2a). When the knee shifts too much toward the outside

Figure 11.2   Pitcher's knee shifting *(a)* inward and *(b)* outward, thus affecting balance.

of the foot, this can cause the pitcher to fall or lose balance the opposite way (see figure 11.2*b*). When performing this single-leg balance test, the athlete will balance on one leg while reaching the other foot out to the side for a toe touch. The goal is to move the foot as far from the center as possible while the opposing knee remains motionless over the laces of the other foot.

Single-Leg Power Assessment

The ability to create and use power in a unilateral fashion while pitching is extremely important. When it comes to pitching, the ability to squat with both legs is less important than the ability to be explosive from one leg to the other. When performing a single-leg power assessment, the pitcher's goal is to load on one leg (see figure 11.3*a*), then push or jump laterally onto the other leg; a measurement is taken of the distance (see figure 11.3*b*). Single-leg trajectory and distance covered translate to power—the greater the distance, the greater the usable power. This type of jump is also called a lateral bound.

Figure 11.3   Single-leg power assessment.

Internal and External Hip Rotation Assessment

For pitchers, deficits in hip rotation are the leading contributors to oblique strains and decreased power or force production. When these deficits exist, they often lead to injuries in the lower back. The ability of the hips to move cleanly—one hip internally rotating while the other externally rotates—allows for force transfer toward the plate. This force is maximized with clean movement. For optimal results, this assessment should be performed by an athletic trainer or physical therapist. The assessment is done by using a goniometric measuring tool to evaluate hip rotation while the pitcher is in a supine position (the pitcher is lying on his back). Any deficits that are found will be highlighted and corrected in the prescribed training program.

Systematic Approach to Training for Ability and Skill

Once we have established a baseline for an athlete, we are then ready to begin the training phase for that athlete. When it comes to training for sport, athletes and coaches must look beyond just standard weight training and muscle building. Muscle building is a part of the process and an end result of an optimal training system. However, a young athlete should not enter the training facility and immediately begin weightlifting. This approach fails to take into account the intricacies that make up the process of athletic development. In this section, I'll break down the training system we use to help our pitchers achieve dynamic, injury-free results and greater overall athleticism and pitching performance. In each workout, our athletes go through the following training blocks:

- Tissue release and lengthening
- Core development and activation
- Prehabilitation
- Movement
- Strength development
- Energy system development (ESD) or work capacity training
- Recovery

Tissue Release and Lengthening

For our pitchers, the daily training process always begins with soft-tissue work. This work may be hands-on with a manual therapist or may include self-therapy using a rolling technique with a foam roller tool, tennis balls, or lacrosse balls. With this rolling technique, the goal is to knead the muscle fibers and free them from any trigger points (i.e., areas of bunched muscle tissue that may inhibit the muscle from becoming neurally innervated and contracting maximally and optimally). Using these simple tools will make the body feel lighter and more stress free. The pitcher begins each training session with these rolling movements, immediately followed by an active stretching routine to enhance lengthening after release. An example of this technique would be to use the foam roller to release an athlete's quadriceps and then go immediately into a side-lying active stretch of the quadriceps and hip flexors for a set of 10. An example using a tennis ball would be rolling out the foot with the ball, then going immediately into an active calf or ankle stretch for a set of 10. We have found that these techniques result in significantly lower musculoskeletal stress and decreased daily pain.

QUICK PITCH

Foam rolling is great for pitchers. Our pitchers use foam rollers daily in their stretching routine and lead-ups to throwing. Foam rolling may hurt at first, but after a period of time, the pitchers can't seem to live without this activity.

Core Development and Activation

Once the pitcher has prepped his body tissue, the next step is to begin the process of chain linking, which we refer to as core development and activation. The purpose of core strengthening is to create a strong, efficient force transfer point between the lower and upper body that is free from energy leakage. The goal of core training is to link the lower and upper body so that ground reaction forces can travel upward. This is an extremely important goal for the throwing athlete because his ability to produce throwing power depends on his ability to use the ground.

We divide our core development training into two parts: stability focus and rotary focus. One important aspect of our program is that we do not include flexion exercises—better known as crunches. The only type of crunch that our pitchers will do is a reverse crunch performed on a bench; the pitcher brings his knees to his shoulders while lying on his back. We never want our pitchers to bring their shoulders to their knees in an isolated fashion because this places higher forces on the lumbar spine region. When addressing the core from the stability standpoint, our pitchers focus on many still, motionless postures that force the athlete to hold a desired position for a prescribed number of seconds or minutes. The most classic example of a core stability exercise would be a pillar bridge. To execute a pillar bridge, the athlete assumes a push-up position, but rather than resting his weight on his hands, his weight will be on his forearms. This is a timed exercise, and the athlete will hold the position for 30-, 45-, and 60-second intervals. For the rotary focus portion of training, our pitchers' off-season work (when throwing volume is low to nonexistent) involves low-level medicine ball throwing and chopping. Once throwing begins, the pitchers' focus switches to antirotation exercises, and rather than focus on chop patterns (which are being reinforced while throwing), the pitchers concentrate on lift patterns, or reverse throwing patterns. The key here is to eliminate pattern overload that can lead to breakdown. Antirotation training consists of an exercise such as kneeling opposites, as shown in figure 11.4; in this exercise, the pitcher assumes a position on all fours and then lifts one leg and the opposite arm at the same time while trying to resist rotating or falling. In a high-rotation sport such as baseball, the pitcher's body has to rotate for him to play; during the in-season period, there is no reason to continually strengthen an already strong and overused movement. At this point, the focus should shift to generating rotation from the hips. The pitcher's training should involve using various total-body pulls to create rotation (this strengthening approach will be discussed further in the upcoming section on the strength training block).

Figure 11.4   Kneeling opposites.

Activation protocols place emphasis on the glute complex as well as the posterior shoulder and scapula. Activation-focused training will begin to "turn on the light switch" in these areas that are typically very inhibited because of our modern-day habit of excessive sitting. After completing the core development training, the pitcher's goal is to prep the glutes and posterior rotator cuff and scapula by using minibands and active movements to activate these regions. By activating the glutes, the pitcher will take pressure off his hamstrings and limit their compensatory action that often leads to strains. He will also increase the recruitment of the glutes, a major contributing muscle group for lower-body power and drive when throwing. Examples of glute activation include miniband walks laterally and side-lying hip extension. An examples of posterior shoulder and scapula activation might include using a miniband to externally rotate the arms with the band wrapped around the athlete's wrist.

Prehabilitation

The prehabilitation training block is designed based on the initial baseline assessment. Prehab consists of the corrective exercises that the assessment determined are needed for the individual pitcher. This training block will also include exercises based on typical injury trends. For baseball players, especially pitchers, this segment of training should include an arm exercise program with extreme focus on the scapula rather than solely isolating the rotator cuff. It should also include hip flexor lengthening with lateral flexion to reduce the stress placed on the obliques. In baseball, the most common injuries occur in the shoulder and elbow region, as well as the obliques and hamstrings. Shoulder and elbow issues can often be traced back to a poorly functioning and moving scapula, while hamstring and oblique strains can be traced to an altered hip position caused by overactive hip flexors. Deficiencies in balance and any postural issues (as determined in the assessment) will also be addressed in this training block. For example, if an athlete's feet turn outward during his postural assessment, the prehab training could include a set of side-lying leg abduction with the foot pointed down in order to correct this imbalance. If the athlete has a static balance issue, his training could include doing barefoot reach patterns touching various cones in order to improve this deficiency. Prehab is the training block where the most athlete-specific training will take place based on the needs of the athlete. Prehab can also be considered the injury prevention block.

Movement

Movement training focuses on athletic body control, balance, and coordination. The goal of this training block is to make sure the pitcher "looks and moves" like an athlete. To develop athletically, a pitcher must move well—free of excessive motion—and must be able to control his body at all times. Movement training will focus on starting, stopping, changing direction, skipping, hopping, footwork drills, shuffles, and active and dynamic balance. It will include the implementation of balls and a focus on reaction. Movement training is often completely left out of a program, and it is sometimes incorrectly implemented as "agilities." The training of agilities is often sloppy, poorly coached or supervised, and just a lot of volume coupled with training tools such as ladders and cones. In our program, the goal of movement training is to create precise movement with no wasted motion. The pitchers work on keeping their arms close to the body at all times and maintaining good form and posture throughout the drills.

Strength Development

A catch phrase that we often use while administering our training program is "Earn your lift." We say this because strength development and lifting often take place 25 minutes into a workout, not at the beginning. Before engaging in the strength portion of our program, the athlete must make sure that his body is fully prepped and ready for the intense workout to come.

QUICK PITCH

As mentioned, we often tell our athletes to "earn their lift." The same can be said of throwing. Instead of playing catch to warm up, the pitcher should warm up *before* throwing so that he can maximize development during his time throwing the ball.

Our focus on strength development is not traditional either. The goal of strength development for pitching is to develop integrated total-body strength. With this goal, our program consists of exercises that always involve using the entire body at the same time. Rather than doing biceps, triceps, chest, shoulders, or back separately, the pitchers are performing exercises in which everything is working together all the time. In addition, the exercises usually require the pitchers to use single-leg or split stances so that they become comfortable generating strength and maintaining posture from a smaller base. This requires the pitchers to maximize forces with a very small surface area in contact with the ground.

When our athletes work on strength, the process is constantly evolving, taking the athletes through phases of stability, strength, and power. We use a triad hierarchy of strength development based on the idea that without stability, the athlete can't achieve strength or power—and without strength and stability, the athlete can't achieve power. Stability is the most important part of our strengthening program. When working to achieve stability, the pitchers use all single-leg movements and postures. The use of moderate weight, high reps (15 to 20), and extremely slow movements is also required in this phase.

Once the pitcher's body is stable, gaining strength becomes easy. Because the pitcher has eliminated any extra motion, he has a solid platform on which to build strength. In the strength phase, the pitcher uses heavier weight, moderate rep ranges (4 to 8), and moderate speeds. The goal here is to recruit muscle fiber—as much as possible to sustain work. As the pitcher moves into the power phase, he then lifts moderate weight, uses rep ranges of 5 to 10, and lifts as fast as possible. In a power phase, the goal is to recruit as much muscle as fast as possible. Working through these phases allows for great adaptation. This process is based on the age-old principles of *progressive overload*. Each time the athlete trains, the variables of weight, sets, or reps should be adjusted to stimulate growth. This is progressive overload.

In addition to the use of single-leg or split stances and total-body movements, a key component of our strength development training is getting the hips to move and create power, especially rotary power. In the strength phase, there is a tremendous emphasis on loading the glutes and then unloading them into upper-body rotation. We want to teach all our athletes to throw from their hips, not just their arms. The loading and unloading of the glutes in an efficient and effective manner will contribute to increased force generation and power. Most important, though, it will help reduce injuries due to compensatory force production. The goal is to not have secondary muscles performing a primary function.

Energy System Development or Work Capacity Training

Also known as conditioning, the energy system development (or work capacity) block is designed to help the body sustain work over a prescribed period of time. The development of work capacity will decrease the stress placed on the body, assist in the reduction of fatigue, and allow for maximum performance over a longer duration. Work capacity training can have several focus points: aerobic, anaerobic, or a combination of both. For a sport such as baseball, developing aerobic fitness is something done during the off-season. This is often called base building. Developing aerobic fitness allows for a base of training. When aerobic fitness is achieved, it takes longer for fatigue to set in, and the body's ability to buffer the by-products of work, such as lactic acid, is enhanced. An athlete's ability to build higher levels of anaerobic fitness is also enhanced when he has already built an aerobic base. The triad of energy system development is built as follows:

aerobic → anaerobic → combination

This illustrates that the athlete must build an aerobic base before he can build anaerobic and combination energy systems. After building the base, he can build the upper tiers of the triad. Aerobic training is typically of longer duration (15 minutes or longer) at lower intensities (heart rates of 60 percent or less). Anaerobic training is much more explosive; the sets last 1 minute or less, are performed at higher intensities (at least 75 percent), and require much more rest to recharge reserves in between.

Combination training is a medley of anaerobic intervals done over a specific time or distance with specific work-to-rest ratios of 1:2, 1:3, 1:4, 1:5, and 1:6. These ratios specify how much work will be done compared to the amount of rest. For example, a 1:2 ratio could refer to a 15-second burst sprint followed by 30 seconds of rest. A 1:4 could be a 15-second burst sprint followed by 1 minute of rest. Pitching requires durational work along with the ability to be explosive throughout that duration. In our training program, we try to ensure that pitchers are developing that ability while being very specific regarding when they perform high-volume or high-intensity days. For most starters, the heaviest work day will be the day after their starts. For relievers, it will be a day that they are "down" or not pitching. During the in-season period, our pitchers drop aerobic work except on recovery days, and most of their training consists of anaerobic and combination days. In our training program, we continually manipulate the ratios, intensities, and durations to keep the pitcher's body in a constantly adapting state. During the season, workouts are typically cycled between low-, moderate-, and high-intensity days. These days are broken down as follows:

- *Low intensity:* Aerobic based, 15 minutes or more, recovery day option
- *Moderate intensity:* Combination day, interval based, shuttle focus, low recovery times
- *High intensity:* Anaerobic day, sprint and explosion focused, full recovery between sets

Recovery

Each training session concludes with a recovery protocol. The objective of recovery is to start the healing process. This process focuses on soft-tissue techniques similar to the tissue release and lengthening phase at the beginning of training. It can also include a postworkout massage, hot or cold water therapies, individual or team swim, rope or partner stretching, yoga, meditation, or relaxation breathing. These techniques are all used to relax the body and stimulate a hormonal release that prepares the body for the repair process as well as for its next workout. During the baseball season, recovery is just as important as training, especially for a pitcher, because of the repetitive stress that comes with the game. Every fourth or fifth week during the season, all players perform a full week of recovery protocols and low-intensity conditioning to promote recovery. These players always come back from the week feeling fresh and revitalized. At first, players are often hesitant to do this because they think they are losing something, but once they participate, they realize that their body needed it.

When planning a training program, pitchers and coaches need to understand the steps and how each step builds from the previous one. The training program described here is extremely progressive and sequenced to allow the body to maximize its athletic development. Remember, athletes who only work one spoke on the wheel of training are going to come up short in the end. Those who only focus on their strengths are also going to come up short. For their athletic training, pitchers must implement an integrated training approach that works side by side with the skill aspects of the game. If they want to play, they must train.

In-Season Throwing Routines

For a pitcher, a primary goal during the season is to stay sharp for his outings and to maintain what he added to his arsenal in the off-season. Many pitchers are afraid that if they come out of the gates too quickly, they may jeopardize their stamina and effectiveness at the end of the season when their performance counts the most. The pitcher fears running out of gas, or worse, injuring himself. On the other hand, if he doesn't throw and train hard enough or often enough, the pitcher becomes ineffective and therefore doesn't help the team as much as he can. Indeed, there is a delicate mix of variables that a pitcher must contend with in order to perform optimally.

At the start of every season, I ask my pitchers these questions: Why does the development of a pitcher have to stop once the season begins? What law is a pitcher breaking by continuing to add bullets to his arsenal through hard work? Who says that pitchers can't continue throwing hard (perhaps even gaining velocity throughout the season), running hard, and lifting hard as long as they manage it intelligently and intuitively so that it fits their individual needs? After hearing my spiel, most pitchers shrug their shoulders and say, "I have no idea, but I sure would like to improve each season." Well, nothing is requiring pitchers to stop working hard to develop during the season except that old familiar excuse in baseball: "It has always been done this way."

QUICK PITCH

My good friend Mark Calvi told his 2010 South Carolina Gamecock pitching staff that they needed to "prepare for the end." I thought this was a brilliant way to look at and train for the rigors of the season. Essentially, Coach Calvi was telling his pitchers that the work they put in during the off-season was only as good as how they approached their in-season work. This strategy paid off for the Gamecocks—they were NCAA champions in 2010 and 2011.

So far this book has covered numerous areas of pitching. Many of these subjects follow conventional baseball views, but others are more outside-the-box type of thinking that may go against traditional views. The following suggestions for in-season training have more of an outside-the-box type of feel to them with a dash of traditional methodology sprinkled in. The information in this chapter has been split into two categories: starters and relievers. A typical throwing week is described for the two types of pitchers, as well as the type of throwing that each might pursue. Individual differences and needs should be addressed, and the pitcher and coach should be aware that alterations are typically needed throughout the season. Coaches should let past experience and intuition be the guiding forces behind implementing any alterations.

Starters

The starter's in-season routine needs to satisfy two main purposes. The first purpose is that the routine must genuinely prepare the pitcher for his next start. Preparation breeds confidence, so whatever the pitcher chooses to do in between starts must give him a sense of security. The second purpose of the routine is that it must help the pitcher continue to develop the skills that he needs to improve on. This is how the pitcher continues his evolution, and he should always be looking for ways to improve both skill and ability. These two underlying goals coupled with the games themselves help form the in-season cycle that orchestrates the pitcher's development. The traditional view of pitcher training is to "grease the grooves," get a feel, and then maintain. My view is much like Coach Calvi's in that I believe the pitcher must continue to work diligently on building, honing, and perfecting his craft. That is where true development lies. Figure 12.1 shows the phases that a pitcher should pass through during the season. These phases are designed to help the pitcher develop a structured routine throughout the course of the season and build purpose into the various training regimens that he will cycle through. After competing, the pitcher will evaluate thoroughly what went well and what went wrong, coming up with a basic plan that identifies the things he must work on before his next start. After evaluating, the pitcher then passes into the repair phase; in this phase, he focuses on readying his arm and body for his next outing. This phase is short but extremely important, and it deals primarily with the ability portion (athleticism) of pitcher training. The third phase is the preparation phase in which the pitcher works on the skill elements of his game. This includes bullpen sessions for command and feel as well as mechanical adjustments or pitch development if needed.

The starter's practice week and bullpen routines are designed to help satisfy the pitcher's needs on many fronts. The ultimate goal is to prepare the pitcher for his next start, but many other elements and individual needs enter into the cycle. The following are a few ideas that can help in defining what might work best for a pitcher.

Starter's Practice Workweek

Baseball is played at numerous levels, and each level will vary in the number of games played, the length of the season, the innings played per game, and the limitations

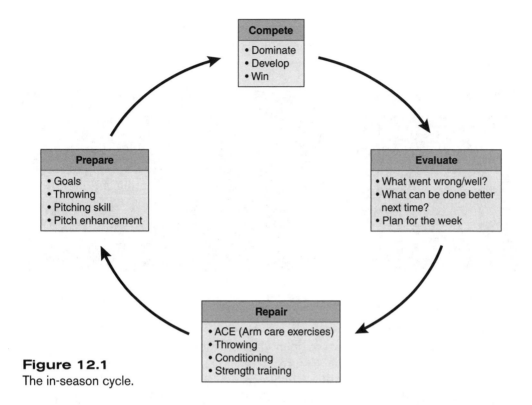

Figure 12.1
The in-season cycle.

that are sanctioned by the league. Therefore, it would be impossible to provide a plan for the pitcher's week that would apply to each level. Instead, as an example, we'll use a college season and the preparation of the collegiate pitcher. Adjustments can then be tailored to fit the needs of each age group. In the college game, a team generally has three pitchers who are designated as starters for games played on the weekend. These pitchers will usually throw competitively one time per week and will have the remaining days to recover and prepare for the next outing. One or two other pitchers may be designated as weekday starters; their function would be to start a game during the midweek and then perhaps pitch in relief on the weekends. These pitchers would obviously have a shorter time to fully recover, so their training needs will be different than those of the weekend starter. As mentioned earlier, the goal of each pitcher is to find what prepares him best for the next start, so individual needs will vary. Some pitchers will feel prepared with one bullpen session in between starts, while others may feel the need for two bullpen sessions. Either option is fine; the important thing is organizing the schedule to best suit the pitcher.

Before throwing a bullpen, whether on game day or a practice day, the pitcher should first prepare his arm to throw by using a general warm-up, resistance tubing exercises, pitcher stretches, and throwing routines as explained in chapter 10. As mentioned earlier, routines are like "home," and they help ensure that the pitcher is ready to pitch, both physically and mentally.

Following are three options for pitchers to choose from when designing their work schedule in between starts. Remember that each pitcher is unique in what works best for him in between starts. Aspects such as how the pitcher's arm responds to mound throwing and what scenario makes the pitcher's arm feel best on game day are considerations that must be addressed.

QUICK PITCH

To maximize the effect of his throwing, the pitcher should warm up to throw, not throw to warm up. This is a distinction that cannot be emphasized enough. Too often, a pitcher goes out to throw without any prior warm-up or preparation before starting to throw. This does not maximize his development because he is working on cold muscles. Injury can result from this, much as it can in strength training, and it cuts down on ROTT (return on training time)—the pitcher will spend a greater amount of time getting ready to maximize his throws as opposed to *being ready* to maximize his throws.

One Bullpen Between Starts

Depending on the number of days the pitcher has between starts will factor in on what day he decides to throw his bullpen. The one bullpen per week is probably the most common bullpen schedule. Figure 12.2 is an example of a workweek schedule for a pitcher who throws one bullpen in between his starts. Notice that the schedule includes some type of throwing almost daily; the volume and intensity of the throwing will increase as the pitcher nears his time for a bullpen and his next start. This example also provides flexibility so that individual needs can be met.

Figure 12.2 Sample Week With One Bullpen Between Starts

Friday	Competition—start
	Postgame—resistance tubing exercises (same as tubing exercises done before the game)
Saturday	Evaluation—write out what went well and what went wrong; plan for this week or the next start
	30-minute distance run at easy to moderate intensity
	Day 1 ACE routine
	Light throwing per tolerance of individual (e.g., some pitchers may throw to 90 feet while others stay around 60 feet)
Sunday	Full-body lift
	Day 2 ACE routine
	Easy long-toss routine—air under ball; throw as far as tolerated (no compression phase)
	Long sprint—pole to pole for time
Monday	Long-toss routine
	Skill work—drills; mechanical points of emphasis; pitch development
	Medium sprint—60 yards with rest (up to 15)

Wednesday	*Bullpen Session*—throw 30-45 pitches Burst sprint—15 yards or less at maximum intensity with rest (up to 15)
Thursday	Light day—perform drills or emphasize a skill element
Friday	Competition—start

Two Bullpens Between Starts

A weekly schedule that includes two bullpen sessions between starts is designed for the pitcher who lacks feel for a certain pitch, needs mechanical adjustments, or simply likes to break up his throwing into more than one bullpen per week. This type of workweek was made popular by Leo Mazzone, longtime pitching coach of the Atlanta Braves, who believed that throwing more in between starts helped his pitchers stay sharper. It would be difficult to argue that Mazzone was wrong; his Braves staff produced three of the most dominant pitchers of the 1990s (Greg Maddux, John Smoltz, and Tom Glavine) and was routinely at the top of the National League in most pitching categories. Figure 12.3 is an example of a workweek schedule for a pitcher who throws two bullpens in between his starts.

Figure 12.3   Sample Week With Two Bullpens Between Starts

Friday	Competition—start Postgame—resistance tubing exercises (same as tubing exercises done before the game)
Saturday	Evaluation—write out what went well and what went wrong; plan for this week or the next start 30-minute distance run at easy to moderate intensity Day 1 ACE routine Light throwing per tolerance of individual (e.g., some pitchers may throw to 90 feet while others stay around 60 feet)
Sunday	Full-body lift Day 2 ACE routine Easy long-toss routine—air under ball; throw as far as tolerated (no compression phase) Long sprint—pole to pole for time
Monday	Long-toss routine *Short bullpen session*—throw for skill development (15-25 pitches) Medium sprint—60 yards with rest (up to 15)
Wednesday	*Short bullpen session*—throw for skill development (15-25 pitches) Burst sprint—15 yards or less at maximum intensity with rest (up to 15)
Thursday	Light day—perform drills or emphasize a skill element
Friday	Competition—start

One Start and One Relief Appearance

Most major-league teams have a defined starting rotation and middle- and short-relief corps that do not drastically change during the season. This is not necessarily the case in college or high school baseball; at those levels, extenuating circumstances such as frequent makeup games and shortages of pitching are the rule rather than the exception, and two-way players are quite common. In these circumstances, a pitcher's weekly schedule may involve making one start and one relief appearance. Instead of a bullpen in the middle of the week, the pitcher would get a "tune-up" inning by pitching in relief a few days before his scheduled start. This routine isn't the best option compared to the others, but it is useful in certain situations. One example might be when a pitcher's previous start was short and rocky. In this case, his arm should be considerably fresher, assuming his pitch count wasn't too high, but his confidence will most likely be lower. Throwing this pitcher back into the fire can help him regain confidence and feel; therefore, a midweek inning could very

Figure 12.4 Sample Week With One Start and One Relief Appearance

Friday	Competition—start Postgame—resistance tubing exercises (same as tubing exercises done before the game)
Saturday	Evaluation—write out what went well and what went wrong; plan for this week or the next start 30-minute distance run at easy to moderate intensity Day 1 ACE routine Light throwing per tolerance of individual (e.g., some pitchers may throw to 90 feet while others stay around 60 feet)
Sunday	Full-body lift Day 2 ACE routine Easy long-toss routine—air under ball; throw as far as tolerated (no compression phase) Long sprint—pole to pole for time
Monday	Long-toss routine Skill work—drills; mechanical points of emphasis; pitch development
Tuesday	Relief appearance in game Resistance tubing exercises
Wednesday	Dumbbell or Bodyblade exercises Light throwing per tolerance of individual (e.g., some pitchers may throw to 90 feet while others stay around 60 feet) Long sprint—pole to pole for time Full-body lift
Thursday	Light day—emphasize a skill element
Friday	Competition—start (or the start may be pushed back to Saturday or Sunday depending on the number of pitches thrown and whether extra rest is needed)

well get the pitcher back on track for his next full outing. Figure 12.4 is an example of a workweek schedule for a pitcher who makes one start and one relief appearance.

Starter's Bullpen Routines

I receive many calls and e-mails regarding the best ways to approach pregame bullpen routines, and generally the questions are the same: How many pitches should I throw and how should I mix my pitches together? My answer is also always the same. First, the pitcher should throw pitches that he really throws well and should throw them to the places (locations) where he will be throwing to in the game. Second, the pitcher should mix his pitches together in a sequence that he might normally use in the game. Next, he should throw the pitches that he "rents" and throw to locations that might not be his strong suit. And lastly, he should finish by mixing all pitches together, either through simple mixing or through a more gamelike situation with the catcher calling strike or ball after each pitch. In chapter 7, we discussed implementing a plan for the pitcher's attack based on the strengths and weaknesses of his pitches and locations. This plan should be used as a template to create an individual bullpen routine for the pitcher.

Let's assume that the pitcher has gone through all of his routine preparatory work and is ready to begin the bullpen. The first step in any bullpen, no matter what time of year the pen is thrown, should be to define the purpose behind the bullpen. What does the pitcher want to get out of this pen? The purpose can be vague or specific, but the pitcher must have some sort of intent or goal in mind before starting. At our baseball field, I often designate certain bullpen areas for certain aspects of training during throwing sessions. The visitor's pen is used for pitchers to work on mechanical issues, grip changes, and other technical aspects. The pen on the home side of the field is used to work on precision, target awareness, and throwing strikes. This defines the lines for the pitcher and the coach, and it further emphasizes what needs to be done during the performance.

QUICK PITCH

Each bullpen session should be designated as a "training bullpen" or a "trusting bullpen." This establishes what the pitcher's mind should be focusing on. In the training mode, the pitcher can think, make adjustments, and change movements. In the trusting mode, he should be target aware and should replicate his game focus. When the bullpens are designated as training or trusting, the pitcher is liberated from trying to do two things at once, and the coach knows when to intervene and when to stay out of the way.

Normal Non-Game-Day Bullpen

The non-game-day bullpen is a bullpen designed to ready the pitcher for his next start. It will include the various pitches he throws and he will throw in different sequences to calibrate timing of the pitches and a feel for the release point of the various pitches. This is what we consider his "preparation for the game" bullpen; the bullpen where he "greases" the grooves, feeling his pitches and delivery. Figure 12.5 is an example of a workweek schedule for a non-game-day bullpen session.

Figure 12.5   Sample Non-Game-Day Bullpen Session

Catch play	Resistance tubing and stretching exercises should be done before this throwing routine.
"Down the hills"	Pitcher steps and throws while on the mound. This helps him understand the angle of the mound and learn the terrain of the mound; he should finish like a pitcher and strive to throw strikes.
Throwing: 40-45 pitches	Stretch–3 fastballs; middle and down Windup–3 fastballs; middle and down Stretch–3 fastballs glove side (for right-handed pitcher, glove side would mean away from right-handed hitter or in to left-handed hitter) Windup–3 fastballs arm side (for right-handed pitcher, arm side would mean in to right-handed hitter or away from left-handed hitter) Stretch or flex step–alternate fastballs glove side with changeups arm side (6 total) Windup–6 changeups; middle and down or down and arm side (can go to glove side if skilled) Stretch or flex step–alternate fastballs glove side with breaking balls glove side (6 total) Windup–3 breaking balls; middle and down or glove side and down Short break (at this point, the pitcher has thrown 30 pitches) Stretch–runner on first; sequence of fastballs and changeups (4 total) Windup–sequence of fastballs and breaking balls (4 total) Stretch–1-2 hitters where catcher calls pitches (stand-in hitters are welcome here)

Pitch-Specific Bullpen

The pitch-specific bullpen means exactly what its name suggests; the pitcher chooses one pitch, usually one that needs attention, and simply works on it until he feels more comfortable or can further master the pitch. This bullpen works quite well for "feel" pitches such as the changeup or the curveball, but it is also a good way to work on fastball location. Because time is usually short and a pitcher needs to work on as many aspects of his game as possible, the pitcher will normally use this bullpen only occasionally. During this bullpen, the pitcher should throw one fastball for every two or three of the pitch he is working on because every pitch is rooted in the fastball. Figure 12.6 is an example of a workweek schedule for a pitch-specific bullpen.

Bullpen for Working on the Stretch With Runners

A primary goal for every pitcher should be to develop the ability to pitch as well out of the stretch as he pitches out of the windup. Very rarely does a perfect game

Figure 12.6   Sample Pitch-Specific Bullpen (Breaking Ball)

Stretch	3 fastballs; middle and down
Windup	3 fastballs; middle and down
Stretch	3 breaking balls at 45 feet; work on spin—these do not count in overall counted pitches
Windup	3 breaking balls at 45 feet; work on spin—these do not count in overall counted pitches
Stretch	Alternate fastball and breaking ball (16 total); short break at 8 pitches
Windup	2 breaking balls and 1 fastball for 5 sets; 10 breaking balls and 5 fastballs for 15 pitches
Stretch	2-4 breaking balls (throw fastball if needed)
Windup	2-4 breaking balls (throw fastball if needed)
	Total: 40-42 pitches

occur, so the pitcher needs to be prepared to pitch effectively out of the stretch. This takes practice because many pitchers become distracted with runners on base. In this bullpen, the pitcher uses any of the previously-described bullpens, but performs them out of the stretch. The pitcher adds looks to first or second, varies the cadence, mimics throwing with runners on, etc. The pitcher goes through the steps of checking the runner, varying head looks, varying timing, and then delivering the pitch. This bullpen can be particularly effective for the younger pitcher who seems to get spooked when runners are on base. If nothing else, the pitcher becomes comfortable with moving his head back and forth, varying his timing, and most important, picking up his target when he decides to deliver to the plate. This type of bullpen also serves as the perfect vehicle for working on the slide step or flex step move to quicken the pitcher's motion to the plate.

Game-Day Bullpen

Every pitcher must remember to use his game-day bullpen wisely so that he is ready to pitch. In addition, the pitcher must learn to either take the bullpen out to the game with him (good bullpen) or leave it behind (poor bullpen). This is a mental consideration more than physical, but it will keep the bullpen in perspective and keep the pitcher in the proper frame of mind. Many great games have been pitched on the heels of a poor performance in the bullpen. I remember hearing a story about Nolan Ryan and how he quit his bullpen halfway through his routine because nothing seemed to click. That day he went out and pitched his fifth career no-hitter! Obviously, he left the bad bullpen behind when he took the mound. Nothing stops the true competitor from giving it his very best.

The game-day bullpen should be very specific to the needs of the individual pitcher. He should practice what he does well first, mix pitches effectively to gain a feel of the release point for each pitch, and then practice things that need work. The pitcher should start by throwing the fastball down the middle and then follow up with pitches to locations that he will use in the game. Once the pitcher establishes control with the fastball in those areas, he should work on other fastball locations; he needs to get the feel of "showing" those pitches so he can use them in the game (see The Pitching Plan in chapter 7). Next, the pitcher should work on secondary pitches such as the breaking ball or changeup both separately and in tandem with the fastball. The entire routine should stay between 35 and 45 pitches, enough to "grease the grooves" and prepare the pitcher. Figure 12.7 is an example schedule for a game-day bullpen session.

Figure 12.7 Sample Game-Day Bullpen

Stretch	3 fastballs; middle of plate
Windup	3 fastballs; middle of plate
Stretch or flex step (choose one)	2 fastballs to glove side of plate and 2 fastballs to arm side of plate
Windup	Alternate fastballs to arm side with breaking balls to glove side of plate for 6 pitches
Stretch or flex step (choose one)	5 breaking balls (Can practice 0-2 count breaking balls during this segment)
Stretch or flex step (choose one)	5 changeups to various parts of the plate; practice various lengths of holds at first base and looks at second base
Windup	Mix fastballs, breaking balls, and changeups together for a total of 8 pitches, or "work hitters" by having the catcher call the pitches; pitcher attempts to throw strikes and uses the count accordingly
	Total: 40 pitches

QUICK PITCH

Every pitcher has staples of his delivery. These are the movements or positions in space that keep him connected, and when they are absent, this can create havoc. Pitchers should work on their staples every day. This can be in the form of a drill, work during catch play, or the first few pitches in a bullpen. Working on these movements and positions will help the pitcher "line everything up" so that he is consistent in his delivery and with his pitches.

Finally, note that there is no universal answer regarding the amount of rest that a starting pitcher needs. Rest is largely individual and should be considered in conjunction with the way the pitcher trains. If the pitcher has trained his arm to handle the stress that game pitches place on it, the pitcher will most likely bounce back quicker, and the arm will be ready sooner. With that in mind, the coach is responsible for ensuring that his pitchers get adequate rest, even though it may sometimes be tempting to throw a pitcher on shorter rest for a big game.

Working on Skills and Drills

Over the years, I have developed a series of drills that the pitcher will work through during the week as preparation for his next start, as well as a series of drills that can be broken into pieces to work on specific problem areas. This is the pitcher's toolbox; he can further evolve through the drills, or he can use the tools to fix a faulty area. Drills are much like movies—some are very good, and some not so good. Some of the best drills that I've seen or created were formed out of need and on the fly when a pitcher had a problem that could not be addressed by something already in use. Coaches and pitchers should test their creative faculties when it comes to implementing drills. Drills should be as specific as possible and should use speed changes (slower and faster) to ingrain and enhance the movement.

One specific technique that seems to have great transfer (i.e., it shortens the learning loop and is specific to the problem) is a technique called backward chaining. The idea behind backward chaining is to start working just past the point of the problem area, work backward through the trouble spot, isolate and solidify the movement, and then finish the remainder of the skill. So, if the problem area is the release point, the drill would start just after the release point, isolating and solidifying what a pitcher is trying to feel in the release point portion of the delivery. Drills like this have been the most beneficial addition to our training program in the last several years.

Another training tool that has proven to be very beneficial is called chunking, as described by Daniel Coyle in his book *The Talent Code.* For our purposes, chunking is taking several skills or drills and chunking them together in a circuit-type setting so that they will transfer faster to the actual skill of pitching. Instead of the traditional method of keeping skills separate from the activity—that is, working on a drill outside of pitching—the skill or drill is implemented as part of the bullpen or scrimmage session.

Although there isn't an ideal model in baseball for rest periods between games (or anything else for that matter), a coach still needs to have guidelines. I've set the following guidelines for our starters:

- If a pitcher throws 50 to 75 pitches in an outing, he must take two days of rest (with adequate amounts of arm care applied)
- If a pitcher throws 75 to 100 pitches, he must take at least three days of rest
- If a pitcher throws 100 or more pitches, he must take at least four days of rest.

This formula can be applied to early-season or "spring training" protocols as well, when the pitcher is building his throwing and pitching foundation for the year. If a pitcher throws 60 pitches in a scrimmage, he would rest for at least two days before throwing in another scrimmage. At that time, because he is building for the season, he would be allowed to add 15 more pitches to his total (now he will throw 75 pitches) and so on, following similar guidelines as the spring progresses. For our starters, the goal going into the first spring game is to have thrown 100 pitches in a day at least two times. If this has occurred, the starting pitchers should be prepared to throw 80 to 85 game pitches in their first outing of the spring.

Relievers

The reliever's role is to shut down the opponent's offense for a short duration. For the closer, this might mean one inning, while a middle reliever may work two or three innings. Relievers must pitch on shorter rest; they have very little time to make the adjustments that a starter often has the luxury of making. A reliever often has to adjust when the game is on the line. He lives and dies by the sword, and he must keep the game and his performance in proper perspective. The role of the reliever is vital to a team's success!

Reliever's Practice Workweek

Because of the nature of the reliever's job, the preparation and routines that he prescribes to must be extremely flexible. The reliever must be able to bounce back quickly; therefore, his ACE routines and throwing in between mound appearances must be short yet purposeful. His routines should be geared toward getting ready—truly ready—as quickly as possible. *Truly ready* means that not only is he physically ready for action, but mentally as well. After the game, win or lose, the reliever must have a short memory. He must be able to forget any poor performance and temper the joy of a triumphant one; he must be ready for tomorrow. Figure 12.8 is a sample workweek schedule for a relief pitcher.

Reliever's Bullpen Routines

During the season, the reliever may not have a great deal of time to spend on bullpen work. This is often because of the recovery periods that a reliever might need (depending on the number of appearances and pitches thrown previously). Another reason is that he faces the possibility of pitching multiple times in a short period. Whatever the case, the reliever must spend his bullpen time wisely and with purpose, but he must also use this time to better himself for the "big picture."

Feel Good Bullpen

The feel good bullpen is designed to help a reliever stay sharp by quickly practicing key pitches in key areas. At the same time, this bullpen keeps the reliever ready for action by not causing him to throw too much in the bullpen. As the name implies, this bullpen is designed to make the pitcher "feel good"—that is, feel confident and ready. A pitcher can use this pen the same day that he is "on call" to pitch; in this case, he would do it before the game starts. This bullpen can also be used after the game is over if the reliever didn't get a chance to pitch but still needs work. Either

Figure 12.8   Sample Reliever Week

Friday	Competition–pitch two innings (36 pitches) Postgame–resistance tubing exercises (same as tubing exercises done before the game)
Saturday	Evaluation–write out what went well and what went wrong; plan for this week or the next relief appearance Dumbbell or Bodyblade exercises Light throwing per tolerance of individual (e.g., some pitchers may throw to 90 feet while others stay around 60 feet)
Sunday	Competition–pitch two innings (45 pitches) Postgame–resistance tubing exercises (same as tubing exercises done before the game) Full-body lift
Monday	Evaluation–write out what went well and what went wrong; plan for this week or the next relief appearance 30-minute distance run at easy to moderate intensity Day 1 ACE routine Light throwing per tolerance of individual (e.g., some pitchers may throw to 90 feet while others stay around 60 feet)
Tuesday	Day 2 ACE routine Full-body lift Easy long-toss routine–air under ball; throw as far as tolerated (no compression phase) Skill work–drills; mechanical points of emphasis; pitch development
Wednesday	*If pitcher pitched in previous game:* Dumbbell or Bodyblade exercises Evaluation–write out what went well and what went wrong; plan for this week or the next relief appearance *If pitcher did not pitch in previous game:* Perform flat-ground or feel good bullpen session; could also perform a short-box bullpen where the catcher moves up to 45 ft, instead of 60 ft 6 in, to preserve the pitcher's arm. Full-body lift
Thursday	Light day–emphasize a skill element
Friday	Start cycle over

situation works fine because this pen is always predicated on need. The bullpen is usually organized as a block pen, meaning that each pitch is worked on separately (as a separate block). But a feel good bullpen could easily be executed by focusing on pitch sequences or by working on only one pitch as long as it addresses the needs of the pitcher. This type of bullpen should be limited to between 15 and 25 pitches if possible. The pitcher should be working on strengths and weaknesses, feel of each pitch, location, and mechanical points in unison. Good focus and gamelike concentration should be at a premium during this bullpen; velocity is not important. Figure 12.9 is a sample of a 7-7-7 feel good bullpen that can be done during practice, before a game, or after a game.

Figure 12.9 Sample 7-7-7 Feel Good Bullpen for Relievers

7 fastballs	Throw fastballs at various locations out of the windup, stretch, and flex step.
7 changeups	Throw changeups at various locations out of the windup, stretch, and flex step.
7 breaking balls	Throw breaking balls at various locations out of the windup, stretch, and flex step.
	Total: 21 throws

Flat-Ground Bullpen

It has been well established in baseball circles that flat-ground throwing will reduce the stress placed on the arm as opposed to throwing off of a mound; therefore, flat-ground throwing is another useful tool that a reliever can use to hone his skill. Our relievers usually perform this bullpen right after they play catch before the game. This helps give them a sense of security if their name is called shortly after the game begins. A flat-ground bullpen can closely mimic a normal bullpen as far as pitches, locations, and feel. The only difference is that the pitcher is performing flat versus sloped throwing. Again, this is a simple yet highly effective way of preparing the reliever for the game without wear and tear on the arm. Figure 12.10 is a sample flat-ground bullpen that can be done before a game.

Figure 12.10 Sample Flat-Ground Bullpen for Relievers

Stretch at 45 feet	Working on a downhill angle, the pitcher wants to emphasize gaining leverage with the delivery, finding his release point out front, and throwing balls low to his target (7-10 throws).
Stretch at 60 feet	Working on a downhill angle, the pitcher follows the same points of emphasis as at 45 feet; different fastball locations can be employed (7-10 throws).
Windup at 60 feet	The pitcher emphasizes rhythm of the delivery; he can either mix fastball and changeup or isolate changeup work (7-10 throws).
Stretch or flex step at 60 feet	The pitcher can either mix fastball and breaking ball or isolate breaking ball work (7-10 throws).
	Total: 28-40 throws

Game-Day Bullpen

For a reliever, feel good bullpens will be the starting point for each game-day bullpen. If player or coach thinks that something should be added because of an extended layoff, a mechanical problem, or a location or feel problem with a certain pitch, then the feel good bullpen could be expanded to include something more specific to address the need. Because this bullpen is a bit more nontraditional, a sample will not be provided here—coaches need to individualize the game-day bullpen based on what they value in their pitchers. I instruct our pitchers to establish their best pitch at their favorite location first and then move to their second and third pitches. At the lower levels, a pitcher is usually a reliever because he is deficient in areas of his game—he may lack command or pitchability, or perhaps he only possesses one good pitch. With this in mind, the coach should keep it simple for the reliever and have him practice what he really does well before going into the game. Developmental skills can be acquired during practice times or in the off-season.

Rest periods may be the single most important aspect in helping the reliever perform optimally. Coaches sometimes get so wrapped up in counting pitches for the starting pitcher (and prescribing rest) that they forget to track the workload of the reliever—the consecutive days that a reliever has thrown, how many pitches he threw in the game, and how many pitches he threw in the bullpen before getting into the game. Though it is true that the reliever will throw significantly fewer pitches than the starter, throwing a high number of pitches in the bullpen while preparing to go into the game—especially on consecutive days—could potentially be more injurious to a pitcher's arm than a once-a-week start. This fact must be accounted for if a coach wants to prevent injury and gain optimal performance from his staff. Regarding rest for a relief pitcher, here are a few general guidelines to keep in mind:

- If a relief pitcher throws fewer than 20 pitches in a game, he can throw the following day.
- If a relief pitcher throws 20 to 35 pitches in a game, he needs one day of rest before pitching again.
- If a relief pitcher throws 35 to 50 pitches in a game, the coach should decide whether the pitcher needs one day or two days of rest before pitching again. This will depend on the pitcher and how he arrived at this pitch total (i.e., whether he had easy innings or difficult innings).
- If a relief pitcher throws 50 to 65 pitches in a game, the pitcher needs at least three days of rest before pitching again.

Also note that during games, the goal is to get the reliever in the game before he has warmed up for a third time in the bullpen. If the pitcher has warmed up more than three times, the coach should consider the number of pitches he has thrown in the bullpen and whether the reliever will be effective in the game. Has he thrown too much to be effective? The coach should also consider whether or not the pitcher risks injury with this type of warm-up.

Organization is the key for a coach who wants to keep his pitching staff running on all cylinders. This might not be difficult to do at the younger levels because teams play fewer games and pitching staffs are smaller, but it can be challenging if coaches have to deal with two-way players and limited practice time. Staying organized at the collegiate level becomes much more difficult, though, for the simple reason that the college coach usually has a larger staff. A coach might find it easy to keep his number 1, 2, and 3 pitchers organized because they are pitching the bulk of the innings and are a large component to the team's success. It is usually numbers 8, 9, and 10 on the staff who suffer and seem to be forgotten. Coaches need to remember this: Pitcher number 8, 9, or 10 may be asked to step up in an important game and do something extraordinary. The coach must also remember that pitchers 8, 9, and 10 may someday be 1, 2, and 3; therefore, a foundation must be set for their success.

THIRTEEN

Year-Round Programming

Many baseball people have said that champions are made in the off-season. Even with all of the planning that a coach does to ensure high-quality practices, good conditioning work, and effective weight training routines, the burden of improving from average to good—and from good to great—often falls on the shoulders of the player when he is working on his game alone. It is during this "alone time" that the player works through the concepts that he has been taught and starts to fit them into something that works for him, something that makes sense to him and his game. The player learns and assimilates, giving himself the opportunity to become a champion. He takes what is complex and simplifies it.

The off-season is also a time when the pitcher becomes more self-assured as he plans his destiny. There is just something about working hard when no one is watching. It solidifies the pitcher's purpose, justifies his sacrifices, and clarifies his goals. He knows that he is in control of his own destiny and is accountable for his actions. Through hard yet smart work, the pitcher will feel prepared for the challenge of the season. And if a pitcher is truly prepared, then how can he fail?

Parents, players, and coaches regularly ask me how often (how much) a pitcher should perform certain activities (programming) during the off-season. They also ask how pitchers can fit all of the various components of an off-season program into a schedule that will make it all work for them. These are good questions, but they are not easy to answer. They are questions that every coach and player would like to know the answers to, because the answers would make players more efficient and consistent and would help them develop faster. In other words, these are not just questions; they are *the* questions that must be answered for development to occur.

Another issue is whether a pitcher should take time off during the off-season. Is it necessary for a pitcher to actively rest his body from the rigors of the game? Is it necessary for the pitcher to actively rest his mind from the game and pursue other interests? My mother once told me that I should never let baseball completely define me as a person. She thought that I had much more to offer the world than simply pitching a baseball, and that a man can wear many hats and find interest in things other than baseball. This was sage advice, and I would offer the same to any young pitcher because it has served me quite well.

So, how does a pitcher approach the off-season in a way that will give him the best opportunity to satisfy his needs for the season as well as the need to get away from the game and gratify other areas of his life? One of the foundational elements discussed earlier in this book was balance. In baseball and in pitching, people think of balance as a crisp, precise movement through space and time and something that is important for the physical and athletic development of the pitcher. As mentioned earlier, balance can also be thought of as a means to becoming a complete pitcher; all areas of pitching are important, and a pitcher's weaknesses must become his strengths if he is to achieve balance. Finally, an additional meaning of balance is that a player must be able to strike a middle ground between baseball and life. This is an important concept that cannot be overlooked in a pitcher's approach to the off-season.

Creating an Off-Season Program

For the off-season, pitchers need to devise a simple yet smart plan for themselves and then have the courage and discipline to carry it out to completion. The program for the off-season must be concise and easy to follow, and it should build in allowances for the downtime or rest periods that allow the pitcher to grow in other areas. The program should be specific to the individual pitcher and his needs. Too often, plans for off-season programs are so broad in their nature that they become counterproductive or useless because they do not specifically address problem areas that a pitcher may be encountering. One size fits all does not apply when it comes to programming. Following a concise and individualized plan is the recipe that makes the "soup taste better."

The most important part of developing a plan for an off-season program (and this applies to in-season programs, too!) is to define what the pitcher would like to achieve, the time frame involved, and how the pitcher will measure his improvements. Setting goals creates a template for the pitcher to follow from start to finish, and it also provides a record for what he has accomplished and what he may need to change in the future. Through the goal-setting process, the pitcher creates a blueprint for success and a diary of accomplishments. The act of setting goals is not a difficult concept to understand, and many people set goals or write down to-do lists on a daily basis. Writing out goals lends credence to their worth. They become visible to their owner, and because they are visible, the owner places importance on them. That alone—placing intent behind the message—is a good starting point for the pitcher.

Many research articles suggest that goals should be attainable and process oriented. Goals should not be so low that the goal becomes too easy to achieve, but at the same time, they should not be so high that they are impossible to accomplish. In addition, goals should not be too outcome driven (e.g., wins and losses, ERA); rather, they should be goals that the owner has control over, such as control of himself or the pitches he throws. When it comes to pitching, the goals must be realistic to some degree, but all types of goals have a value. I tell my pitchers that it is okay for them to dream about what could be and what they would like to happen, as long as they are taking care of the day-to-day process-oriented goals. This is referred to as double vision, having one eye on the ultimate dream while the other steadies itself on the daily tasks required to achieve that dream. It is much like setting a five-year plan (ultimate goal) in action by following through on the daily goals necessary to achieve the dream. It is the best of both worlds.

Once a pitcher's goals have been established, it is time to create a detailed plan that will help the pitcher follow through on what is expected. During my college years, I took many courses on teaching methods and education. In those courses, I was taught how to plan using a three-step method: the block plan, the weekly plan, and the daily plan. This method has been used for decades by teachers of all types, and it is extremely useful in helping a pitcher design an off-season plan.

Step 1: Create a Block Plan

The pitcher's first step in implementing an off-season plan is to create a schedule of events for the applicable time frame. This could vary from a six-week period to a three-month period depending on what type of off-season the pitcher has. The block plan is the general overview of the off-season plan and can be as simple as sketching basic ideas of what will happen in the allotted time on a calendar. Figure 13.1 is a sample of what this might look like for a college pitcher on a winter break. The block plan becomes the road map of what the pitcher hopes to accomplish in the long term and what measurements he might take to determine progress. The block plan can be as generic or as detailed as the pitcher would like it to be, but keep in mind that the weekly plan is designed to take over for the block plan in terms of defining tasks and providing detail. I like to keep the block plan fairly simple, listing things such as bullpen days and the theme of the bullpen, strength training and conditioning days and the theme or rep scheme during a certain time frame, and off-days where no training occurs.

Step 2: Create a Weekly Plan

The weekly plan is more specific than the block plan. Though it follows the theme set forth in the block plan, the weekly plan gives more specific information regarding what the pitcher will be doing by assigning short-term, specific goals for the pitcher to meet. Whereas the block plan gave a generic theme or schedule, the weekly plan provides further details on what the pitcher is trying to accomplish. The weekly plan should also designate appropriate times for measuring progress. Figure 13.2 is a sample of a weekly plan for all of the pitchers on a team. The overall time frame is broken down into weeks (in this example, the off-season is eight weeks), and specific training or tasks are assigned to each pitcher based on his role, his strengths and weaknesses, and his short- and long-term goals.

Step 3: Create a Daily Plan

The most complete part of the off-season plan is the daily plan, which details the activities and goals for each day. The daily plan is very specific and can feature hour-to-hour details, or perhaps even minute-to-minute details. The block plan that was funneled into the weekly plan is now funneled into a daily plan. This is where the rubber meets the road. Measurements should be recorded in this area of the plan so that the pitcher can determine progress and make adjustments accordingly.

Figure 13.1 Sample College Pitcher's Off-Season Block Plan for Winter Break

19	20	21	22	23	24	25
	Long-toss routine Velocity training routine Postsession lifting	ACE routine Dumbbell or Bodyblade exercises Medicine ball work Conditioning work	Long-toss routine Velocity training routine Postsession lifting	ACE routine Medicine ball work Stretching and flexibility work Conditioning work	Long-toss routine Velocity training routine Postsession lifting	DAY OFF
26	**27**	**28**	**29**	**30**	**31**	**1**
DAY OFF	Long-toss routine Velocity training routine Postsession lifting	ACE routine Conditioning work	Long-toss routine Velocity training routine Postsession lifting	ACE routine Drill work (delivery) Stretching and flexibility work Conditioning work	Long-toss routine Pickoff work Postsession lifting	DAY OFF
2	**3**	**4**	**5**	**6**	**7**	**8**
Cross-training (e.g., play basketball, jog 2 miles)	Long-toss routine Velocity training routine Postsession lifting	ACE routine Conditioning work	Long-toss routine Postsession lifting	ACE routine Drill work (pickoffs and delivery) Stretching and flexibility work Conditioning work	Velocity training routine Postsession lifting	Throwing (50 on flat ground or 30 on mound)
9	**10**	**11**	**12**	**13**	**14**	**15**
ACE routine	Drill work (delivery)	Throwing (40 mound) Pickoff work	FIRST DAY OF SCHOOL			

Figure 13.2   Sample College Pitcher's Off-Season Weekly Plan

Monday	OFF
Tuesday	Stretch; Long-toss routine (30 min); weighted ball training (5 oz, 7 oz, 4 oz, 5 oz); lower-body weight training
Wednesday	Stretch; dumbbell/Bodyblade exercises; core work; short-distance sprints (15x)
Thursday	Stretch; Long-toss routine (33 min); weighted ball training (5 oz, 14 oz, 7 oz, 4 oz, 5 oz); full-body weight training
Friday	Stretch; Day 1 ACE Routine; 30-min run; flexibility work
Saturday	Stretch; Long-toss routine (35 min); weighted ball training (5 oz, 21 oz, 14 oz, 7 oz, 4 oz, 5 oz); lower-body weight training
Sunday	Stretch; dumbbell/Bodyblade exercises; skill and drill work
Monday	OFF

Figure 13.3, *a* and *b*, provide two sample daily plans that outline all of the types of activities that could occur during a practice session for pitchers. Measurements can include radar gun readings in bullpen sessions, long-toss distances, weight increases in strength training, time decreases in conditioning exercises, or video comparison from week to week (or even day to day) to evaluate mechanical adjustments or pitch enhancements.

Figure 13.3   Sample College Pitcher's Off-Season Daily Plans
Figure 13.3*a*   Sample Daily Plan 1

2:00 p.m.	Early training (prepractice warm-up, resistance band exercises, pitcher stretches)
2:30 p.m.	Third-base dugout meeting with notebook
2:45 p.m.	Stretching and flexibility (with cleats)
3:05 p.m.	Catch play routine: 1:25 at each distance (no compression for easy long toss pitchers); changeup work–drill at 45; breaking ball work–drill at 45; perfect 10 (review 1-5 and teach 6-10)
3:35 p.m.	Review eyes and fastball grips; add split
3:45 p.m.	Review feet setup with stretch; add windup (rocker), knees, glove position, and starting position
4:15 p.m.	Square drill
4:35 p.m.	Cuts and relays
4:45 p.m.	Fly-ball communication
4:55 p.m.	Bullpen to explain the rest of the day
5:05 p.m.	30-pitch bullpen (filmed); conditioning, PFP on field, shag, arm care in lab
5:50 p.m.	2-pitch game
6:00 p.m.	Duties
	Conditioning: 6 30-second poles with 1 minute of rest in between

Figure 13.3b Sample Daily Plan 2

2:00 p.m.	Early training (prepractice warm-up, resistance band exercises, pitcher stretches)
2:30 p.m.	Third-base dugout meeting with notebook
2:50 p.m.	Stretching and flexibility (with cleats)
3:20 p.m.	Catch play routine: 1:15 at each distance; compression; changeup work at 75-90 feet; breaking ball work at 45-55 feet; perfect 10
3:50 p.m.	Fastball training; knee work
4:00 p.m.	Training the eyes; knee work
4:15 p.m.	Setup; wind and stretch dry work
4:40 p.m.	Square drill
5:00 p.m.	Team defense
5:20 p.m.	Begin bullpens
6:15 p.m.	2-pitch game

Making Adjustments to the Plan

Any athlete who wants to improve must be able to look back and identify what adjustments he needs to make in his training program in order to increase his return on training time (ROTT). After every baseball season, I spend a few weeks evaluating my coaching skills as well as my pitching staff's process—that is, our system. I want to find out, both subjectively and objectively if possible, what works well within our system and what changes are needed for the future. If I can tighten the learning loop or simplify the system in any way that will shorten the time it takes for our pitchers to improve, then a greater ROTT is possible. This technique can be used in every area of one's life and is not limited to baseball or pitching. Extraordinary (not saying that I am) people use this to facilitate improvement in many if not all facets of their lives; it is most likely a major reason why they are considered extraordinary.

Yearly Programming for Specific Groups

By now, it should be clear that baseball pitchers need time within a calendar year to recuperate from throwing a baseball. They must implement a strategy that specifies what to train, when to train, and how much to train in order to maximize ability and to develop as a player. Many aspects go into training the pitcher, and the player and coach often find themselves trying to fit those aspects into a short amount of time. The pitcher needs to balance all of the training aspects and find ways to gain greater return on training time; therefore, the block plan, weekly plan, and daily plan should form the basis of what a pitcher will do in a given year. And because all age levels and skill levels have different time constraints, playing seasons, and practice limitations, the following sections outline various calendars that may be used for youth, high school, and collegiate pitchers.

QUICK PITCH

Let common sense prevail when determining how much rest a pitcher needs at the end of the season. If a young pitcher has logged a good number of innings with relatively no downtime from competing, he should probably go a solid month without getting on a mound. Each pitcher should develop a calendar for when he is competing and when he is training. At younger levels, the calendar should have more training time and more rest periods than competition time built into it. Training techniques that help a pitcher develop throwing skill and throwing ability—weighted ball, long toss, flat-ground work, mound work—are useful and should be included outside of the competition calendar.

Youth Calendar

Several studies by Dr. James Andrews have concluded that a large number of injuries occur in youth league baseball because of high weekly pitch totals and because pitchers pitch competitively for a high number of consecutive months. We live in an ultracompetitive society where club and summer baseball are being played 12 months of the year, especially in warm climate states.

Another phenomenon today is that children seem to specialize very early in a single sport rather than play multiple sports. In the past, many young people grew up playing football in the fall, basketball in the winter, and baseball in the spring and summer, repeating this cycle year after year. Today, parents and players tend to pick one sport and spend a large amount of money on equipment, lessons, and league fees. They hope that this will help the player become the next "great" in that sport. In my opinion, there is a serious flaw in this ideology. Specializing in one sport at an early age can limit the athletic ceiling for athletes by not letting them be exposed to playing various sports. An example of the benefit of this exposure would be the agility and leaping skills, as well as other fine motor skills that are developed by playing basketball and can transfer onto the baseball diamond. Playing football promotes a combination of speed, agility, and power that is impossible to replicate in a weight room or in an agility drill, not to mention the emotional and physical benefits associated with being able to "take a hit." Specializing in one sport may provide some advantages, especially in the area of skill enhancement (throwing accuracy or pitch development); however, the best strategy is to build the athlete first—the baseball player will develop soon after.

Figure 13.4 is a sample calendar for a youth baseball pitcher. This calendar includes seasonal throwing and rest periods, as well as allowances for competing in multiple sports.

Figure 13.4 Sample Youth Calendar

January	February	March	April
Ability building (throwing, long toss, and strength and conditioning) _____ Participation in other sport (if so, no ability building this month)	General fitness; no throwing _____ If participating in other sport, begin ability building here instead of January	Ability building Skill building Mechanical adjustments Pitch development Team defense (bunts, PFPs)	Ability building Skill building Possible game cycle
May	**June**	**July**	**August**
Team building (team defense, building the pitch count, scrimmage) Possible game cycle	Games Game cycle	Games Game cycle	General fitness; no throwing
September	**October**	**November**	**December**
Games Game cycle _____ Participation in other sport	Games Game cycle _____ Participation in other sport	General fitness; no throwing	Ability building (throwing, long toss, and strength and conditioning) _____ Participation in other sport

High School Calendar

Almost every state has its own rules and regulations regarding how much contact a coach can have with his players during the off-season, so it would be difficult to design a true calendar that applies to all high school athletes. A better approach is to start with the traditional playing season and work forward from there. This way, we can implement a block plan of three main components: playing season, summer season, and off-season.

Though the time frames for the high school calendar will vary widely because of differing schedules and geographical considerations, this sample should provide enough information to help design the calendar of a high school pitcher. Adjustments might be necessary for the high school pitcher who plays a second or third sport, as well as one who plays a second position, though recommendations have been built into the calendar for those instances. Figure 13.5 is a sample calendar for a high school pitcher.

Figure 13.5   Sample High School Calendar

January	February	March	April
Ability building	Bullpen work	Everything from February plus scrimmage schedule and building pitch count. Games begin later in March.	Games
Skill building	Skill building (PFP, pickoffs, team defense)		Game cycle (compete, evaluate, repair, prepare, compete)
Mound work	Scrimmage		
Arm care	Role development		
	Arm care		
	Conditioning		

May	June	July	August
Games	2-3 weeks downtime for general fitness (no throwing). Summer baseball begins later in June.	Games (summer baseball)	General fitness; no throwing
Game cycle (compete, evaluate, repair, prepare, compete)		Game cycle (compete, evaluate, repair, prepare, compete)	System training

September	October	November	December
Ability building (long toss, weight training, system training) to develop a base for throwing and conditioning	Ability building (long toss, heavy strength training, heavy conditioning for agility and speed, plyometrics); no mound work	Ability building (add velocity enhancement)	Ability building and skill building; mound work is acceptable
		Skill building (mechanical adjustments, pitch development); mound work is acceptable	Last week of December OFF

College Calendar

The collegiate calendar (see figure 13.6) will look very different from the youth and high school calendar. The calendar for the college pitcher offers less downtime for the pitcher and much more interaction between player and coach during the off-season, as long as this time is in compliance with NCAA bylaws and regulations. I have continually made adjustments to this calendar over the years, trying for a better return on training time and generally making the plan as efficient as possible.

Figure 13.6 Sample Collegiate Calendar

January	February	March	April
Preseason throwing Long toss Bullpen work Skill work (command) Weight training (4 times per week) Heavy conditioning Arm care Ability building and skill building	Bullpen work Skill work (PFP, pick-offs, team defense) Scrimmage Build pitch count Role development Arm care Weight training (2-3 times per week) Conditioning	Games Game cycle (compete, evaluate, repair, prepare, compete)	Games Game cycle (compete, evaluate, repair, prepare, compete)

May	June	July	August
Games Game cycle (compete, evaluate, repair, prepare, compete)	Games Game cycle (compete, evaluate, repair, prepare, compete) Season ends; 2 weeks of downtime	Games (summer baseball) Game cycle (compete, evaluate, repair, prepare, compete)	Games (summer baseball) Game cycle (compete, evaluate, repair, prepare, compete) Season ends; 2 weeks of downtime

September	October	November	December
Fall baseball begins General conditioning Weight training introduction Foundation and systems training Throwing Arm care Bullpen work	Fall baseball Team defense Team pitching Foundation (arsenal) Plan Scrimmage Arm care Weight training (5 times per week) Conditioning	2 weeks with no throwing Ability training Long toss Heavy strength training Heavy conditioning (agility, speed, plyometrics) Velocity enhancement with skill component (mechanical adjustments; pitch enhancement)	Continue with ability training Long toss Velocity enhancement Strength and conditioning Skill work (mechanical adjustments; pitch enhancement) No throwing last week of December

I am not a proponent of the training periodization schedule that most major-league and minor-league pitchers follow, even though many collegiate programs have adopted the same type of schedule. A periodization schedule may be appropriate for the professional player, but it may not fit the needs of the collegiate player. A typical major-league season is 162 games long with a mind-boggling travel schedule and games almost every day for the better part of eight months. Starting pitchers may throw between 200 and 250 innings and pitch on shorter rest than the collegiate pitcher. Also, the major-league pitcher is generally older than the collegiate pitcher and has more experience and more repetitions at his disposal. With that in mind, once the season is over for the big-league pitcher, a long duration of rest is needed so that the pitcher's arm, body, and psyche can fully recover. Because the collegiate pitcher throws fewer innings in a given year, plays considerably fewer games, travels less, and has a longer rest period in between pitching bouts, a shorter rest cycle can be safely implemented. The sample plan contains built-in rest cycles spread out much like a deloading cycle in weight training: heavy bouts of training, followed by a deloading rest cycle, followed by yet another cycle of training. This has worked quite well for our pitchers, and the pitchers' arm strength seems to increase as the season progresses.

QUICK PITCH

Note that there is a big difference between training for pitching and competition pitching. If a pitcher has pitched competitively for nine consecutive months with no downtime and little training time, a recovery period will be necessary. If short bouts of rest are coupled with adequate training time—weight training and preparing the arm to handle the stress of pitching along with intermittent periods of recovery between seasons—the pitcher may be equipped to continue a throwing/pitching program.

Weight Training for Pitchers

Weight training and conditioning were covered in chapter 11, so we won't get into details about training protocols here. However, commonsense measures should be addressed before setting up a pitcher's training plan. For example, in an out-of-season week, the pitcher may throw a bullpen on Tuesday and Friday. He is in a phase of his training where he is lifting four days a week, two upper-body days and two lower-body days. If possible, the pitcher should perform his upper-body lifting on nonthrowing days, or at the very least, he should throw his bullpens before heading into the weight room. This will ensure that the quality of the bullpen is not jeopardized and that muscle fatigue or soreness will not hinder his throwing, giving the pitcher the greatest chance of staying injury free. Proper sleep and nutrition will also optimize the chance for growth and progress.

Building the Athlete, the Pitcher, and the Team

Another important concept is the idea of building the athlete first and then building the pitcher. From both a mechanical and training perspective, this falls into the same category as skill versus ability, throwing preceding pitching, and physical assessment and correction. The pitcher cannot become what he wants to become without implementing these concepts. As mentioned before, to become a better pitcher, the player must first become a better thrower. Without symmetry, mobility, and stability in the right areas, the pitcher has no chance to change his mechanics or alter his physique without risk of injury or without getting worse instead of improving. Building the athlete starts when the athlete isn't competing. It is during the off-season that he has the most time to work on physical skills that will soon translate into baseball ability. He can do so in a safe environment, without having to test his mettle against an opponent in competition. In time, the player's improved athleticism will show up in his baseball skills—improved explosiveness turns into a faster arm, which turns into a livelier, more explosive fastball. And, because the pitcher has increased body strength, he is now better equipped to control his body, his livelier arm, and his more explosive fastball. Development has occurred.

Related to building the athlete and the pitcher, another important concept is building the team. Not only are champions made in the off-season, but good teams become good teams in the off-season as well. One might think that this is a topic strictly for coaches, but that is hardly the case. Good teams always have a good leader, and the leader often emerges from the off-season. The team leader is often the player who puts in the work, who assimilates and learns, and who becomes confident in himself and in his game through working on his own.

In the collegiate setting, the off-season is also a time when teams develop unity. Note that team unity is different from team chemistry. The chemistry of a team is built during the playing season, largely because most adversity strikes during the course of the season, not before it. Chemistry happens as a result of individuals being able to set aside personal feelings for the greater good of the team. For example, though a pitcher may not be happy with his current role or the amount of playing time he is receiving, he accepts it for the good of the team, and strives to reach a higher level personally. More than anything else, he wants the team to win. Good chemistry is very difficult to achieve because the ego of the player has to be checked at the door, which often goes against human nature.

Unity, on the other hand, is much easier to attain because it deals with friendships and camaraderie among teammates, both of which can happen on and off the baseball field and do not stand in the way of individual goals. Team-building activities build interpersonal trust and respect among teammates. These activities can be simple in nature because all that is required is time and communication. For example, players can connect while eating a team meal together; sometimes the smallest instances of friendship and being a good teammate have a great impact on team unity.

The goal of team-building exercises is to unify the team by building relationships. If these relationships strengthen to the degree that each member of the team can set aside personal feelings for the greater good of the team (check the ego), then team chemistry during the season can be very strong.

Successful people in all facets of life seem to manage their time better than those who aren't quite as successful, and managing time wisely for the pitching athlete is no different. Generally, for example, pitchers who make it past the minor leagues and into the major leagues are the ones who trained smarter and harder than their colleagues. They kept their eye on the prize (the big leagues) yet also managed to stay in the present moment. They stayed focused. They stayed consistent. They kept their double vision. They planned their work and worked their plan.

AFTERWORD

Believe it or not, there is life outside of baseball. As an athlete or a coach, we often define ourselves by the sport that we play. It becomes so much a part of us that forget what the game is truly about—joy. Baseball should bring joy to your life. It should be a very nonthreatening feeling to come to the ballpark, strap up your cleats, and play the game with joy and passion. Fun. Some time ago, I listened to a sport psychologist talk about the mental game at a clinic, and found myself wondering why we needed psychologists and mental techniques to conquer fear in the game of baseball. Fear of what? Please don't misunderstand. This fellow was a sharp person with incredible ideas about the mental game, but it did make me wonder where our game is going. Fear doesn't exist when the game is played out of joy and passion. There is no need for a technique because a wonderfully designed nothingness is present. That is joy. Don't you remember how excited you were for your first game? How excited you were to be there with your friends, learning the chants and nuances of the game? Can you remember seeing your first big league game with your mom or dad? Keeping score, watching batting practice, and watching the precision, power, and grace of the players? That is joy, and that is how the game should be played. No fear, because there is nothing to fear. It is simply me versus you. Fun.

I hope you will find value in something that was said to me long ago and has stuck with me through the years: "The game always knows." The message is very clear—you get exactly what you put into this game. I truly believe that the game will take care of the people who take care of it. This is done by honoring its traditions, teaching its values, and respecting the proper way to play the game. It is staying humble when you win and staying hungry when you lose. It is about putting in the work required for the opportunity to be good and understanding that it might take even more. It is about doing things right. In the end, it is about *you*.

I hope that this book demonstrates the joy and passion I have for pitching. It is my hope that something here made you think differently about what you currently know about throwing a ball. I hope this book will prompt you to try something new. Most important, I hope that this book will help you improve. My favorite part of baseball, and in particular pitching, is that there is *always* more to know. New thoughts, techniques, and innovations of pitching are being invented and implemented consistently, and what is new today is often old news tomorrow. It is up to you as the player or coach to decide what you can use and discard the rest.

REFERENCES

Cressey, E. 2010. Clearing up the rotator cuff controversy. www.ericcressey.com [January 31, 2010].

DeRenne, C., B.P. Buxton, R.K. Hetzler, and K.W. Ho. 1994. Effects of under- and overweighted implement training on pitching velocity. *The Journal of Strength and Conditioning Research* 8(4): 247-250.

The National Collegiate Athletic Association. 2010. 2011 and 2012 NCAA Baseball Rule Book. Indianapolis, IN: NCAA.

Peterson, D. 2009. Youth baseball: Good news and bad news. LiveScience.com [June 12, 2009].

INDEX

PLEASE NOTE: Page numbers followed by an italicized *f* or *t* indicate that there is a figure or table on that page, respectively.

A

abilities 7-9, 9*t*, 219-225
ACE. *See* arm care exercises
Andrews, James 249
arm
    circles 182, 182*f*
    positioning, during upper-body finish 55
    strengthening exercises 171-212
arm action 41-46
    classic 43, 43*f*
    classic, with EC 43, 44*f*
    horizontal W 44, 44*f*
    inverted L 45, 45*f*
    inverted W 45, 45*f*
    scapular loading in 46-47, 47*f*
    training 52
arm and glove synchronization 52-53, 53*f*
arm care exercises (ACE) 192-205, 192*f*-193*f*,
    194*f*-195*f*
arm slot 41-42
    change 106
    determination 55, 80
    pitch type and 81*t*
    spin angle for 42*f*
arsenals, considerations for 79-84
assessments 171
    hip rotation 218-219
    points 217*f*
    posture 216-217
    single-leg balance 217-218, 217*f*
    single-leg power 218, 218*f*
athlete building 254-255
athleticism 213-215
Athletic Pitcher program 190

B

back leg
    riding down of 71, 71*f*
    sweeping of 24*f*
backward C extension 74, 74*f*
backward pitcher exercise 181, 181*f*
backward side-to-side exercise 179, 179*f*
backward straight-arm hypertension 176, 176*f*
balance 9-10, 9*f*, 214
    connection and 10
    eyes and 16
    improving 64
    lower body and 60-62
    single-leg assessments of 217-218, 217*f*
balks 140. *See also* best moves
ball sections 99*f*
barehanding 153*f*
baselines 214-219

base runners, multiple 150*f*
base stealing 134-135
bat speed 127-128
batting orders 117*t*, 120*t*
batting practice 93-94
bent-arm external and internal rotation 175, 175*f*
best moves 140
Bodyblade exercises 195-200
breaking balls 99-103
breathing, before pitches 14-15
bullpens
    feel good 238-240, 240*t*
    flat-ground 240, 241*t*
    game-day 235-238, 236*f*, 240-242
    normal non-game day 233-234, 234*t*
    one, between starts 230, 230*t*-231*t*
    pitch-specific 234, 235*t*
    routines, for relievers 238-242
    two, between starts 231, 231*t*-232*t*
    for working on stretch with runners 234-235
bunts 151-153, 151*f*

C

cadence, varying of 135
carryover biceps curl 204, 204*f*
catchers
    qualities of 107-109
    responsibilities of 109-111
    working with 111-113
changeups 94-99
    circle grip for 96*f*
    drills 96-99
    pitchfork grip for 95*f*
choking 14-15
circle grip 96, 96*f*
college calendar 251, 252*f*
comebackers 149-150
connection 8
    balance and 10
    setup positions and 20
coordination 214
core
    development and activation 220-221
    initiation 63*f*
Corral, Fred 23
counts 129-131
coupling 74-75, 75*f*
curveballs 100-101
    grip 100*f*, 101*f*
    pressure drill 100-101
    spike grip 103*f*
cutoffs 153
cutters 89-91, 89*f*

cycled approach 37

D
deceptive qualities 104-106, 104*f*
DeRenne, Coop 190
diagonal movement series 199-200, 199*f*-200*f*
double lift and throw drill 68
dumbbell exercises 200-210

E
elbow climb 43, 44*f*
elbows-in triceps extension 205, 205*f*
energy system development 224
eyes
    balance and 16
    good *versus* bad 16*f*
    before pitches 15-18
    training 18

F
fastballs 84-94
    bat speed and 128
    batting practice 93-94
    extra 93-94
    four-seam 85-86, 85*f*
    split-finger 88, 88*f*
    two-seam 86-87, 87*f*
finish
    coupling during 74-75, 75*f*
    glove-side action during 50*f*
    upper body 53-56, 54*f*
first base
    comebackers to 149-150
    covering 149*f*
    pickoffs at 137-143, 137*f*, 138*f*, 142*f*
5-3 move 154-155
flex step 34-35, 35*f*
focus 15-18
foot plant, with glove-side action 49*f*
foot positioning
    for first-base pickoffs 137*f*
    next to rubber 23-24, 23*f*
    at start of stretch 21-23, 21*f*
forearm fly-out 48
forkballs 88
forward pitcher exercise 180, 180*f*
forward side-to-side exercise 178, 178*f*
foundation 3-11, 4*f*
front-leg action 71-72, 72*f*

G
Gambetta, Vern 192
game situation 118
glenohumeral internal rotation deficit (GIRD) 185
glove-side action 47-50
    closing of 50*f*
    drill 51
    during finish 50*f*
    foot plant with 49*f*
    high 105*f*, 106
    pinch and swivel 48-49, 48*f*
    pull and tuck 47-48, 48*f*

H
hand positioning 28-32
hands-knees exercise 39
head positioning 19-20, 54*f*
high school calendar 250, 251*f*
hips, setting of 68-70, 69*f*
hip positioning 25-26
    with front-leg action 72*f*
    open *versus* closed 26*f*
hip rotation assessments 218-219
hitters
    awareness of 121-123
    stance 126-127, 127*f*
    stride 126-127
    swing 123-129
    traits of 115-116
    types 117*t*
hit the spot drill 18-19
"hooking the foot" 25, 66, 66*f*
House, Tom 48, 52, 190, 192

I
injuries 169-171
in-season cycle 229*f*
intent 7
intentional walks 154, 155*f*

J
Jobe exercises 170
joy 4-5

K
kneeling opposites 221*f*
knees
    back 63*f*
    lift 66-68, 67*f*
    positioning 25-26

L
landing 17*f*, 72-73, 73*f*
leaning 16-17, 17*f*
left-handed pitchers
    first-base pickoffs for 141-143, 142*f*
    pickoff exercises for 143-144, 143*f*-144*f*
leg lift 26-28
    efficient 27*f*
    hooking the foot and 66*f*
    overrotation during 28*f*
leverage 65, 65*f*, 69*f*
loading 53
lower body
    balance and 60-62
    components 61*f*
    considerations, for youth league 75
    mechanics 59-60
    momentum and 60-62
    posture and 62-64
    rhythm and tempo of 60

M
Marshall, Mike 190
matching 52
Mazzone, Leo 231

mechanics
  lower body 59-60
  stretch 20-30
  training progression and 8
  windup 30-33
mental game 157-158
mental toughness 159
me *versus* me and me *versus* you mentality 6, 160-161
modified hand bump exercise 32
momentum 60-62
mound, caring for 14, 15*f*
movements
  gap 33-34, 160
  leaking 71, 71*f*
  small 33-34
  total-body 223
  training 222

N
Nyman, Paul 190

O
overhead triceps extension 177, 177*f*
overthrowing 94

P
pace 159-160
pain, levels of 186
partner push drill 64-65
PFP. *See* pitcher's field practice
pickoffs 136-148
  best move 140
  bottom-of-the-set 140, 140*f*
  daylight 145-146
  exercises 141, 143-144, 143*f*-144*f*
  at first base 137-143, 137*f*, 138*f*, 142*f*
  inside move 146-148, 147*f*
  out of hand 138, 139*f*
  pitching *versus* 135-136
  at second base 144-148, 145*f*, 146*f*
  set and hold 141
  top-of-the-set 139, 139*f*
pitches
  before 14-20
  owning *versus* renting 80-81
  pickoffs *versus* 135-136
  types 79-80, 81*t*
pitchability 159-160
pitchers. *See also* left-handed pitchers; right-handed pitchers
  building 254-255
  strengths 118
  stretch exercises 182-185
pitcher's field practice (PFP) 148-156
pitchfork grip 95, 95*f*, 152*f*
pitching plans 118-121, 120*t*
pitchouts 136, 153, 154*f*
posture
  assessments 216-217
  lower body and 62-64
  of spine 19*f*
  upper body 39-40
pot stirs 183, 183*f*

power 213
  single-leg assessments of 218, 218*f*
practice
  relievers 238, 239*t*
  routines 162-163
  routines, for starters 228-233
prehabilitation 222
pre-mechanics 13
presence 159-160
pressure zones 119
prevention 214
Price, David 161
programming 243. *See also* training
  block 245, 246*f*
  for college calendar 251, 252*f*
  daily 245, 247*f*
  for high school calendar 250, 251*f*
  off-season 244-245
  weekly 245, 247f
  yearly 248-253
  for youth league calendar 249, 250*f*
progressive overload 223
pronation 55, 55*f*, 87, 212, 212*f*
prone external rotation 209, 209*f*
prone four-step extension 208, 208*f*
prone horizontal abduction 207, 207*f*
prone shoulder extension 206, 206*f*
push-up plus 210, 210*f*

R
recovery protocol 225
relays 153
relievers 238-242
  bullpen, routines for 238-242
  practice 238, 239*t*
resistance tubing exercises 172-181
return on training time (ROTT) 248
rhythm 38, 60
right-handed pitchers
  first-base pickoffs for 138*f*
  pickoff exercises for 141
Rivera, Mariano 90
rocker step 30-31, 31*f*
rotary training 220
ROTT. *See* return on training time
ROUR principle 190
routines 162-165
  catch play 187, 187*t*
  long-toss 188-189, 189*t*
  postgame 164-165
  practice 162-163
  practice, for starters 228-233
  pregame 163
  prepitch 163-164
  for reliever's bullpen 238-242
  starters 228-238
  throwing 186-189
  velocity training 190, 191*t*
rubber
  foot position during stretch on 21-23, 21*f*
  foot positioning next to 23-24, 23*f*
running game 134-136

S

Sandy Koufax exercise 24-25
scapulae 46*f*
scapular loading, in arm action 46-47, 47*f*
scooping 152*f*
scouting reports 216
second base
    comebackers to 149-150
    pickoffs at 144-148
set position stance 22-23
setting the hip drill 70
setup positions 20-33
shin angle 70, 70*f*
shoulder abduction series 197-198, 197*f*-198*f*
shoulder flexion series 196-197, 196*f*-197*f*
shoulder rotation 41
side-lying external rotation 210, 210*f*
sidewinders 106
sinkers 91-93, 91*f*, 92*f*
skills 7-9, 9*t*, 213-215, 219-225
sleeper stretch 185, 185*f*
sliders 102-103
    action 102*f*
    fat-finger 103*f*
    grip 102*f*
slide step 34-35, 34*f*
slow-medium-fast arm interaction exercise 53
Spahn, Warren 115
speed 213
spike curveball grip 103*f*
spine
    angle, for arm slot 42*f*
    posture 19*f*
    during upper-body finish 54
stability 214, 220
stalling 63*f*, 64
stance
    hitters 126-127, 127*f*
    for set position 22-23
starters
    with one relief appearance 232-233, 232*t*
    practice routines 228-233
    routines 228-238
straight-arm abduction 202, 202*f*
straight-arm flexion 201, 201*f*
straight-arm horizontal abduction 174, 174*f*
straight-arm horizontal adduction 173, 173*f*
straight-arm scaption 203, 203*f*
strength 213, 222-223
stretch
    foot positioning at start of 21-23, 21*f*
    mechanics 20-30
stride 71-72, 72*f*
    of hitters 126-127
strike zone 82-84, 83*f*
Strom, Brent 49
suicides 152-153
superstitions 157
swing
    of hitters 123-129
    plane 128-129
    speed 127-128

T

T-drill 40
teacups 184, 184*f*
team building 254-255
tempo 38, 60
3-1s 148-149
throwing
    across body 24*f*, 105
    intermediate 150*f*
    in and off plate 125*f*
    overhead 151*f*
    routines 186-189
    uphill 69
throwing arm direction 106
tissue release and lengthening 219
toe-arch relationship 22*f*
training 10-11. *See also* programming
    for ability 219-225
    arm action 52
    cycled approach to 37
    eyes 18
    movement 222
    progression 8
    rotary 220
    for skill 219-225
    strength 222-223
    velocity 190, 191*t*
    work capacity 224
trusting 10-11

U

unloading 53, 73*f*
upper body
    considerations, for youth league 56
    finish 53-56, 54*f*
    posture 39-40
    rhythm and tempo of 38

V

velocity training 190, 191*t*
Verstegen, Mark 192

W

weight distribution 25-26
weight training 253
windup mechanics 30-33
Wolforth, Ron 190, 192
work capacity 213, 224
wrist
    deviations 211, 211*f*
    exercises 211-212
    pronation 212, 212*f*
    supination 212, 212*f*

X

X grip 87, 87*f*

Y

youth league
    calendar 249, 250*f*
    considerations for 56, 75

ABOUT THE AUTHOR

Derek Johnson, named college baseball's National Pitching Coach of the Year in 2004 and National Assistant Coach of the Year in 2010, is widely considered one of the top pitching coaches in the country. In October 2012, he accepted a position with the Chicago Cubs as their minor league pitching coordinator. Before his appointment with the Cubs, he spent 11 years as pitching coach at Vanderbilt, three as associate head coach. While at Vanderbilt, four of his last five staffs led the Southeastern Conference in earned-run average (ERA). His staffs were also ranked nationally at number 15 (2003), 7 (2004), 17 (2005), and 13 (2007). More than 25 of Johnson's past pitchers have been drafted.

Under Johnson's tutelage, Vanderbilt participated in the College World Series in 2011, led by eight players who would later be selected in the Major League Baseball draft, including first-round picks Sonny Gray and Grayson Gravin. The 2011 pitching team led the Southeastern Conference in ERAs and strikeouts. In 2010, the Commodores allowed the fewest home runs in the league, led by Sonny Gray, who was named Baseball America's Summer League Player of the Year (the Commodores' third win in five years). For his efforts with this team, Johnson was named the ABCA/Baseball America Assistant Coach of the Year.

Johnson's 2007 crew led the SEC in eight statistical categories, including ERA (3.55), strikeouts (632), opponents' batting average (.238), complete games (7), and runs allowed (266). Vanderbilt hurlers also threw a school record 606.2 innings in 67 games with 13 saves. Six pitchers from that 2007 staff were drafted and signed into the professional ranks, led by number-one overall pick David Price (Tampa Bay Devil Rays) and the eighth overall pick, Casey Weathers (Colorado Rockies).

Johnson lives in Nashville, Tennessee.

Cody Crowell, Ty Davis, Tyler Rhoden, and Stephen Shao also were drafted and signed, further elevating Johnson's reputation of developing pitchers and honing their skills during their collegiate careers.